Bion, Intuition and the Expansion of Psychoanalytic Theory

Bion, Intuition and the Expansion of Psychoanalytic Theory illuminates how Bion's work on intuition has changed the landscape of contemporary psychoanalysis through his understanding of its supra-scientific and non-sub-scientific condition.

Based on the work of the biannual Bion conference, this book includes contributions from the most eminent voices on Bion's work. The global cohort of contributors in this volume examine topics such as dream work, the Infinite Unconscious, the Spectral model of the mind, the realm of the minus and observation and intuition. Each chapter explores different elements arising from Bion's insistence on learning from experience and establishing the difference between knowing and becoming as an experiential process of the mind as a container in relation to its contents of sensations, feelings, dreams and thoughts.

This book will be of key interest to analysts and analytic therapists of all schools and is an essential resource for those that follow the work of Bion.

Antònia Grimalt, M.D., is a training and supervising analyst for the Spanish Society (SEP-IPA) and the Spanish Federation of Associations of Psychotherapists (FEAP), as well as a child and adolescent training analyst for the former Hans Groen Prakken Institute (EPI). She is former chair of the Forum for Child Psychoanalysis (FEP) and is a member of the Ed. Monografies de Psicoanàlisi i Psicoteràpia. She has taught on the works of Klein and Bion at multiple universities and has edited works on Bion, Pere Folch, Matte Blanco and Ricardo Lombardi in both Spanish and Catalan. In 2020, she chaired the International Bion Meeting in Barcelona.

The Routledge Wilfred Bion Studies Book Series

Series Editor
Howard B. Levine, MD

Editorial Advisory
Board Nicola Abel-Hirsch, Joseph Aguayo, Avner Bergstein, Lawrence J. Brown, Judith Eekhoff, Claudio Laks Eizerik, Robert D. Hinshelwood, Chris Mawson, James Ogilvie, Elias M. da Rocha Barros, Jani Santamaria, Rudi Vermote

The contributions of Wilfred Bion are among the most cited in the analytic literature. Their appeal lies not only in their content and explanatory value but in their generative potential. Although Bion's training and many of his clinical instincts were deeply rooted in the classical tradition of Melanie Klein, his ideas have a potentially universal appeal. Rather than emphasizing a particular psychic content (e.g., Oedipal conflicts in need of resolution; splits that needed to be healed; preconceived transferences that must be allowed to form and flourish, etc.), he tried to help open and prepare the mind of the analyst (without memory, desire or theoretical preconception) for the encounter with the patient.

Bion's formulations of group mentality and the psychotic and non-psychotic portions of the mind, his theory of thinking and emphasis on facing and articulating the truth of one's existence so that one might truly learn firsthand from one's own experience, his description of psychic development (alpha function and container/contained) and his exploration of **O** are "non-denominational" concepts that defy relegation to a particular school or orientation of psychoanalysis. Consequently, his ideas have taken root in many places . . . and those ideas continue to inform many different branches of psychoanalytic inquiry and interest.[1]

It is with this heritage and its promise for the future developments of psychoanalysis in mind that we present *The Routledge Wilfred Bion Studies Book Series*. This series gathers together under newly emerging and continually evolving contributions to psychoanalytic thinking that rest upon Bion's foundational texts and explore and extend the implications of his thought. For a full list of titles in the series, please visit the Routledge website at: www.routledge.com/The-Routledge-Wilfred-Bion-Studies-Book-Series/book-series/RWBSBS.

Howard B. Levine, MD
Series Editor

Note

1 Levine, H.B. and Civitarese, G. (2016). Editors' Preface, *The W.R. Bion Tradition*, Levine and Civitarese, eds., London: Karnac 2016, p. xxi.

'This book sheds light on the phenomenon of intuition, so essential in psychoanalysis, but sometimes so forgotten. Through several individual articles, intuition is studied in numerous vertices that form a precious whole, a real gold mine where one glimpses precious nuggets to be collected. All this raises intuition to its true epistemological stature in the construction of knowledge about the unconscious mind and in science in general.'

Ruggero Levy, *SPPA – Porto Alegre, Brazil*

'In this brilliant and wide-ranging collection of papers, Bion's concept of intuition functions as a portal to the infinite and emergent aspects of human experience. Drawing on philosophy, music, poetry, dreaming, and neuroscience, these essays elaborate Bion's most enigmatic concepts – the language of achievement, the mystic, caesura, and negative capability – yet ground these theoretical discussions in sensitively described personal and clinical moments of transformation and becoming. This collection repositions psychoanalysis once again as a revolutionary endeavor, one that traverses the splits between the group and the individual, the self and the other, the known and unknowable. Enigmatic, allusive, and yet profoundly intuitive of what it means to be human and to feel and think in the face of the terror of the unknown and always changing, this collection is itself a memoir of the future of psychoanalysis.'

Thomas P. Helscher, *Ph.D. FIPA, Training and Supervising Analyst, Los Angeles Institute and Society for Psychoanalytic Studies (LAISPS), USA*

'*Bion, Intuition and the Expansion of Psychoanalytic Theory* brings together some of the most influential international scholars of Wilfred Bion's thought. At the centre of the book is the concept of "intuition", around which revolves a sophisticated theoretical and clinical elaboration. But readers will find that this new valuable contribution deals with several other exciting topics that are changing the landscape of contemporary psychoanalysis. I can only recommend it to all psychotherapists, psychoanalysts and scholars of human sciences.'

Giuseppe Civitarese, *author of Sublime Subjects. Aesthetic Experience and Intersubjectivity in Psychoanalysis (2017), Routledge, and Training Analyst of the Italian Psychoanalytic Society (IPA), Italy*

Bion, Intuition and the Expansion of Psychoanalytic Theory

Edited by Antònia Grimalt

Routledge
Taylor & Francis Group

LONDON AND NEW YORK

Cover image: Joan Miró, Bleu II, 1961 © Successió Miró, 2021

First published 2022
by Routledge
4 Park Square, Milton Park, Abingdon, Oxon OX14 4RN

and by Routledge
605 Third Avenue, New York, NY 10158

Routledge is an imprint of the Taylor & Francis Group, an informa business

British Library Cataloguing-in-Publication Data
A catalogue record for this book is available from the British Library

Library of Congress Cataloging-in-Publication Data
A catalog record for this book has been requested

ISBN: 978-1-032-27578-9 (hbk)
ISBN: 978-1-032-26949-8 (pbk)
ISBN: 978-1-003-29339-2 (ebk)

DOI: 10.4324/9781003293392

Typeset in Times New Roman
by Apex CoVantage, LLC

To my sons and grandsons

Contents

Acknowledgments

Intuition

**"The intuitive mind is a sacred Gift.
And the rational mind is a faithful Servant.
We have created a Society that honors the servant.
and has forgotten the Gift."**

We want to thank Quantic Physics Prof. Ignacio Latorre for his help to clarify the former quotation not properly attributed to Albert Einstein:

Albert Einstein died in 1955. The earliest evidence known to **QI** linking Einstein to this expression appeared in the 1976 book *The Metaphoric Mind: A Celebration of Creative Consciousness* by Bob Samples.[1] The author did not claim he was quoting Einstein; instead, Samples was presenting his personal interpretation of Einstein's perspective. Boldface has been added to the following excerpts:

> The metaphoric mind is a maverick. It is as wild and unruly as a child. It follows us doggedly and plagues us with its presence as we wander the contrived corridors of rationality. It is a metaphoric link with the unknown called religion that causes us to build cathedrals – and the very cathedrals are built with rational, logical plans. When some personal crisis or the bewildering chaos of everyday life closes in on us, we often rush to worship the rationally planned cathedral and ignore the religion. **Albert Einstein called the intuitive or metaphoric mind a sacred gift. He added that the rational mind was a faithful servant. It is paradoxical that in the context of modern life we have begun to worship the servant and defile the divine.**

Several researchers have been unable to locate a statement by Einstein matching this expression, though Einstein did speak highly of intuition. Samples articulated his opinion about Einstein's beliefs more than once.

All the components of the local Organizing and Scientific Committee spent many hours of their time for two years and a half, meeting and dreaming the Bion

2020 XI Conference into being: a patience and constancy which deserve plenty of gratitude to Esperança Castell, Josep Oriol Esteve, Elena Fieschi, Lluis Isern, Jose Antonio Loren, Carmen Miranda, Montserrat Pol, Mabel Silva, Carlos Tabbia, Maria Alicia Vinent. In special, the valuable suggestions by Giorgio Corrente with his long experience in the organization of Bion Congresses. Special mention deserves my small Bion study seminar (E. Castell, LL. Isern, M. Pol, M. Silva, A. Vinent) with their constant deep work in discussing the Congress papers.

All my gratitude to Howard B. Levine, the Bion Series Routledge's editor, for his great help in providing guidelines for the selection and working through of the papers to be published. To Chris Mawson (recently passed away) and Nicola Abel-Hirsch for their help to find the quotation from Bion in New York and Sao Paulo. Finally, I would like to stress the enthusiasm that the theme of the Congress aroused, reflected in the quantity, quality, and depth of individual papers we received, twice as many as we had been able to include in the time and space available. We are grateful to all the contributors.

Note

1 1976, The Metaphoric Mind: A Celebration of Creative Consciousness by Bob Samples, Quote Page 26, Addison-Wesley Publishing Company, Reading, Massachusetts. (Verified on paper).

About the editors and contributors

Jaume Aguilar i Matas is a doctor in medicine, psychiatrist, and full member of the Spanish Psychoanalytic Society. He has worked for many years in the neuro-psycho development of cerebral palsy in children and has directed for some years the Department of Mental Health of the Hospital of Sant Pere Claver in Barcelona. Recently, he has developed a musical work as a composer. The two published CDs can now be found in the web at www.jaumeaguilar.cat.

João Carlos Braga is a full member, training analyst and supervisor at the Brazilian Psychoanalytic Society of São Paulo and Psychoanalytic Group of Curitiba.

Gisèle de Mattos Brito is a psychoanalyst, full member and training analyst of the Psychoanalytic Society from Minas Gerais (SBPMG), Brasil; full member of the Psychoanalytic Society from São Paulo (SBPSP), Brasil; Former president of SBPMG; Professor and supervisor. Since 2009, has coordinated Bion's Supervisions Seminars at the Society of São Paulo. Co-editor with Howard Levine and Junqueira Mattos, the book *Bion in Brazil – Supervisions and Seminars* (Karnac, 2017). Author of many book chapters and scientific papers published in regional, national and international psychoanalytic reviews.

Alessandro Bruni, M.D., was originally a biologist. He gave his dissertation thesis on altered states of consciousness with Nobel Prize recipient Daniel Bovet, prof. of psychopharmacology at Rome's University La Sapienza. He has been working in private practice in psychoanalysis and groups from 1980. He is now a psychoanalyst, training and supervising analyst of the Italian Psychoanalytical Society (SPI), founding member and training analyst of the Italian Institute of Group Psychoanalysis (IIPG) (of Bionian trend), member of Synaptica – Mind-body Research Center, supervisor in public health services in many Italian cities.

Robert Caper, M.D., is a psychoanalyst in private practice in New York City. He has lectured and taught extensively in North and South America, Europe and Asia and is the author of numerous psychoanalytic papers and four books: *Immaterial Facts: Freud's Discovery of Psychic Reality and Klein's Development of His Work, A Mind of One's Own, Building Out into the Dark,* and most recently *Bion and Thoughts Too Deep for Words.*

Arnaldo Chuster, M.D., is a member of the Brazilian Psychiatric Association and Rio de Janeiro Psychiatric Association; a psychoanalyst and training and teaching analyst at Rio de Janeiro Psychoanalytic Society, IPA; professor at W. Bion Institute in Porto Alegre; has authored eight books in Portuguese about Bion's ideas and a book in English, *A Lonesome Road: Essays on the Complexity of Bion's Work*.

Ignacio Gerber is a psychoanalyst practicing in São Paulo, Brazil. Previously, he was a full professor of soil mechanics and foundation engineering at Mackenzie University, also in São Paulo. Author of about 5,000 projects of foundations of large structures, he began his psychoanalytic training in 1980 at the Brazilian Society of Psychoanalysis of São Paulo, of which he is currently an effective member and teacher. He has books and articles published in Brazil and other countries. He is also an amateur musician active as a cellist and choir conductor.

Antònia Grimalt, M.D., is a training and supervising analyst for the Spanish Society (SEP-IPA) and the Spanish Federation of Associations of Psychotherapists (FEAP), as well as a child and adolescent training analyst for the former Hans Groen Prakken Institute (EPI). She is former chair of the Forum for Child Psychoanalysis (FEP) and is a member of the Ed. Monografies de Psicoanàlisi i Psicoteràpia. She has taught on the works of Klein and Bion at multiple universities and has edited works on Bion, Pere Folch, Matte Blanco and Ricardo Lombardi in both English and Catalan. In 2020, she chaired the International Bion Meeting in Barcelona.

Howard B. Levine is a member of APSA, PINE, the Contemporary Freudian Society, on the faculty of the NYU Post-Doc Contemporary Freudian track, on the editorial board of the *IJP* and *Psychoanalytic Inquiry*, editor-in-chief of the *Routledge Wilfred Bion Studies Book Series* and in private practice in Brookline, Massachusetts. He has authored many articles, book chapters, and reviews on psychoanalytic process and technique and the treatment of primitive personality disorders. His co-edited books include *Unrepresented States and the Construction of Meaning* (Karnac 2013), *On Freud's Screen Memories* (Karnac 2014), *The Wilfred Bion Tradition* (Karnac 2016), *Bion in Brazil* (Karnac 2017) and *Andre Green Revisited: Representation and the Work of the Negative* (Karnac 2018). He is the author of *Transformations de l'Irreprésentable* (Ithaque 2019).

Carmen C. Mion, M.D., is a full member, supervisor and training analyst at SBPSP, at FEBRAPSI, at FEPAL and IPA. Professor at the Institute of the SBPSP and at the Postgraduation Course of Psychoanalytic Psychotherapy on the Discipline "Bion's Contribution to Psychoanalysis" at the UNIPE, University at Sao Paulo. Chair of the Psychoanalytic Training Study Group linked to the Scientific Board at the SBPSP. Graduated as a neurologist at the Medicine School at the University of Sao Paulo (USP) and postgraduate in the Department of Psychiatry at the University of Iowa College of Medicine with Prof. Nancy Andreason. Member of the Comissión de Educacion of FEPAL, 2008–2012.

Member of the IPA's Education and Oversight Committee from 2012–2017. Member of IPA Task Force for Evaluation of the Relationships between IPA and the Components Societies and Study Groups from 2015–2017. Private practice with adults and adolescent patients, supervisions and study groups on Freud's and Bion's theories.

Simona Morini is associate professor of philosophy and decision theory at Università IUAV di Venezia. Her research and publications concern the nature and characteristics of non-demonstrative rationality and the analysis of ways of conceptualizing uncertainty in different research fields: probability theory and statistics, decision and game theory, scepticism and, in general, epistemology, history of ideas and ethics. Among her books is *Il rischio. Da Pascal a Fukushima* (Bollati Boringhieri, Torino 2014). Her latest publication is "Reinventare la politica. Tecnologie civiche e gestione della complessità" in L. Taddio, G. Giacomino (a cura di), *Filosofia del digitale* (Mimesis Edizioni, Milano 2020).

Lia Pistiner de Cortiñas, Ph.D., is a lawyer, psychologist and training and supervising psychoanalyst, full member of SAP (Argentine Society of Psychoanalysis). Full member of the International Psychoanalytic Association (IPA). Post-graduate professor of the Faculty of Psychology of the Buenos Aires University and of seminars on Bion's ideas and work, and of theory of psychoanalytic technique at the University Institute of Mental Health (IUSAM) of APDEBA (Psychoanalytic Association of Buenos Aires) and seminars of post-Kleinian authors in SAP.

Annie Reiner is a senior faculty member and training analyst at The Psychoanalytic Center of California (PCC) in Los Angeles. Her work was greatly influenced by Wilfred Bion, with whom she studied in the 1970's. She is widely published in journals and anthologies and the author of three books – *The Quest for Conscience & The Birth of the Mind* (Karnac 2009), *Bion and Being: Passion and the Creative Mind* (Karnac 2012), and *Of Things Invisible to Mortal Sight: Celebrating the Work of James S. Grotstein* (Ed.) (Karnac, 2016).

Goriano Rugi, M.D., is a psychiatrist and psychoanalyst with training functions of the Italian Group Psychoanalysis Institute, and former director of the Psychoanalysis School of Milan (I.I.P.G.). He lives and works in Verona. He has published works in Italian and foreign magazines and edited the volumes *Il Sapere e lo scarto*, Edizioni Kappa, 1985; *Il Campo gruppale*, with E. Gaburri, Borla, 1998; *La dimensione estetica nella clinica*, Alpes, Rome. For the types of FrancoAngeli he published, *Trasformazioni del dolore* (2015) and *Diagnosi e disturbi mentali* (2018).

Paulo Cesar Sandler, M.D., M.Sci., H.M. Fa.B., honorary associate, Accademia Lancisiana, Rome, training analyst, SBPSP, psychiatrist at IMREA – Hospital das Clinicas, São Paulo Medical School of University of São Paulo; author of many books about Bion, including the world reference dictionary of concepts,

The Language of Bion, the three-volume series *A Clinical Application of Bion's Concepts*, and the two-volume series *An Introduction to A Memoir of the Future, by W. R. Bion* by Routledge. Dr Sandler is also the translator of Bion's works into Brazilian Portuguese and co-organizer of the first international meetings about the work of Bion, at first held within the Congresses of IPA (from 1992 to 2002) and later independently organized in many cities in the world. He also is the author of many papers dealing with clinic and transdisciplinary works drawn from Freud and Bion's observations.

Renato Trachtenberg (Brazil) is a psychiatrist, full member, training and supervising analyst for the Brazilian Psychoanalytical Society of Porto Alegre (IPA). He is full member of the Buenos Aires Psychoanalytical Association (IPA) and full member of the Psychoanalytical Studies Center of Porto Alegre. He is co-author of the books *The Seven Capital Envies* with Arnaldo Chuster (Artmed, Porto Alegre, 2009 and Lumen, Buenos Aires, 2010) and *W.R. Bion: The Complex Work* with Arnaldo Chuster and Gustavo Soares (Sulina, Porto Alegre, 2014). He has also written articles and papers for many psychoanalytical journals, magazines and books.

Introduction

Antònia Grimalt

Like Freud and Klein, Bion mythologized a great existential conflict within each of us. Freud saw the struggle between instinct and civilization, and Klein between love and hate. Bion described a deep tension between a basic need for emotional knowledge and the human tendency to avoid meaning, because emotional knowledge so often brings painful realizations and the conflict between feeling emotions or getting rid of them. The analyst, as well as the patient, ambivalently approach thinking that may cause mental pain and may propel unconscious decisions to evade, modify, or even pervert the process of making meaning. Nascent thought raises the potential for pain because it alerts the individual to a painful "missing." Absence of the object (including the object of knowledge such as the complexity of one's feelings) stimulates thinking to the extent to which one is able to tolerate frustration.

The primary pre-conflict love–hate area, linked to the knowledge of the object and reality, poses the dilemma between ambivalent vivid emotions and its absence. At the primitive levels of construction of the experience, there appears in the first place the dialectic between feeling and thinking emotions or getting rid of them, evacuating emotional experience. At these archaic levels, the pain caused by the absence of satisfaction can be experienced as a void, a nothingness. The pain provoked by the absence of the object cannot be differentiated from its absence and is replaced by a non-emotion. The absence of emotion (emptiness), non-emotion (or area of negativity), would be analogous to "past" and "future" that remain in the place where the present was, before time was annihilated: the area of non-existence is created (Bion 1962). This area does not function as a static void but as a voracious object that devours meaning and sucks into the void. Then space is not an area where human relationships could develop, nor the notion of time through interplay presence ↔ absence. It is rather the presence of an inhuman absence that must be expelled from the consciousness at any cost: Static Splitting and Transformation in Hallucinosis come into play (Grimalt 2007).

Bion's life, permeated by the experience of two cultures, was marked by traumatic experiences of separation and loss. The early separation from the parents and living together within the emotional anonymity of a boarding school may have induced distance and emotional withdrawal as a defense against the pain

DOI: 10.4324/9781003293392-1

of loss. He became a specialist in the psychology of voids and present absences, giving it such relevance that we can easily equate it to the appearance of negative numbers in the history of mathematics (Lopez Corvo 2002). An ineffable realm of minus, immaterial counterpoint of any materialized reality but experience-able, intuitable and usable, as Paulo Cesar Sandler raises in his paper. Thought is established on the emptiness of a thing, always implying a binocular vision that includes its presence and its absence.

Bion's insistence on learning from experience establishes the difference between knowing and becoming as an *experiential process* of the mind as a "container" *in relation to* its contents of sensations, feelings, dreams, and thoughts: a *bi-modal relationship* (Bion 1962b) as a foundation of the capacity to think. He was asking the reader, in the very act of reading, to live an experience of "meeting" with the text, beyond the rational or logical, allowing what is intuitively relevant to emerge through a vision that clarifies obscurities and obscures clarification.

He illustrated Kant's statement, "Intuition without concept is blind, and con-cept without intuition is empty," in a very explicit way:

> The individual is intuitive but does not match it with any concepts. If Klei-nian theory has anything to do with the real facts, infants must be marvelous Kleinians because they know all about what it feels like, but they have no concepts, they cannot write any of these great books – their concepts are blind. Later on, they have forgotten what it is like to feel terrified; they pick up these words, but the words are empty – "I'm terrified": You have to notice that it is an empty phrase, it is a concept, it is only verbal; the intuition is missing. If we can draw attention to this fact, then possibly the concept of terror and the feeling could be married. The analytic procedure is an attempt to introduce the patient to who he is, because whether he likes it or not that is a marriage which is going to last as long as he lives. When the patient talks about terror, he really knows what he is talking about. It is useless for the ana-lyst to talk about some psychoanalytic theory unless he can say, "This is it."
>
> Bion in New York and Sao Paulo (the complete works
> of W.R. Bion | volume viii p. 274)

When there is no co-operative mental intercourse, a theory or idea is a sterile, concrete fact that can be stored in the mind as a memory but is no longer ame-nable to fluid use in creative thinking. In describing the difficulty of defining a psychoanalyst, Bion (1975, quoted by A. Reiner p. 27) said, "You could say the mental experience and the sensuous experience had been making love to each other – hence the psychoanalyst."

In a Supervision in Brazil:

> I think that the difficulty is how to harmonize or how to marry our ability to think with our ability to feel. Now it is no good becoming so intellectual that we do not have any feeling at all. On the other hand, there is the problem that

if we allow ourselves to be feeling people, then how is it possible to avoid a situation in which our capacity to feel overwhelms our capacity to think? So, I think that there is always this sort of *storm* going on inside us. Sometimes the waves of thought rise so high that our capacity to feel is submerged. Sometimes our capacity to feel rises so high that our capacity to think is submerged!

This is the sort of thing that happens to me, or any of us, when we lose our abilities to think, because of the experience of panic, fear . . . or lose our capacity to fear, so that we do extremely dangerous things, like waging war.

Junqueira de Matos, Bion in Brazil (2017, p. 23)

Bion dedicated his life to accomplish, to forge a new and effective language for what he did call sometimes "the game of psychoanalysis". *Intuition* seems capable of doing the job: the analyst within the inevitable turmoil of emotions needs to be quick and instinctive or intuitive so as to weave and contain with the patient the analytic object. The passion for truth underlies and informs the genuine intuition and receptivity, which overlaps trust in exploring the unknown.

In their interesting paper on Bion's supervisions in Brazil, João Carlos Braga and G. de Matos Brito point out intuition as the concept most implicitly present in Bion's clinical thinking but also the least explicit. There, the theme of intuition is sometimes addressed directly, but what is most interesting is that one can follow Bion exercising his own intuition to identify and elaborate facets of psychic reality. The authors identify and correlate the presence of intuition in different states of mind corresponding to the evolutionary periods of Bion's thinking: intuition evolving in a state of mind proper to the dimension *of knowing*. Intuition evolving in a state of mind proper of *being in unison with reality*. Intuition as an experience of *receptiveness to thoughts without a thinker*.

The interesting dialogues between Bion and Myself in *A Memoir of the Future* (Bion 1991, I. 43) illustrate the complexity of conceptualizing, describing, and contrasting intuition with other terms.

ALICE: Your intuition seems to be like what is left when the thought has disappeared.
ROLAND: Or like the thought when the concept has gone.

In the *Past Presented* (Bion 199, II.4), there appears a character which Bion calls Du as a formulation of an *imaginative conjecture* representing an idea striving to escape from the confines of Roland's mind.

H. Levine considers in his chapter how Freud's clinical experience forced him to acknowledge that constructions may function dynamically in the analytic process and the cure in the same way that the recovery of a once-repressed traumatic childhood memory did. The terms "construction" and "conviction" refer to ideas (constructions) and feelings (convictions) as end products of psychic processes arising spontaneously. A construction would be a presumptive formulation or understanding, an "imaginative conjecture", that comes to the analyst's mind unbidden in the midst of the analyst's reverie. As is any intuition, a construction is an extension in the domain of myth a necessary dimension of the analyst interpretation pointed out by Bion. Construction would be then the ideational outcome of intuition and conviction the affect associated with a sense of rightness, relief and fit.

By giving intuition a central role in the analytical work, Bion freed psychoanalysis from the bonds of a mechanistic vision of science with his bringing the understanding of its supra-scientific – and non-sub-scientific – condition. Making analogies with the realm of electromagnetic waves, Bion raises his hypothesis about the mind:

> I shall suppose a mental multidimensional space of unthought and unthinkable extent and characteristics. Within this I shall suppose there to be a domain of thoughts that have no thinker separated from each other in time, space and style. . . . I shall employ a sign that is as devoid of meaning as I can make it (compatible with retention of its capacity for communicability) Σ **(sigma)**.
>
> . . . I am supposing that there is a psychoanalytic domain with its own reality. . . . These realities are **"intuitable"** if the proper apparatus is available in the condition proper to its functioning.
>
> (Bion 1992, pp.313–315)

The war made an incisive mark on the development of Bion's personality and left traces of permanent disturbance that often appeared as ghosts of memory. The "thalamic terror" involving a never-ending emotional process to bear an intense psychic pain remained active in the mind as an indecipherable and unrepresentable essence, unable to express. His later success in gathering up the pieces of this mental explosion probably helped fuel his impressive creativity, as Annie Reiner points out in her chapter (quoting Bion): "Most people experience mental death if they live long enough. You don't have to live long . . . all you have to do is be mentally alive."

The lessons painfully learned brought Bion to name the struggle to transform and represent the previously unrepresented and unrepresentable – i.e., to preserve the capacity to think by containing catastrophic anxiety in order to manage in life and make it less traumatic and therefore bearable – as a central goal of psychic functioning. As H. Levine says: its necessity follows in part from the fact that a *major task of the human psyche is representation of the previously unrepresentable*. This is an endless task in which the inherently traumatic sensations of being alive and suffering Existence are contained, ameliorated, and made somewhat more tolerable.

In this never-ending processing of trauma, we find Bion (1992), sixty years after Amiens, cogitating:

> Once more the world has reached the kind of place in its journey round the sun which it occupied in the battle of Amiens (August 1918) . . . the ghosts look in from the battle again. . . .

This experience is similar to others I have had in the past, but the similarity refers only to the known facts, not to the unknown. In this respect there are new experiences – unlike any Eight of August of the past – not least when Francesca and I visited Shelley and Keats museum in Rome. We both found it an extremely profound and moving occasion, as if we were indeed participating in an experience in which Shelley was still alive.

Bion 1992 (p. 368)

He was tremendously impressed by Shelley's description of Keats as a greater man. . . .

So much generosity triumphed over hatred and rivalry and envy. These poets and artists have methods of recording their awareness of some kind of influence, stimuli that come from without, the unknown that is so terrifying and stimulates feelings so powerful, not to be described in common terms. They have to be considered to be perceivable only to the extent that the human being has thalamic organs and thalamic experiences and as if the human mind itself, described in physical terms, were a central nervous system developed only as far as the thalamus, thus leaving no real synaptic communication between the thalamus and the subsequent developments of the mind, the neo-pallium, or whatever the appropriate term for it should be.

Cogitations 1992 (8/8/1978, p. 369)

He pointed to embryonic intuition as part of the endowment of a personality to the perception of what he called "embryonic sense of reality, embryonic sense of sense, transformed for use in a non-sensuous domain of thought without a thinker, from thoughts in which a thinker is itself of the essence of thought" (Bion 1991, p. 122).

Poetry was of central importance for Bion all his life, as were music and art. He projected to compile an anthology of poetry for psychoanalysts. Not, he said, for anyone who is merely *called* a psychoanalyst, not the label of certification, but the "real thing". The pieces were to be selected, not for the practice of psychoanalytic virtuosity in giving so-called "psychoanalytic" interpretations, but because a psychoanalytically expanded capacity would fit the reader to have a new experience, however familiar he might think he was with previous experience of the words (F. Bion 1981). Thanks to Francesca Bion, we are able to know what he wrote as an introduction:

It is easy in this age of the plague – not of poverty and hunger, but of plenty, surfeit, and gluttony – to lose our capacity for awe. It is as well to be reminded by the poet Herman Melville that there are many ways of reading books, but very few of reading them properly – that is, with awe. How much the more is it true of reading people. I resort to the poets because they seem to me to say something in a way which is beyond my powers and yet to be in a way which I myself would choose if I had the capacity. The unconscious – for want of a better word – seems to me to show the way "down to descend", its realms have an awe-inspiring quality.

(Quoted by F. Bion 1981)

What is requested from the analyst in order to maintain contact with the psychoanalytic objects is to be capable of standing in intuitive states of mind. A psychoanalytic theory that offers a concept to reify or promote blind or mistaken intuitions may be transformed into a paramnesia, something to fulfill unbearable emptiness, what Bion often called our "bottom of deep ignorance".

If we consider that there is a thing called a mind or a character, is there any way in which we can verbalize it, which is not a complete distortion? The mathematicians talk about "quantum intermediacy", something unknown in between. We can imagine some sort of a screen onto which these various elements project themselves. For example, Picasso paints a picture on a sheet of glass so that it can be seen from either side.

(Bion 1976, p. 318)

The practice of psychoanalysis is largely dependent on intuition of what has been felt within the moment of discovery. We must be able to transform what we have intuitively felt into a formulation. This formulation, allowing us to link analysis to knowledge, does not pretend to be true in the hard sciences but only true in the emotional sense, as Robert Caper shows us in his chapter.

There are many things, especially in living matter and particularly in the complex manifestations of human thought and activity, that are intangible and that cannot be reduced to mathematical formulations. Intuition and feeling are just as real tools of the mind as the intellect, and they need not to be forgotten. The analyst listens, using his knowledge and his intuition, and should be legitimately concerned with the psychological obstacles within himself. We could describe Bion's intuition as a kind of seeing and knowing that pierces the veil of sense and reveals "non-sense" as a directly lived experience.

Bion argues that the effective interpretation should bridge the gap between knowledge learned and truth lived. Within the context of this gap between reality and unreality, he contends that "The interpretation must do more than increase knowledge" and asks, "Is it possible through Psychoanalytic interpretation to effect a transition from knowing the phenomena of the real self to being the real self?" Interpretations that simply increase knowledge maintain "the inaccessibility of 'O', and "postpone 'O' indefinitely" (1965, p. 147–149). From this perspective, accumulations of empirical knowledge function to occlude truth. Clinically, the analyst can offer interpretations that are true to the facts but block the unfolding at-one-ment with the ultimate emotional truth of the patient: effective and accurate interpretations result in transformations in O (ultimate reality, truth), not simply in K (knowledge). They require a capacity for "at-one-ment" in the analyst.

In Bion's own words, "the more the analyst becomes expert in excluding memory, desire and understanding from his mental activity, the more he is likely at least in the early stages, to experience painful emotions that are usually excluded or screened by the conventional apparatus of 'memory' of the session, analytical theories, often disguised desires or denials of ignorance." His intuition led him to shift attention away from the destructiveness directed at the object through invidious attacks and instead to focus on an attack against the *linking function* that the object represents (Bion 1959). The breakdown of this linking is one of the most characteristic aspects of psychological defense (Bion 1967) and awareness of this in both theoretical and clinical realms. His subtlety was in pinpointing the less obvious but immensely powerful psychotic phenomena that appear in groups.

Thinking requires a negative realization and a process of evolution, for meaning develops over time. As Freud (1912) advised, "It must not be forgotten that the things one hears are for the most part things whose meaning is only recognized later on" (p. 112). Receptivity to the new idea requires tolerating feelings of insecurity, persecution, and depression, recapitulating the good-breast, absent-bad-breast anxieties of early childhood. The consequent mental pain must be understood and accepted as a subjective aspect of the analyst's emotional participation. In parading the same characteristics of ineffability and truth as O, intuition, too, does not seem to allow itself to be captured in one single, clear conceptual definition. The significance of intuitions would lie in their establishing an intimate connection with O, the ultimate psychic reality extending beyond everything the very mind may know (Bion 1965).

It is worth emphasizing that in some chapters, the authors underline the conceptual difference between Intuition and evolution that would appear to fall into the same area of emotional experience. Bion described them as "resembling" (and, therefore, not coinciding with) the transformation Ps⇔D, coming close to it but not the same thing, insofar as Ps⇔D is a factor of the α function and already belongs to K and the sphere of thought (Bion 1963). It is, perhaps, possible to bring out this difference from a phenomenological point of view if we observe intuition's spontaneity and immediacy, qualities that contrast with the taste of *après-coup* experienced in the forms of understanding born of reasoning, conversely. The quest for meaning implies an unsaturated quality. As Bion writes, there is "an evolution, namely, the coming together, by a sudden precipitating intuition, of a mass of apparently unrelated incoherent phenomena which are thereby given coherence and meaning not previously possessed".

According to G. Rugi, the concept of intuition has nothing to do with Bion's so-called "mysticism" but rather with his rejection of the positivist paradigm and the introduction of a new epistemology linked to Bergson, Poincaré, Husserl, and Whitehead, who refuted the positivist position that truth is reached through empirical tests, and he created a movement that provides the possibility of transcending caesuras through binocular vision. Only intuition is capable of facing the problem of grasping the psychic reality that is devoid of known sensory realization. Bion conceives intuition as a holistic cognitive modality, which belongs to the whole system and allows us to get in touch with O, with what happens in the session and the "ultimate reality" of the patient's mind. Intuition and O are therefore closely linked, and the ability to understand the transformations passes through the effective understanding of the nature of O, which however is an elusive concept, in which we feel the presence of many meanings: the idea of origin and zero; of an abstract sign that refers to infinity, divinity, and the Platonic form. Therefore, it takes on different meanings according to its contexts and levels, passing from reality itself, the absolute facts, to the godhead, the noumenon, the infinite, and the absolute truth. He goes on, establishing the difference between insight and intuition: Insight implies an awareness of the logical relationships between a problem and an answer; in intuition there is only a rapid, sudden, feeling of coherence, without any logical, rational connection. It is a presentiment that is felt in the body, a flash of consciousness, which reveals the unknown and maintains the link with the invisible and the infinite. Intuition can therefore precede the insight, but it does not coincide with it.

In *Transformations*, Bion differentiates an "intuitive psychoanalysis" from an "axiomatic psychoanalysis", considering the former more suitable for representing genetic stages and the latter to represent the use made out of them.

Starting from the classical mathematics of Aristotle and Euclid and Isaac Newton's classical physics, which do not admit contradiction (the Positivists references to which Freud had access), Bion boldly entered the contemporary creations of a science that admits ambiguity, paradox, infinity, and the inevitable implication of the observer. As Gerber points out in his chapter, Bion's ideas can be understood within an historical context in which illusory temporal certainties of conscious logic opened themselves to the radical, timeless uncertainty of unconscious logic. Ambiguity and uncertainty broke the limited barriers of rational certainty and confronted it with the Infinite: from Newtonian determinism to the probabilistic randomness of quantum mechanics. The Unconscious is the most striking example of the concrete existence of the "Infinite in Act", which constitutes us as human beings and that the possible apprehension of his interference in the field of the "conscious finitude" is given in an attitude of "Intuitive Attention" of the analyst. In an attempt to illustrate Caesura, a dear term to Bion, Gerber appeals to musical listening between a finite and infinite experience. All auditions are valid and important both aesthetically and intellectually and also emotionally. But there are times when we are captured by the music and forget everything we learned before and that we know now, and we give ourselves to music in a radically pleasurable experience. It has no more composer or interpreter or listener; perhaps we are bold discoverers of a music that exists, waiting to be discovered, infinite.

The model that best approximates the use of observation (finite conscious) and intuition (infinite unconscious) is Bion's proposal of "perception of a germ of an embryonic idea". Similar to binocular vision, there is a moment when observation and intuition come together in the analyst's mind and the "focus" happens: this is the moment when the analyst "sees" (feels, captures) that the impression about the patient or what is going on at that moment that was taking shape, perhaps growing in his mind, suddenly becomes "visible". This is the subject that

Carmen C. Mion considers in her chapter: the development of this process will depend on the analyst's psychic qualities that will be communicated to the patient through the affective channels of communication and their inevitable impacts on the patient's mind. Welcoming the object with freedom, patience, mature compassion, respect, and tolerance enables the growth of the threads forming the meshes of the continent reticulum to be filled with different emotional contents ($♀♂→∞$). In order for dreamlike thoughts and binocular perception to be possible, the analyst must have a tolerance for doubt and a sense of infinity, a certain negative capability as the ability of a man to be in uncertainties, mysteries, doubts, without any attempt to reach fact and reason.

The presence of the analyst's subjectivity acquires greater importance, with all its possibilities and limitations, as the observation ↔ intuition is linked to the analyst's conscious/finite↔unconscious/infinite "binocular vision". The contact barrier, which not only maintains but also gives rise to the differentiation between conscious and unconscious, is formed by alpha-elements presenting one face to conscious and another to unconscious. When Bion presented his alpha-function theory, he introduced the idea that conscious awareness and unconscious capture would occur simultaneously, likewise the binocular vision. At his seminars in Tavistock, he takes up this model as an approximation to the "perception of a germ of an embryonic idea", which at first appears unfocused and somewhat confused and creates a sense of discomfort until the "focus" happens. Although Bion was not explicit, this is the model that best approximates the use of observation (finite conscious) and intuition (infinite unconscious) by the analyst in the analysis room.

From a selection of contributions of the XI International Bion Conference in 2020, this book examines the many ways in which the authors conceive the concept of intuition in their theories and developments. Intuition, as a fleeting concept is a huge theme full of nuances and different ways of associating and differentiating with other concepts in the historical evolution in Bion's thinking. It tries to convey something of what happened but is unquestionably limited by verbal formulations: for something that occurred was a living event, a real emotional experience. So it is *itself* an effort "to make the best of a bad job", trying to transmit something of the aliveness, of what one is able to reflect about this living experience. An experience that, after the pandemic turbulences that followed afterwards, became something to be kept and treasured in mind in front of future uncertain perspectives, in a present cruel and inhuman state of confinement.

The first part of the book will be focused on the panel's presentations. A second part is composed by free communications related to theoretical developments about intuition in Bion's thinking. I proceed to briefly summarize the composition of the three sections.

Intuition . . . beyond (La intuició, . . . més enllà)

After considering the role of intuition in other areas of scientific discovery, we proposed a multidisciplinary panel, offering a plurality of ideas to introduce the theme in the perspective of other sciences. A philosopher, a quantum physicist, and a psychoanalyst and music composer offered us their thoughts.

Simona Morini (philosopher), in "Intuition and the Chinese room", tried to refute the belief that a machine can reach thinking and questioned what means understanding, emphasizing the importance of intuition. In the discussion, the link between understanding and intuition was questioned, as understanding would be a second step in the process of intuiting.

"Quantic physics, the search for the invisible, interpellated scientists and philosophers in a field of speculative thinking, deeply fruitful, which unfolds in several artistic and cultural languages". Its principles are especially adequate to Bion's analogy of a psychoanalytic domain with its own "intuitable" realities: quantum physics breaks the classic physics determinism and introduces *randomness, superposition, interweaving, entanglement, indetermination, paradoxes*. Many terms have been adopted to describe the dynamics of the psyche through analogies.

Jaume Aguilar i Matas, in "Music. Deep unconscious and intuition", considers the mental processes associated with the creation, raising the need of transforming "non-mentalized" sensory impressions. When Bion poses the "opacity of memory and desire", he is asking room for no coherence, because coherence between scattered elements can generate at times a false "selected fact". Starting from Kant's idea that "the intuition without concept is blind", he presents, in a very new format, the creative process of a musical composition: "Besada d'ona" (Wave Kiss), progressively encased in meaning and sense through several contributions and finally through words with a haiku by Jordi Sala. Bion ceased to center his attention on the process of representation and began to focus instead on what happens in this state of non-differentiation, which had never before been represented; the intuition allows us to capture things that we otherwise wouldn't be able to reach.

Wanderer . . . there is no path

Renato Trachtenberg, in "Intuition in a spectral model of the mind. On caesuras, bridges, and other crossings", proposes to include intuition in a spectral model of the mind while working on the topic of caesura and considering intuition as a linking concept. For him, the concept of interference (which he relates with the "entanglement" of quantum physics) is fundamental: the meeting that affects both members of the couple and no of the one to the other. "When looking for causes the what of intuition is missing". In the intuition, it is important to have in mind the psychotic functioning. Bion's model of thinking frees us from causality, evolution, fanaticism, morality, and comparison between ideas or mental states, as the author describes in his spectral model of the mind.

Alessandro Bruni, in "Apocalypse → revelation. The ways of intuition", after an interesting tour around etymological archaeology, proposes two types of exercises for the analyst to stretch his *"mental muscles"*. The first one concerns the mental structure inside the session. He suggests "opacifying" memory and desire and practicing "hallucinosis". And second, a theoretical exercise, working outside the session: the need to assimilate and dispose a suitcase of abstract theoretical elements as light as possible, extracted through an alchemical distillation from those psychoanalytic theories considered most essential and of general proven validity. These are the "*Elements of Psychoanalysis*" proposed in analogy to the "*Elements of Geometry*".

Arnaldo Chuster's chapter, "Psychoanalytical intuition in dream and waking life. Their relations to caesura, imagination and language of achievement", aims at freely investigating links between the *psychoanalytical act* (interpretative work) and the *poetic act* and the mystery that compels us to think and create. His focus on the commensal container/contained relationship leads him to a number of questions, to the point of becoming entangled to correlate intuition, imagination, thought, ethics, poetry, and psychoanalysis from the vertex of complexity. He proposed Intuition as the psychoanalyst's "north star".

Intuition . . . a matter of two

Even though the moment of discovery seems to emerge out of nowhere, it is in fact the fruit of a long suspension in the unthinkable, undreamable, and inarticulate, reflecting a great deal of unconscious work that has taken place by the analytic couple, primarily in the analyst's mind.

Robert Caper, in "Intuition and science", describes how Bion talked of psychoanalysis as a science but did not think there was a need to establish its scientific nature as with other disciplines, like neurosciences. Bion distinguishes between what natural science studies: the inanimate world, and what psychoanalysis studies: the animate world. He "conjectures phenomenologically" that underlying all our perceptions, there is an objective reality that is itself not directly perceivable. On considering Condon's research on *Self-synchrony* and *Interactional synchrony*, he suggests that our intuitions about others operate in the register of song and dance. We resonate unconsciously with the vibes sent out equally unconsciously by others, and our intuition rests largely on sensitivity to these vibes.

Annie Reiner, in "Mystic intuition and the language of dreams", raises the question that mystic is not the antithesis of scientist; Bion talked of the mystic as a synonym of genius. Considering Ferenczi's concept of traumatized "wise babies", she focused on the perspective of envisaging the potentialities and beauty of the patient to aid it at evolving rather than on the pathology. It will be necessary to renounce to the dead self (the deprived, impostor) and go at finding the authentic self, deeper and vital.

Lia Pistiner de Cortiñas, in "A thought without a thing: intuition, negative capability, and psychoanalytic function of the personality: intuition: a memoir of the future?", points to the intuition as one of the factors of reverie an makes many bridges with different concepts of Bion's theory. It is necessary to find in oneself a way to exist, to be real. The intuition is, for the psychic reality, the equivalent of the senses for the sensory reality.

References

Billow, R. M. (2000). From countertransference to passion. *Psychoanalytic Quarterly*, 69(1):93–119.

Bion, F. (1981). Memorial meeting for Dr Wilfred Bion. (1981). *International Review of Psycho-Analysis*, 8:3–14.

Bion, W. R. (1959). Attacks on linking. In *Second Thoughts*. London: Heinemann, 1967.

Bion, W. R. (1962). *Learning from Experience*. London: Heinemann.

Bion, W. R. (1963). *Elements of psychoanalysis*.

Bion, W. R. (1965). *Transformations*. New York: Basic Books.

Bion, W. R. (1967). Reverence and awe. In *Cogitations*. London: Karnac, 1992.

Bion, W. R. (1975). *Bion's Brazilian lectures II*. Rio de Janeiro: Imago Editora.

Bion, W. R. (1976). Evidence. In *Clinical Seminars and Four Papers*. London: Karnac, 1994.

Bion, W. R. (1991). *A Memory of the Future*. London: Karnak.

Bob Samples. (1976). *The Metaphoric Mind: A Celebration of Creative Consciousness*, Quote Page 26. Reading, MA: Addison-Wesley Publishing Company.

De Bianchedi, E. T. (2000). Making the best of a bad job. *Revista de Psicoanalisis Sociedad Psicoanalitica Argentina*, 7.

Freud, S. (1912). Recommendations to physicians practicing psychoanalysis. *S.E.*, 12.

Grimalt, A. (2007). Reversing perspective: Static splitting. *Time↔Timelessness. Psychoanalysis in Europe. Bulletin 61*, Grimalt.

Junqueira de Mattos, J. A., de Mattos Britto, G. and Levine, H. B. (2017). *Bion in Brazil: Supervisions and Commentaries*. London: Karnak.

Lopez Corvo, R. E. (2002). *Diccionario de la obra de Wilfred R. Bion*. Madrid: Ed. Biblioteca. Reiner, A. (2012). *Bion and Being: Passion and the Creative Mind*. London: Karnak.

First Part

Part 1

Intuition . . . beyond

Chapter 1

Tribute to Pere Folch

Antònia Grimalt

The congress event coincided with the centenary of our mentor Pere Folch, one of the founders of the Spanish Psychoanalytical Society. I will reproduce here some lines of his thinking, in connection to his position and creative development of Bion's concepts.

Pere Folch's research into psychoanalytical technique was imbued with Bion's thought. His interest in the analyst's mental processes led him to explore in the minutest detail the interactions with the patient, in which what is not said, either in words or in between words, is formalized or dramatized (enacted); or in the silence that sustains the muted music of interaction, and the process of mutual transformation, between patient and analyst. I would like to draw particular attention at this point to his emphasis on the experiential and the interactive at a time when the prevailing style focused mainly on the patient's intra-psychic conflicts.

In the vicissitudes of his intuitive impressions Folch often had recourse to the artistic vertex to articulate his experience through the music of poetry. In the article entitled "The Lyrical and the Logical in the Process of Interpretation" (Folch 2019), he situates the fluctuations in the receptive, cognitive and expressive style of the analyst between two extremes: the logical and the lyrical, acting in a constant choreography, according to whether what predominates is experience which is contained by conceptual rigor, or a more amorphous resonance, processed through the imagination, with no formalized discourse.

Like a virtuoso violinist, who moves seamlessly from the musical score to the music, Folch moves from clinical practice to poetic creation: he deploys creative intuitions which he communicates in a simple, inspiring, and original manner, while always signaling the differences between these two processes. The poet, swept along or visited by inspiration and by his or her imagination, also needs to give shape and limits on his fantasizing with the rigor of the word and the demands of poetic discourse.

Let me go deeply into this creative process by Folch:

His objective was to highlight stylistic differences between the ways in which analytical work is conducted. These differences begin to appear from the moment the analyst starts listening and persist until the interpretation is formulated. During the course of the countertransferential experience, we become aware of fluctuations

DOI: 10.4324/9781003293392-4

in the way in which we receive, reflect and express ourselves, fluctuations that are more or less moderated but which can give rise to omissions, inopportune interventions. He situates the way in which the analyst is affected by and responds to the patient between two polar opposites: the logical and the lyrical. Folch strives to link his notion of the lyrical and the logical to aspects of schizo-paranoid and depressive mental organization, at the mercy of whatever is on control of it, and, of course to Bion's concept of oscillation between these two types of organization (PS⇔D). The coexistence between logic and lyrical, the conflicts and the alternations between them find a more or less precise echo in the opposition between common sense and unrestrained emotion.

> The interpretative work begins with the analyst's capacity to engage emotionally and the way in which he engages. This capacity, and the way the analyst is affected by his patient, foster the emergence of an unconscious waking dream, in the Bionian sense (1965–1992), which more or less corresponds to the notion of reverie. This would be an initial stage of the work, followed by a second stage consisting of the communication of this waking dream to the patient. But this reverie, this dream, just like the nocturnal dream, undergoes a secondary review, which will serve to shape the third stage, the formal interpretation. Freud (1900) conceived the secondary revision (dream-work) as a means of making the content of the dream comprehensible, and sufficiently rational, depending on the requirements of the secondary process; at the same time, he regarded this revision as complementing the interpretation of the dream, so as to assuage and render tolerable to the conscious mind the phantasy that is latent in the dream.
>
> Folch 2019 (3rd vol.)

From the listening stage to the voicing of the interpretation, the mental activity of the analyst follows a trajectory that is comparable to that of anyone who dreams, whether asleep or awake. It is affected and impacted by the patient; an impact, a day residue, which becomes meaningful in the mobilization of an unconscious phantasy. This unconscious phantasy charts a complex pathway towards presence, towards consciousness, towards that which the conscious mind can tolerate. If an interpretation derives from the analyst's waking dream, – and has been worked on by his alpha function, that has transformed the impact made upon him by the patient, how is the protean, evanescent emotional experience of the session visualized internally and then expressed in words? Folch asks.

This question suggests me the concept of primary links (L, H, K) which Bion considers the emotional key of the session (in analogy with the musical pentagram key). In particular, the analyst's capacity to perceive the prevailing emotional quality of the atmosphere of the session, the "key of the session", is important as well as the quality of his own internal setting, whether it is L, H or K and what sign it has, introducing when necessary movements and inversion of sign. In which emotional key the analyst registers and transforms the emotional impact that an unconscious phantasy mobilizes? When speaking of the tropisms as primary links Bion (1963) raises the problem that if these do not find a receiving object that registers, contains and transforms, they will disappear in the void. The analyst is in charge of this process of containing and transforming the archaic tropisms deployed by the patient in the session: the emotional links of love (L), murder (H) or knowledge (K) to be contained and transformed. And all in all, it makes me think of what Folch raises about the analyst's reception and transformation Key would be related with the emotions that rule the countertransference and his capacity to contain them to give space to the reception and transformation of the patient primary links (Grimalt 2021).

Along with receptivity what is important is the quality of the emotional links between analyst and patient (or analyst, patient and supervisor), the very source of the quality of the psychic contact. It does not matter that they are L, H or K, provided they are living, true and not negative (-L, -H, -K) or null (no L, no H, no K). These links necessarily permeate also the relationship that an analyst has with his own analytic function. How much do we trust our method? How much love or hate do we bring to our work or how much indifference, routine, compromises? It does mean working *without desire but not without passion.*

The dream and the reverie of the analyst have some features in common with processes that are at work in the patient. It is true that our technique, and the technique that we would like our patients to learn, have many things in common; in fact, we think that the more free-floating our attention is, or the closer it is to the state of grace which Bion (1967) believed was characterized by the absence of memory and desire, the freer the thought and the associations of the patient become. However, although whatever the patient expresses in their words and silences is acceptable, and indeed welcome within the setting, the same is not true of the analyst, who must learn to remain silent and to speak only when it is opportune to do so. This is one of the many senses in which the interaction between the patient and the analyst is asymmetrical: the latter is responsible for using the knowledge he possesses in the service of the patient.

> There is a professionalism in the phantasizing of the analyst which distinguishes him from the patient's position. There is also a professionalism in our use of words which, in certain respects, is not dissimilar from that of the poet, which Freud draws attention to in 1907.
>
> Like the poet, we work "with working hands-on word" (Vinyoli 1973), and at good times in the performance of our tasks we can say with him "I patiently sift to the debris and then I build again".
>
> One of the relevant aspects to bear in mind with regard to the internal attitude of the analyst is the gestation and development of the interpretative work, culminating in the articulation to the patient. The present comments mainly concern what we could understand as matters of style: the receptive, cogitative and expressive style of the analyst. They address how we engage emotionally with the patient (**resonating time**); how we process in

our reverie that which has affected us (**transformation time**); and how we communicate or express the thoughts that our reverie has brought to mind (**expressive time**).

Folch 2019 (3rd vol.)

In highlighting the lyrical and the logical, Folch is referring to two contrasting nuances of the analyst's receptive, elaborative and expressive style. The poetic/lyrical way of engaging would be, initially, expressed through the analyst's intimate emotional resonance. It may be characterized by a certain anarchy, whether calm or agitated; the analyst's attention is dispersed and, indeed, prefers heterogeneity. His resonance is rich in unsuspected reflections, which discovers a secret affinity between those things revealed by the symbols. It is a state of mind in which living an experience takes precedence over understanding it.

In contrast with this poetic manner of engaging, there is a tendency to organize and hierarchize, to impose descriptive or rational sequences on the diverse stimuli that affect us. In line with Bion, Folch describes the obstacles in this process, pointing to the predominance of the desire to understand, that constrains the expansive development of the lived experience. However, it should also be borne in mind that they need each other. Lyrical expansion scatters and naturally cries out for thought to organize it. Likewise, the poet who is carried away by, or visited by, inspiration and, by the messages received through his phantasy, needs to give form and limits to his phantasizing via the rigor of the word and the strictures of the poetic discourse.

Some poets, such as Carles Riba (1953), speak of a lyrical process which begins with a message drawn from preconsciousness, or which has reached the conscious mind as a dreamlike offer, but which, in order to become a poem, must allow itself to be subjected to a conscious endeavor, in the painstaking vigilance of thought, with linguistic resources being exploited to the full.

Folch, P (2019, OC Vol III, p. 134)

In this way Folch highlights the stylistic contrast between logical processing as an ordering, syntactical and rational function on the one hand and another way in which experience and word are actualized, a more effusive way in which syntactical ordering gives way to semantic disruption, to the unexpected and to metaphorical leaps. At different stages of the interpretative work, the lyrical and the logical poles vie with each other for predominance in the mind of the analyst. Logic strives to give shape to the intuition in the form of discursive thought. If logic were to predominate, the analyst's interventions could be interrogating, maybe intrusive. They could be too influenced by rationalistic reductionism, intolerant of contradiction and paradox. By contrast, when the lyrical predominates, the unconscious permeates the phantasy-imbued intersubjectivity of patient and analyst. The lyrical and the logical, in their interaction and correspondence, could be likened to the cyclical beating of the heart, to paranoid-schizoid diastole and a depressive organizing, retreating systole around which a selected fact may crystallize (this does not mean that Folch is equating logic with a depressive integration of the inner experience, as he later clarifies).

The logical and the lyrical could be loosely compared with the frequently recalled *sense-versus-sensibility binary*, not only denoting behavior styles, but rather ways of being emotionally affected, that is, receptive styles. Sensibility would be closer to the language of poetry, sense to the world of logic. The coexistence of sense with sensibility, or logic and poetry, is complex.

> The poet J. V. Foix (1936) was particularly interested in this binary, and one of his poems alludes to it explicitly: "If only I could make reason and folly agree".
>
> G. Janer Manila seems less anxious about this when he writes "the folly that one can put into poetic play". When it is driven by intuition, sensibility reminds me of what Bion refers to as the mad/sane part of the personality.
>
> Paul Valéry (1937) also approached this idea when, in the opening class of his course on Poetics at the Collège de France, he said of the soul that "disorder is the condition of its fecundity: it contains the promise of this fecundity, which depends more on the unexpected than on the expected, more on what we do not know than on what we know".
>
> Folch, P (2019, OC Vol III, p. 134)

Logical style or poetic style are not mutually exclusive: it's really about the predominance of one over the other but without ruling out the opposite style. Thus, both styles remain interwoven. When the influence of either the logical or the lyrical is overwhelming, we are dangerously close to psychopathology. Thus, an obsessive personality may exhibit a predominance of the logical, while when in a passionate state, in certain depressive states or narcissistic structures, the lyrical attitude cannot easily be tempered by logical discourse.

The coexistence of logical and lyrical styles can also involve conflict: the logical imposes strict constraints on the poetic, or the latter becomes a sort of mischievous child which needs logic to take care of it, as Folch in his metaphorical style points to. At best, the logic and the lyrical veins can coexist in a successive or reversible container–contained relationship, in a Russian doll–like formation. This coexistence, the alternating succession of the logical and the lyrical would correspond to a good PS⇔D synergy in the Bionian sense. Undoubtedly it would be appropriate if, during the interpretative work, there were a time for poetic predominance and a time for logical predominance, a time for lyrical expansion of inner experience, of resonance and a time for verbal communication. In fact, in verbalizing an interpretation one must not only express simply and clearly what one wants to say in relation to one's waking dream; it must also adapt to the lexical and discursive ability of the patient. One must do this on occasion even when one senses the patient's reluctance to listen and understand. And it goes without saying that any inclination towards embellishment on the part of the analyst is entirely inappropriate. Choosing exquisite language betrays an enacting of a narcissistic countertransference.

> The poetic and the interpretative tasks are different. We might be affected poetically in the initial phase of the interpretative work, just as a poet is affected by external reality or by their own dreams. An analogy can be drawn between the way one is affected by reading a poem and the way one may afterwards discuss the meaning of a poem. Similarly, whilst one is affected by the development of a session, or by the creations of a patient (like the 7-year-old child I was treating who made a plasticine duck with four legs, bursting with movement, which symbolized the anguish-free mobility which the four sessions had achieved for her), the way we speak about the creation must be measured. Our attention should be focused on clarifying the situation that we are confronted with, and are sharing with the patient, clouded as this may be by their defense mechanisms and by our deficiencies.
>
> At other times, the poetic language of the patient, the increased use of metaphor in his discourse, triggered by an anguish which draws everything, including the analyst, into it, makes us less receptive than we would like to be.
>
> Folch, P (OC 2019, Vol III, p. 139)

But the interpretative task of the analyst differs from the meticulous, often prolonged activity of the poet, who may become lost in the process of sculpting words. The poet, though he may round off each stage of poetic creation, may have an indefinite period of time in which to write. Analysts, by contrast, have to articulate their waking dreams in the fleeting moment of a session when communication is most appropriate, when it is most likely to be effective. However, if the differences between the poetic expression and the third stage of the verbal interpretation are great, the analogies and coincidences are evident in the first and second stages, which Folch tries to delimit within the interpretive process as a whole:

The first stage (in line with Bion's proposal: without memory and desire) is conceived as a period characterized by ignorance, in which progressive or sudden elucidations are always so partial that they leave ample space for mystery. Here there might be certain aspects in common with the way the poet is affected. The poet is open to the dream, as Freud writes, and the poets themselves have explained in greater depth. Yet if the poet can "open (his) eyes wide to the dream", the analyst can only do so partially or intermittently, like the hare that sleeps with one eye open. To put it more precisely, he has to inhabit a complex simultaneity: He must be open to reverie *and* offer an observant, receptive presence in the continuous present of the session in relation to what the patient says and does. The analyst must be present in these ways both when the patient's communications are clearer and during those foggy moments when the analyst and the patient are, to express it once again in the words of a poet, "the hosts of the same mystery" (Carles Riba 1937).

Such moments are poetic, but they also call for more descriptive, rational reflection upon the scene that patient and analyst are enacting in the course of their interaction. Folch suggests that it is at this point that the logical takes over. Then, cognition is distilled from an emotional experience. New horizons of experience can be glimpsed and new uncertainties too. These will then also have to be addressed, perhaps lyrically. Of course, logic should not become a straitjacket for poetic expression, nor should the poetic message be reduced through the application of theory.

The second stage of the interpretative work affords us, in a rather more reflective or enquiring manner, a closer awareness of the meaning of our reverie: the most poetic and regressive aspects of the analyst's reverie interlock with the beginning of a logical orientation, reaching towards a reflection that has more to do with the secondary process. It should be said that the analyst, when he allows himself to become immersed in his dreamlike meandering, is in a rather symmetrical situation to the patient. In the analyst's waking dream, which develops out of the day residues of the patient's reflections, he discovers correspondences with that which the patient is explaining or inferring. It would seem that both patient and analyst need to metabolize the direct, here-and-now relationship by connecting to situations that are remote in time and place in order to then revert to what resembles as closely as possible what is happening in the session. These are moments when the poetic predominates, but as it develops, it also calls for a descriptive, rational reflection on the scene that patient and analyst are enacting in the course of their interaction. We need to identify variance in the logical quality of the receptive and expressive style and should in particular reflect upon the most viable ways to acquire the ostensive insights.

The third stage begins with the interpretation as it takes shape in the mind of the analyst and ends with the formulated interpretation. Sometimes the analyst will prolong this stage. He may have a clear formulation in mind but may not quite be able to arrive at an interpretation with which he is satisfied. Possible interpretations may not withstand his criticism and may be only accepted once they have already been confirmed by further material from the patient. The analyst finds this delay difficult to deal with. He is constrained by the need to feel sure that he is right before offering the interpretation to the patient. During this time, it is the logic of the analyst's cogitative style that predominates. At other times, on grasping the meaning of an internal situation that the patient dramatizes, the analyst might too quickly communicate the "truth" that he has grasped or constructed. These are moments of lyrical predominance that lack logical moderation.

When the lyrical and the logical do not interact appropriately, in the mind of the analyst, the unconscious tension might lead the analyst to betray himself with a lapse that is unhelpful to the patient. The difficulty of harmonizing intuition – which arises unexpectedly – with a minimally logical language, capable of making it comprehensible, though without defining it, causes a *lapsus linguae* or a failed act. There are shocking slips of the tongue, especially when we are interpreting. Folch, in his honest position, argues that it is a cold comfort to say that at least we are honest enough to show the symptoms. We must take advantage of them to work on the counter-transferential motivations.

Apart from the unconscious activity which determines the secondary revision of the analyst's waking dream, his conscious reception, to the insight he has achieved is also important: the degree of conviction or doubt, of credibility or incredulity, with which he experiences this insight. The unformulated interpretation enters, in the mind of the analyst, into a dynamic that is not always lineal, ranging from belief and the hope of gaining greater knowledge . . . to skepticism and doubt. If, as Britton (1998) says, the interpretation is the belief of the analyst, the degree of conviction, ambivalence and uncertainty seems to be decisive in the rhythm of the formulation, in the tone, and even the grammar of the formulated interpretation.

> If the correspondences that we can establish with our reverie (activated by the projective identification from the patient) and our imagination, seem largely credible to us, the time that passes between the discovery of a selected fact and the formulation of an interpretation will be short. The interpretation will be articulated without much caution and in the indicative tense. However, if our belief in the unconscious element we have discovered is less certain, our choice of words will reveal this; we will tend to word in subjunctive or conditional tense. The delivery formality of the interpretation will also be affected, by our degree of conviction. This will be heard, for example, in more sensual aspects of the interpretation such as emphasis, tone of voice, prosodic variation. For example, a lack of clarity in what we have understood can cause us to adopt an excessively exhortative tone. By contrast, when what we want to say presents itself to us internally as a clear insight that might bring new knowledge to light, the verbalization of it does not need any rhetorical device to enhance its expressive force.
>
> Folch 2019 (3rd vol.)

The analyst's communicative style may depend on the degree of verbal improvisation or intra-psychic prefiguring of the interpretation before it is articulated. Some analysts report that when they begin to interpret, they hardly know what they will end up saying. It is as if the words organize themselves during the act of speech itself. At a certain moment during the session, the analyst may simply find himself speaking.

> Here we find a certain similarity with the activity of the poet. Frequently, the poet does not know what he wants to say until he actually says it. Carles Riba (1937) asks himself whether the word goes before or after the experience. He says that we do not believe until we have said what we believe. Thus, "I believed therefore I spoke", as opposed to "I spoke therefore I believed".

More recently (Ferran Carbó 1990), we find the wonder of the poet on realizing that the "found" word tells him what he wanted to say. To put this in Freudian terms, only the representation of the word can make us conscious of the representation of the thing.

Folch 2019 OC (3rd vol.)

Returning to the clinical situation, when the analyst allows himself to be in a state of reverie and finds, in his waking dream, correspondences with that which the patient is explaining or implying, he finds himself in a symmetrical situation to that of the patient. As previously stated, in order to further understand what is happening in the session, both analyst and patient need to metaphorize their direct relationship in the here and now in situations that are displaced in space and time.

A good coexistence of the lyrical with the logical is necessary in the formulation of an interpretation. Such coexistence may ensure that the interpretative message is sufficiently rational but unsaturated enough to leave room for the patient to be inspired by it. Such an interpretation can animate or bring greater liveliness to the patient's subsequent communications. As I see it, this harmonious marriage of the logical and the lyrical can be expressed quite dramatically. Such dramatic expression may see analyst and patient actualize, most vibrantly, the patient's self-internal objects' unconscious drama. This actualization entails bringing into the realm of the present the unconscious that is intuited in the analyst's reverie and expressed through his word.

Folch concludes that a happy coincidence occurs when a good synergy between the logical and the lyrical in thought and feeling of the analyst makes it possible to link the patient's relational scenarios (external and internal) with their continued enactment during the session. A good coexistence of the lyrical with the logical in its formulation will allow the interpretative message to be sufficiently ordered rationally but unsaturated enough for the implicit concomitances that it awakens in the mind of the patient to animate the liveliness of the patient's communication. Such an interpretation can animate or bring greater liveliness to the patient's subsequent communications. As I see it, this harmonious marriage of the logical and the lyrical can be concretely expressed through drama in the formulation of the interpretation. This moment experienced by analyst and patient becomes a vibrant actualization of the unconscious drama between self and internal objects. This actualization entails bringing into the realm of the present the *unconscious intuited in the reverie and constructed through the word.*

Even if Folch basically speaks of reverie in this paper, I think his spirit is not so far away from Bion's recommendation of the freedom of allowing imaginative conjectures to be accepted in the intuitive process as the paper full content expresses.

A second aspect of Folch which deserves to be highlighted was the critical capacity with which he called into question idolatrous idealizations.

The title of a paper, "The Bionian Pill or a Coherent Theoretical-Technical Diagram?" (Folch 2018), ironizes concerning the escape from dogma and addresses the complexity and the infinite tensions and contradictions of primary symmetries in a universe characterized by constant emotional turbulence and expansion:

This paper was a prolific Bionian dialogue, which he shared with a group of his colleagues. He considers clinical observation in relation to the oscillating nature of the quality of psychic functions and suggests that the oscillation Ps⇔D

> . . . does not go from a creative pole to a destructive one. What is truly creative is the oscillation itself in the operation of the psychic functions. In this case, the vital collapse does not lie in one or other extreme of this pendulum swing, but in the lack of a pendulum swing, in blockages, in cantonment, in the excessive range of the oscillation, whether at the PS or the D extreme.

What are the conditions in the mind of the analyst that stimulate the PS⇔D oscillation, and what is it that maintains it when it languishes or becomes blocked? Folch replies, I quote:

> Bion's concept of the absence of memory and desire would favor an adequate oscillation in the mind of the analyst – a beneficial PS⇔D oscillation – where his or her floating attention, always held in suspense by virtue of training, would avoid visiting certain corners of the past or future, and would perform its oscillations from the immediacy of the present moment during the session. It is only this deliberate, obstinate attachment to the present that should be recommended as a means of approaching unconscious experience, in which there is no past, no future and no conditional, where everything is present continuous, were thinking and doing are one and the same thing.
>
> Pere Folch OC (2018 Vol. 2 p. 445)

Then he has recourse to the following lines of the poet

> No memory moves my thoughts.
> Now the present steals everything I bring to it.
> Now I only have eyes to see afresh.
> And a heart that submits to the new vision.
> JM de Sagarra[1]
> Pere Folch OC (2018 Vol. 2 p. 447)

Nevertheless, the to-and-fro swing is an ideal image. In the course of the experience,

> the rhythm and symmetry are very fragile, "tempo" is frivolous, the viscosity or fluidity subject at every moment to the wind that blows inside and outside the psychic reality.
>
> Pere Folch OC (2018 Vol. 2 p. 452)

To conclude, Folch gives us a schema for positive and negative PS⇔D oscillation, based on the one hand on Binocular Vision and on the other on the Sectorial Approach – Perspective Reversal, a schema which he explains in detail and with which he sets out to answer some questions and raise many more.

Note

1 Josep Maria de Sagarra, a prolific early 20th-century Catalan writer.

References

Bion, W. R. (1963). *Elements of Psychoanalysis*. London: Heineman.

Bion, W. R. (1967b). Notes on memory and desires. In W. R. Bion (1992) Cogitations.

Britton (1998). *Belief and Imagination: Explorations in Psychoanalysis*. New York. Routledge.

Carbó, F. (1990). Joan vinyloli: EScriptura poètica i construcció imaginària. Inst. de filologia Valeniana. Publicacions. Abadia de Montserrat.

Foix, J. V. (1936). *Sol i de dol*. Barcelona. L'amic de les arts p. 26.

Folch, P. (2018). Píndola Bioniana o diagrama coherent teòric tècnic? *A Obres Completes* (Complete Works) Vol. 2. Barcelona, Ed. A. Grimalt, Monografies de Psicoanàlisi i psicoteràpia.

Folch, P. (2019). Lírica i lògica en el treball interpretatiu. *A Obres Completes* (Complete Works) Vol. 3. Barcelona, Ed. A. Grimalt, Monografies de Psicoanàlisi i psicoteràpia.

Freud, S. (1900). *The Interpretation of dreams*. S-E. 4-5.

Grimalt, A. (2021). La trobada amb Bion en la clínica psicoanalítica de Pere Folch (in Press).

Riba, C. (1937). Un nu i uns ulls. A O.C., 3, Critica 2, pp. 251–252.

Riba, C. (1953). Comentari a l' "Elegia de Bierville". IN O.C., 3. Critia 2, pp. 251–252.

Valery, Paul. (1937). Oeuvres, I, p. 1340 ss. Paris Gllimard.

Vinyoli (1973). encara les paraules. Barcelona Ed. 62 (1975). Ara que és tard. Barcelona Ed. 62.

"Shapes of Silence"

"Shapes of Silence" was the music and lyrics dedicated to Folch's memory. A mourning process on absence and permanent loss, it can be found at www.jaumeaguilar.cat/en/musica-i-paraules/figures-dun-silenci/.

> So much absence
> shapes the silence.
> that draws us closer to you!
>
> The unloaded amphora
> held so many desires:
> we made them ours.
>
> Quivering leaves
> in the new air:
> old conversations are brought back.

Not all is longing
and weariness: remember
the shared joy of being alive.

Now the joy is
to embody the words
that we exchanged and joined.

We come to a great feast:
for the blooming fields,
for the harvest.

Like the highpoint
of the cherry tree when it overflows
with fruit and sap.

Like lavender
that welcomes buzzing bees
and scents the air.

The wave breaks.
Water's song
moves away from the rock.

A new day awakes lighting our pupils. You liven up a world.
Under the arid sun
the trying effort
we made to nurture new visions.

Our voices so doubtful
and a presence
that bears down on us.

And the frost, at dawn,
a tangible presence
crafted in darkness.

We ask no more of you.
If we raised questions
you would be silent.

The sea never
Ceases to overflow.
Rivers never die.
They are never lost.

Lyrics by Jordi Sala
(Translated from the Catalan by Sam Abrams)

Chapter 2

A philosopher's perspective on intuition

"Intuition and the Chinese room"

Simona Morini

A man in a room receives questions written in Chinese on a piece of paper that is slid under the room door. The man does not know a word of Chinese and does not even know that the strange signs are questions in another language. However, he consults a manual that tells him exactly, in his language, which signs to write on the paper to send back out of the door. Thanks to the "intelligence" contained in the manual, the signs he draws on the paper are answers to the questions sent. The Chinese person outside the room can therefore believe that the person inside knows Chinese (as happens in the Turing test to evaluate the intelligence of machines) even if he does not understand it and does not even understand what he is doing. Looking only at the exchange of sheets, it seems that two people are communicating in Chinese. But in fact, no real understanding of Chinese is required for the process to work. John Searle (1980b) believes that the moral of the story is that artificial intelligence does not involve an *understanding* process, at least according to the way the word is commonly used. Alternatively, one can think that the process of understanding does not consist of anything mysterious and insightful but of nothing more than the application of rules and dumb procedures.

This thought experiment – conceived by John Searle in 1980, in an essay that generated an endless controversy between philosophers of mind, artificial intelligence specialists and cognitive scientists – raises the problem of the nature and possibility of artificial intelligence and is directed against the thesis of "strong artificial intelligence" according to which "the computer is not merely a tool in the study of the mind; rather, the appropriately programmed computer really is a mind, in the sense that computers given the right programs can be literally said to understand and have other cognitive states"[1] (Searle 1980a; Searle 1982; Lepore and van Gulick 1993; Wakefield 2003). Searle's argument also prompts us to reflect on what it means to understand, know and learn. His thesis is that an artificial intelligence program can give an external observer the impression of being intelligent, for example of knowing how to use language, even though it has no real ability to do so.

But what does "understanding" mean? How can one be "intelligent" without understanding? What do the understanding of a sentence, a language, a problem, a subject, a person have in common? The philosophical debate on these questions

DOI: 10.4324/9781003293392-5

is, again, endless. There seems to be in understanding something typically human, or at least typical of the living. And also a character of immediacy, a time and a mode different from the time and mode of knowledge.

That is where intuition seems to come into play. There are things we understand immediately, without thinking. "Thought", wrote Henri Poincaré, "is a flash between two long nights". For the most part, it is a question of establishing connections or correlations between disparate objects, phenomena or elements. Intuition has the same characteristics of emerging phenomena that in some way are products of complex or chaotic systems: "flashes" that we can hardly foresee or control. There are other things that we understand with time, such as languages or other subjects of study. Here the times are longer, but the act of understanding is always somehow sudden and involuntary. You cannot teach or learn to understand, you just understand. In the example of the Chinese room, we could say that the man "knows" (or seems to know) Chinese because he can formulate the answers correctly from a series of instructions. But to be able to say that he understands Chinese, he should not only learn the words and rules of the language but also relate them to each other to express his own thoughts or to know how to connect them to the context in which a conversation takes place, to interact with other people who speak the same language. It is precisely this operation of *connecting with the context* that machines, through learning the meaning of words and rules, have so far been able to do only with difficulty.

In science, intuition is the basis of the ability to formulate hypotheses. Henri Poincaré, a scientist often quoted by Bion, maintained that the task of science is to formulate hypotheses capable to "unite elements long since known, but till then scattered and seemingly foreign to each other, and suddenly introduce order where the appearance of disorder reigned".[2] *Suddenly*: even in the formulation of hypotheses, understanding seems to be the result of intuition. If, however, anyone can formulate hypotheses in the most diverse fields, the characteristic of science is that of not accepting hypotheses that have not been "controlled" in the light of facts or experiments. It is the task of method (namely of a system of rules shared and refined over time) to justify or falsify the assumptions on the basis of the observations and data collected and to logically deduce the consequences. In order to have science, intuition must be followed by control and demonstration. Hence, once the scientific method has been applied, we should be able not only to understand but also to *understand why*, that is, to arrive at that knowledge of the causes which, starting from Aristotle, is the ultimate end of theory.

Psychoanalysis has often been criticized by scientists and philosophers of science precisely because it is not "controllable" (not *falsifiable* according to Karl Popper), and on the other hand – says Bion commenting Poincaré in several points of his work – the analyst, just like the scientist, observes a mass of "elements long since known, but till then scattered and seemingly foreign to each other" to give an interpretation. Interpretation is thus one of those "facts worthy of attention" that, according to Poincaré, "suddenly introduce order where the appearance of disorder reigned", thus making the complexity of phenomena accessible. The psychoanalyst thus helps the patient to find, thanks to his ability to formulate hypotheses, one of these unifying facts. However, while this "intuition", which is at the origin of the scientific process, is a non-problematic datum for the scientist, the psychoanalyst's interpretation is entirely addressed to the subjective conditions that make intuition possible, i.e., the "ideational" act. In Bion's words, "it is true to say that in actuality a stream of elements exists, some of which are seen to unite at a moment that, like the elements themselves, is selected by the predisposition of the observer",[3] but while the stream of elements is real and constant, the choice of the elements to be united and the particular moment in which they are united (i.e., the intuition which is at the origin of understanding) depends on the observer's predisposition and, in particular, on that process that Melanie Klein calls "synthesis of the depressive position", which is at the origin of the symbolic and abstraction capacity followed by the calculation and the method of scientific deduction. In Bion's words, "The ideational system I shall regard as relatively primitive and belonging principally to the mental dynamics by which ideas, related to objects, are formed. The scientific deductive system I regard as more sophisticated and related to the (. . .) establishing of knowledge in a form that is permanent and indestructible".[4] While, therefore, the weakness of psychoanalysis would be the lack of a scientific method and control, the weakness of science would lie in the irreducible subjectivity of the "ideational system" and therefore of intuition. Hence, Bion's thesis that "the scientific method itself lacks the 'objectivity' that is widely attributed to it, and may indeed spring from very deep-seated elements in the personality which sewed fulfilment".[5] Therefore, if the method is problematic for psychoanalysis, which formulates hypotheses that perhaps work but are not controllable, intuition (the ideational process) is problematic for science.

But what kind of science are we talking about? Many years after Searle's mental experiment, Poincaré's observations and Bion's reflections, science has changed considerably, especially as a result of the extraordinary amount of data that can be collected, the extraordinary power of computers (traditional or quantum) and the very rapid progress in the field of artificial intelligence. Let us take the case of translation in the Chinese room experiment. As long as we have tried to teach machines to translate as we would teach a human, that is, through the symbols and rules in the boxes and in the manual in the Chinese room, perhaps even trying to get them used to drawing information from linguistic behavior, no significant progress has been made. Since we have used their ability, all artificial and precluded to human intelligence, to learn by comparing avalanches of documents written in different languages and discovering correlations and regularities within them, that is learning more or less in the same way that the corrector of our mobile phone learns our language – progressively recording the corrections we have made – we have obtained results that are not perfect but definitely better. In addition, the machines used the same method to learn all the languages, without having to resort to the specific rules and characteristics of each one. Not differently, Google has conquered and revolutionized the world of advertising based on an enormous amount of data and simple mathematical algorithms without knowing anything about the functioning and rules of advertising. Bion himself, writing in his *Cogitations* about the possibility of measuring something people "feel", observes that "it is found that things, inanimate objects, are sensitive to temperature though they do not feel 'heat or cold'. What about love and hate? Are they not 'Prejudices'?"[6]

Machines, when they learn "in their own way", learn "better" – in terms of results, at least – even without understanding. These results are largely due to the success that deep neural networks have achieved in recent years. Deep learning does not represent a significant innovation in terms of the development of new computational architectures. Its advances are largely enabled by the use of more sophisticated mathematics. Moreover, the original purpose of deep learning had less to do with cognition than with engineering intent. Nevertheless, the impact on cognition has been impressive (Perconti and Plebe 2020). In many areas, such as visual recognition and language translation, previously unknown results have been achieved, and very often computer performance has surpassed that of humans.

In a much discussed article entitled "The End of Theory: The Data Deluge Makes the Scientific Method Obsolete",[7] the former director of *Wired*, Chris Anderson, reflecting on the characteristics of the Petabyte Age, on the change of scale determined by the dizzying increase of data we can collect on reality and by the new distributed calculation methods, talked about "the end of theory" or at least about overcoming the scientific models through which it is possible to know reality and formulate hypotheses on the causes and effects of phenomena.

Not unlike what medicine and other "minor" sciences have always done, today's machines are in fact able to find significant correlations and formulate hypotheses about reality that "work" even without knowing why and often without being able to control the results they produce. Every scientist learns to distinguish correlations from causes and to look for a model able to explain data. In the traditional conception of science, "data without a model is simple noise", observes Anderson. And yet the traditional scientific approach – formulating hypotheses, elaborating a model, controlling – is limited: an avalanche of data allows machines to make discoveries and formulate hypotheses, which, even if they are not controllable, and therefore do not produce scientific "knowledge" in the traditional sense, can advance what we know about the world. This also applies to physics and to many other sciences. To give an example used by Anderson, Craig Venter, sequencing the DNA of entire ecosystems, such as ocean water or air, discovered the DNA (and therefore the existence) of thousands of species of bacteria and other microorganisms never observed before and that possibly we may never be able to observe in the future. Of course, we know nothing about the morphology of these new species or their behavior. We only have a statistical blip – a sequence which, being different from all the other sequences in a database, must represent a new species and that we can correlate with other species on which we have more information. Also, in physics, many hypotheses are formulated starting from the data without it being possible, for reasons of cost and complexity, to make experiments that confirm or deny them. Despite this, science is progressing prodigiously.

Recent artificial intelligence no longer regards intuition as an obscure field of research to be excluded. On the contrary, a thriving field of research has emerged called precisely "Artificial Intuition" (Diaz-Hernandez and Gonzalez-Villela 2015; Perez 2018; Sloman 1971). Artificial Intuition enables systems to instantly identify threats, problems as well as opportunities without knowing, especially in unsupervised networks, what exactly they are looking for or being told to look for. Artificial Intuition is mostly used today in finance and banking, cybersecurity and retail and pharmaceuticals. Two different approaches have been taken on the subject. On the one hand, there has been an attempt to model how intuition is believed to work in humans (Chik D. and Dundas, J. 2011). On the other, the aforementioned non-human-like deep-neural-network route has been taken. That is, we have attempted to achieve the result of immediate understanding of the relationships in a given field of observation through inferential statistical techniques and predictive coding. The results are surprising, and it must be acknowledged that just as computers do not need an understanding of things in the human-like sense to successfully perform tasks that we are accustomed to associate with understanding, so too computers can be shown to have intuitive abilities without simulating any abilities that we would be inclined to attribute to a romantic genius.

Can we come to the conclusion that the capacity of the machines to discover patterns and to "unite elements long since known, but till then scattered and seemingly foreign to each other" means that they can have "intuitions"? And again, how can we accept these "intuitions" that are rather distant from our normal cognitive processes (no matter how we define them) and that we cannot control, justify or falsify using the "traditional scientific approach"? Should we conclude with Anderson that "correlation takes precedence over causation and science can proceed without consistent models, unified theories or mechanistic explanations"? Without causes? If we are pragmatists, yes, and this clearly would imply that science can go on – like psychoanalysis and other "soft sciences" – without any pretense of "objectivity" or truth. But this would also imply that discoveries don't necessarily spring from what we would call a "brain" but can be obtained by a new and different cognitive process.

I am sure that this conclusion is quite disappointing for everyone – for scientists because they are deprived of causes and objectivity and will probably have to revise their methods when confronted with artificial intelligence and for psychoanalysts because machines think and discover things in their own way, and we still don't know if they could dream or have an unconscious.

This kind of discussion depends on an idea of science (and of mind) that algorithms and artificial intelligence are every day changing and reshaping radically. The very problem addressed by Searle's thought experiment, "is an appropriately programmed computer really a mind?" sounds different if we consider the possibility that a complex world can require a different notion of "understanding" and can be handled only by an "extended mind", where, as noted by Clark and Chalmers in their seminal article, "a human being is linked with an external entity in a two-way inter-action, creating a *coupled system* that can be seen as a cognitive system in its own right. . . . If we remove the external component the system's behavioral competence will drop, just as it would if we removed parts of its brain".[8] The same can be said of an "extended mind" in which human beings are connected non only with "an external entity", but with other human beings and "minds", forming a "collective intelligence" capable of "understanding" the world "outside the heads" of every single individual. An interesting example is the creation of Cluster Laboratories like the Cluster Exploratory, a research program involving six universities using IBM and Google highly distributed computing resources (consisting of 1,600 processors, sev-eral terabytes of memory and hundreds of terabytes of storage) to analyze massive amounts of data and to find patterns in natural and social phenomena.

This is going to change not only science but also the way we think. We still don't know how. All forms of technologically based cognitive extensions require a long period of technological, psychological and even neurological adaptation. Early forms of writing, for example, were heavily influenced by the traditions and practices of the previous era, when information was communicated orally (the first texts were composed in "continuous writing", retaining the continuity of speech). In his book *Orality and Literacy. The Technologizing of the Word*, Wal-ter Ong has convincingly shown that "writing has transformed the human mind more than any other invention." In the beginning, writing was defined as "inhu-man" because it recreated *out* of the mind what could only exist *in* it. The same happened with print and is happening today with the web, which is still strongly influenced by the traditions and practices of the written and printed word but could take new and different forms.[9]

"Our mind is frail – Poincare wrote – as our senses are; it would lose itself in the complexity of the world if that complexity were not harmonious; like the short-sighted, it would only see the details . . . incapable of taking in the whole".[10] The "mind" of machines is not frail, it "understands" and "thinks" differently and has capacities that allow it to detect regularities and formulate hypotheses and predictions even if the complexity were not "harmonious" but totally chaotic (and this is, unfortunately, the case today). We need these capacities and new forms of artificial intuition that will become part of the cognitive tools that will evolve in order to deal with chaos and complexity. The interaction between man and technology touches the depths of the psyche and is part of the evolution of consciousness. All this seems to me to be part of the definition and evolution of "human nature", not an alternative to it.

Notes

1   Searle, J. (1980), p. 2.
2   Poincaré, H. (1993), p. 30.
3   Bion, W. (1992), p. 7.
4   Ibid., p. 5.

5   Ibid., p. 7.
6   Ibid., p. 2.
7   Anderson, C. (2008).
8   Clark, A. and Chalmers, D. (1998), pp. 8–9.
9   As an example, see Tim Berners Lee "semantic web", and the discussion about it in.
10 Poincaré, H. (1993) as quoted in Bion, W. (1992) p. 284.

References

Anderson, C. (2008). "The End of Theory: The Data Deluge Makes the Scientific Method Obsolete", *Wired* (www.wired.com/2008/06/pb-theory/).
Bion, W. R. (1992). *Cogitations, New Extended Edition*, Karnac Books, London.
Chik, D. and Dundas, J. (2011). "Implementing Human-Like Intuition Mechanism in Artificial Intelligence", arXiv preprint arXiv:1106.5917.
Clark, A. and Chalmers, D. (1998). *The Extended Mind*. Analysis Wiley Online Library.
Diaz-Hernandez, O. and Gonzalez-Villela, V. (2015). "Analysis of Human Intuition towards Artificial Intuition Synthesis for Robotics", *Mechatronics and Applications: An International Journal*, 1: 23.
Halpin, H. and Monnin, A. (eds.). (2014). *Philosophical Engineering: Towards a Philosophy of the Web*, Wiley Blackwell. New York.
Lepore, E. and van Gulick, R. (eds.). (1993 March). *John Searle and His Critics*, Wiley-Blackwell. New York.
Perconti, P. and Plebe, A. (2020 October). "Deep Learning and Cognitive Science", *Cognition*, 203.
Perez, C. E. (2018). *Artificial Intuition: The Improbable Deep Learning Revolution*, Createspace Independent Publishing Platform.
Poincaré, H. (1993). *Science and Method*, Dover Publications, New York.
Searle, J. R. (1980a). "Intrinsic Intentionality", *Behavioral and Brain Sciences*, 3: 450–457.
Searle, J. R. (1980b). "Minds, Brains and Programs", *Behavioral and Brain Sciences*, 3: 417–457.
Searle, J. R. (1982). "The Chinese Room Revisited," *Behavioral and Brain Sciences*, 5(2): 345–348.
Sloman, A. (1971). "The Role of Intuition and Non-Logical Reasoning in Intelligence", *Artificial Intelligence*, 2: 209–225.
Wakefield, J. C. (2003). "The Chinese Room Argument Reconsidered: Essentialism, Indeterminacy, and Strong AI", *Minds and Machines*, 13: 285–319.

Chapter 3

Music. Deep unconscious and intuition

Jaume Aguilar i Matas

Introduction

The aim of this chapter is to explain the importance of non-mentalized sensoriality in the creation of initial musical ideas, out of which the composer will gradually develop his increasingly complex technique. What is more, from a text attributed to Mozart on his process of composition, he emphasizes the importance of elaborating musically the objects that have overcome their partial character and achieved the status of total artistic object, which, in line with the conception put forward by Hanna Segal, enables the artist to feel the reparation of the damaged object. Then it goes on to analyze, on the basis of Bion's dictum about the need to approach the patient without memory, desire, understanding and coherence, the role played by incoherent elements during the course of the analytical relationship and the importance of not treating them as subordinate to the prevailing or determining discourse, as this could create a false selected fact. On the basis of unsubordinated and apparently incoherent elements of modern musical structure, it examines the role played by incoherent musical units in modern music and its relationship with the music inspired by certain aspects of quantum physics. It also analyses the incoherence of musical elements from within a fractal conception. Finally, it comments on aspects of a composition of my own for a string and soprano quartet and the unconscious elaboration of certain parts of it. The composition in question, "Besada d'Ona", can be found on the web at www.jaumeaguilar.cat.

At the superior margin of the web, moving over "catalan" you can find the English translation of this haiku:

> "*Besada d'ona la mar necessitada de terra digna*": "The kiss of a wave, the sea in such a need of a noble earth".

Music and sensoriality

Martin Nass, 1984, during conversations with more than 100 composers from a range of musical styles, realized that the first musical ideas had their origin

DOI: 10.4324/9781003293392-6

in preferential and extremely idiosyncratic sensory systems (visual, aural, kinesthetic, tactile). For some of them, surprisingly, even tactile sensations of smoothness and roughness could trigger the process that led to a musical idea. When we listen to music, we experience something that has never formed part of the system of symbolic verbal representation and which belongs to the sphere of nonmentalized sense impressions. Music can transport us to a certain state of ineffability, where it is no longer possible to describe sensations and feelings that transcend the linguistic system. It is a state in which subject and object are not clearly differentiated (Siegried Zepf 2013). According to Zepf, the structural similarity between rhythm, harmony and melody on the one hand and certain sensorial mnesic registers is one of the reasons music stirs our sensorial experiences from the very first months of life. This author also argues that the need felt by the fetus to reconnect with sounds which have been interrupted, in order to re-establish the continuity of the archaic auditory sensorial experience, is comparable to the need that we feel, as music listeners, to listen out for certain musical elements which the basic structure of the harmony requires. The need, for example, that a melody that is structured in a dominant chord move towards a fundamental tonic chord, in other words, that it find again the original home from which it had temporarily departed. Anthony Storr (1997) similarly argued that the perception of the harmonious structure of the music, though unconscious, is essential in order to be able to appreciate and enjoy it. From what has been said so far, we can draw the following conclusions: (1) One of the creative composer's essential characteristics is their capacity to retain and develop primary modes of corporal and sensory expression in ever-richer and more complex formulations of their musical language. (2) The composer's ability to recodify their preferred sensorial support systems, whether they be mainly auditory, visual, tactile or kinesthetic, in more complex configurations that imply the integration or articulation of the different sensorial systems, seems another important point to explain the gradual elaboration of the initial musical ideas. (3) When the creative artist enters this mnesic forest of sensations, embodied experiences and affections, they can find a rhythm, a color, a feeling, a corporal experience or a texture which can then be elaborated by their conscious self or perhaps, as Bion might say, can be dreamt by virtue of its alpha function, which is to enable the birth of a potentially creative idea.

Music and motivational systems

In 1914 Freud attributed the public's interest in a work of art to the process of identification with the artist. For Freud, however, the public identifies with the unconscious omnipotent sexual fantasies of the artist, while for Segal, 1957, the most significant unconscious motivation for this identification lies in the need to elaborate the depressive anxieties that our behavior is prompted by, from the depths of our unconscious, with the aim of repairing the damage: the repair of our damaged mental objects. In this sense, the desire to repair implies, above and beyond the need to satisfy unconscious sexual or omnipotent fantasies, an increased awareness of reality: the awareness that we have damaged, by envy or intolerance of frustration, that which is good in others or in ourselves (Klein 1946). Segal, 1991, also wonders why the work of art has such a profound and permanent impact on people. For her, it is precisely the formal and aesthetic qualities of the work of art that is most important, given that what we feel has been destroyed can be repaired by the beauty, plenitude and harmony contained in the formal perfection of a musical, pictorial or literary work of art. By an uncanny coincidence, in a letter attributed to Mozart we find paragraphs of great interest from a psychological perspective with regard to the profundity of a work of art, in this case with reference to his own process of musical composition.

> [E]verything keeps getting bigger and bigger, [he is referring to the process of composition from the initial musical ideas to the expansion and elaboration of those ideas] and I keep making it ever more extensive and clearer. And indeed, whatever the length of it, the whole thing is then ready in my head, so that I can see it all in spirit at a single glance, almost as if it were a beautiful painting or a lovely human face, and I can feel it in my imagination, not as one thing following upon another, as it must later become, but everything at the same time, in a single instant. That is truly a banquet! The task of finding and elaborating then becomes a beautiful, intense dream within my mind, but feeling it in that way, all at once, is obviously the best thing about it. What has taken shape in this way cannot easily be forgotten, and this is perhaps the greatest gift that the Lord God has given to me. When I sit down afterwards to write, I simply select from my brain what was, as I said, already assembled there. That is why writing it down on paper does not take long, for as a matter of fact, it was ready, and very rarely does it become a very different thing from what had already taken shape in my head. Therefore, when I am writing it does not matter if I am disturbed, and all kinds of things can be happening around me; I just keep writing despite everything.

It seems to me that in this paragraph Mozart eloquently expresses the importance of this gift that he received from his process of creation, which has not always followed conscious pathways; it gave him the complete work of art, the artistic object which he was able to grasp all at once in its entirety. An entire object made without a conscious effort, directly born from his deep unconscious. Following Segal it would be an object that survived fragmentation and every episode of attack and destruction and which in its aesthetic perfection repaired that which, unconsciously, he possibly felt to be damaged.

Music's deep unconscious

Vermote (2011) says that Wilfred Bion ceased, at a certain point, to center his attention on the process of representation and began to focus instead on what happens in this state of non-differentiation, which has never before been represented.

He found the unconscious-conscious notion to be too closely associated with the principle of sensory pleasure, while psychic reality is located in the non-sensory sphere. It was for this reason that he introduced the idea of the infinite–finite axis. Transformation in O (TO) can be regarded as a movement on the infinite–finite axis and, therefore, each thought is considered a conquest from the dark and formless infinite: a powerful, vital world which imparts life and from which human creativity is nourished. This, Bion's unrepressed, dark and infinite unconscious, or the infinite and symmetrical/ undifferentiated unconscious of Matte Blanco, shows a strong correspondence with the vision of Marion Milner (1969) when she argues that the unconscious mind, can do things that the conscious, logical mind cannot, being more sensitive to the similarities than to the differences between things (Matte Blanco's symmetrical properties of the deep unconscious?) restoring blood to the spirit, passion to the intuition, as Milner says, quoting Maritain.

All this makes me wonder whether this unconscious need of the artist to be more sensitive to the similarities than to the differences between things, on account of being passionately committed to finding what is familiar in what is unfamiliar, thus creating a subjectivized reality, might have something to do with not psychotic, processes of hallucinosis, which lead the analyst, in a first moment, to see reality with the greatest possible degree of subjectivity. This (Civitarese 2015) is precisely what can enable the analyst to intuit the emotional reality of the analytical relationship. A second stage begins when the analyst can explain what is really happening or happened (Nachträglichkeit) emotionally in the session.

In relation to the initial musical ideas, my view is that we could think of the process of "subjectivization" as a necessary step to explain the transformation of the sensations in a kind of stuff workable in the non-repressed deep unconscious. In accordance with this idea, it should be a possible correlation between the process of subjectivation and the symmetrical properties of the deep unconscious.

Modern music and Bion's "without memory, desire, understanding, coherence"

When Bion proposes to listen to the patient without memory, desire, understanding and coherence, I believe that what he is demanding, among other things, is that we allow for the appearance of incoherence as one of the elements that can enable us to listen, in a renewed and creative manner, to what the patient is saying. I believe that accepting incoherence means accepting incoherent elements from the patient or from the analyst's own mental apparatus. In fact, coherence between the scattered elements which form part of the selected fact, at times, result in a wrong fact being selected, as has been pointed out by some post-Kleinian authors, which tends to confirm the analyst in his or her own favorite theories or in the narrative as it is understood up to that point with regard to the mental structure of the patient in the context of the transference–countertransference binary. In the field of musical composition, there has always been, historically speaking, an impulse towards coherence. In relation to that, Dalhaus (1972) in his paper entitled "Uber den Zerfall des musikalischen Werkbegriffs", says the following: "Each individual musical instant is part of a whole, within which it is determined and to which it owes its meaning, which it would otherwise, be seen as an isolated moment, not have". This text serves to corroborate the fact that musical moments are determined by the whole piece that they belong to. According to this idea, it is disconcerting when music produces the emergence of elements which are not subject to the dominating discourse. A part of the musicians of the 20th century have played with the idea of breaking with the coherent structure of the tonal compositions, in order to elaborate other harmonic structures, unexpected musical figures or dynamics etc.

Bion (1991) in *Memoire of the Future*, argues that language can become a suit of armor that is devoid of meaning. A kind of coffin which prevents the birth of nascent thoughts and emotions. Perhaps the kind of listening that Bion demands might include the negative capability inherent in the fact of being able to have patience when a dream appears or a flash or any incoherent communicative element which we cannot understand or disconcerts us on account of its strangeness without being able to subordinate it to the syntax that has hitherto prevailed in the relationship with the patient. It is a question of living and let live that which it is not advisable to treat, from the outset, as a subordinate element. In fact, Bion thought that the appearance of uncontrolled or even wild thoughts could reflect the hatching of thoughts emerging from the dark regions of the unconscious, or a transformation of O in search of a thinker.

From the 1940s onwards, composers such as Iannis Xenakis, Morton Feldman, György Ligeti, Pierre Boulez, John Cage and Karlheinz Stockhausen, among many others, felt the need to open musical composition to abrupt changes which were felt as a juxtaposition or as incoherence (or perhaps would be better understood as a quantum leap?). Morton Feldman, for example, in his composition entitled *Piano*, after a 15-minute pianissimo, suddenly breaks into a fortissimo, which then gives way after a while to another abrupt change. Some of these types of music have been structured on the basis of quantum physics concepts such as indeterminism and complementarity, which in musical terms translate into the polarity of musical and sonorous states of continuity and discontinuity. The continuous-discontinuous is comparable to the binary wave-particle in accordance with Rocha Iturbide, 2018. In line with Martí-Jufresa, for example, Iannis Xenakis, in his composition entitled *Pithoprakta* (1955–56), makes transitions between continuous states, cumuli of glissandi, and discontinuous states, clouds of pizzicati, between states of order and states of disorder. A significant amount of this music involves a desire to break with the deterministic and causal relationships that characterized classical music prior to the 20th century, with the aim of achieving greater freedom.

In a book by Civitarese, 2017, recently revised by Ruggero Levy, the author suggests that the gap between the mother and the baby, between the subject and the object, between the body and the mind, in so far as it can be dreamt and represented, contributes to our human subjectivity. I wonder whether the transit, which is sometimes brusque, between continuous and discontinuous musical passages, between pizzicato followed by glissando clusters or between abruptly opposed musical dynamics, above and beyond the conscious intentions of the composer, might have something to do with the need to bridge the gap which might trigger the most primary anxieties of fear of death due to the loss of the object. Writing these discontinuities would entail a step towards controlling them and, indeed, representing them in some way. As regards the pace at which certain musical figures appear and disappear, it might also have something to do with the need to control primary anxieties in relation to the appearance and disappearance of the primary objects.

John Cage went to the extreme of producing random compositions in which his aim was to totally eliminate the self of the composer. Nevertheless, the question arises whether this would also result in the elimination of the intersubjective relationship, which means that there is no longer any possibility of the composer's desire that the emotions that have taken shape in his or her mind trigger associations and emotions in the listener, which does not mean imposing on them a type of listening that is dominated by a hallucinatory state. On the other hand, it would appear that however random the music might be, the composer cannot but desire that it will produce a certain effect in the listener or at least in himself. In any case, behind this random music there is always someone who wanted it to be like that.

In a deterministic conception of linear causality, the whole is the result of adding up all the parts, while in a non-linear, fractal conception, the whole is already configured in each part (Terry Marks-Tarlow 2008). In this sense we could say that an apparently disconnected or juxtaposed element of the relationship with the dominant structure of the musical discourse can represent an increase in complexity, which enables the musician to delve more deeply into the whole which is often present within the unconscious. In this sense, the juxtaposition or the incoherence, would in the end be coherent, but only in a sphere of meaning which involves greater complexity in so far as it has incorporated elements from the dark recesses of the deepest unconscious and the most primitive anxieties.

"The Kiss of a Wave" ("Besada d'ona")

The reader interested in listening to this composition can find it at www. jaumeaguilar.cat/en/musica-i-paraules-2/besada-dona-the-kiss-of-a-wave/.

I recommend first accessing the audio and then reading the corresponding text.

This composition for a string quartet with a solo voice is structured on the basis of a tone-semitone scale. It is a series of semitones (1–2), which follow, in a similar way to Bela Bartok, one of the proportions of Fibonacci's numerical series, 2-3-5-8-13-21. There are many moments when the composition develops as a structure of imitative responses in the form of a canon. It has reminded many listeners of the repetitive, oscillating movement of waves. The structure of this composition blurs the tonality and its cadences or typical phrases, thus giving the work an atmosphere of tension and disquietude. One of the musicians asked me why it had occurred to me to compose a work of this nature. At the time, I told him that I had no answer to that question. When I asked the author of the poem, a very close friend and a fellow psychoanalyst, if he was thinking of the Mediterranean tragedy when he wrote the haiku which inspired this composition, he said, "not yet, not at that time". When the musician who conducted the strings Brossa Quartet told me that the sea in this composition was very agitated and raging, and when I heard his and the musicians' interpretation of the score, especially from the 25th to the 32nd bar, where there is a crescendo and a certain acceleration resulting from a group of semiquavers, I could clearly hear and see the sea in a state of rage, demanding that the earth be worthy, crying out for a policy that would prevent the death of so many refugees and immigrants. The musical engineer who mastered the recording of this composition and spent many hours on it suggested to increase the resonance of the final bars as it produced an effect of fading away and gradually disappearing. Might we say, perhaps, on the basis of his proposal, that the cry of the soloist and the musicians expresses the idea that, in the end, it was an ephemeral cry, that everything is liable to fade away and be lost, however resonant it was at the beginning? Just like the lives of these men and women, our own brothers and sisters, who were drowned? By contrast, perhaps it was a cry of those who fight to remain alive and survive? When I look at how the process of composition developed within me, however, I would say that this composition itself wants to live and is crying out for a fuller development. As a matter of fact, now I am developing it further, adding choral parts which constitute a "requiem". I have also asked my friend and colleague, the writer of the text, for new poetic expressions of this humanitarian catastrophe.

I will conclude by saying that I believe this composition has grown in meaning and significance as a result of the voices and the comments of many people who have helped me to add thoughts and words to what was initially *only an intuition*, still linked to the deep unconscious, but desiring to be more fully developed. In any case, many thanks to all those who shared their comments with me.

References

Bion, W.R. 1991. "*A memoir of the future*". London, Karnac.

Civitarese, G. 2015. "Transformations in Hallucinosis and the Receptivity of the Analyst". *The International Journal of Psychoanalysis* 96: 1091–1116.

Civitarese, G. 2017. "*Sublime subjects: Aesthetic experience and intersubjectivity in psychoanalysis*". London, Routledge.

Dalhaus, C. 1972. "'*Uber den Zerfall des musikalischen Werkbegriffs' in Schoenberg und andere, gesammelte Aufsätze zur neuen Musik*". Schott, Mainz, 1978, p. 281.

Klein, M. 1946. "*Notes on some schizoid mechanisms*". Hogarth Press, 1975.

Leuzinger-Bohleber & Pfeifer, R. 2004. "Recordando un objeto primario depresivo. La memoria en un diálogo entre el psicoanàlisi y la ciencia cognitiva". *Libro anual de Psicoanálisis* 18: 79–107.

Marks-Tarlow, T. 2008. *"Psyche's Veil: Psychotherapy, fractals and complexity"*. London, Routledge.

Milner, 1969. *The Hands of the Living God* (New York: International Universities Press, 1969).

Rocha Iturbide. 2013–2019. *"La composición musical a través de una concepción cuántica del sonido II"*. www.sulponticello.com

Storr, A. 1997. *"Music and the mind"*. Harper Collins, Editor.

Vermote, R. 2011. "On the Value of 'Late Bion' to Analytic Theory and Practice". *International Journal of Psychoanalysis* 92/5: 1089–1098.

Zepf, S. 2013. "Where Are We When We Listen to Music?". *Journal of Neuropsychoanalysis.*

Part 2

Wanderer there is no path . . . the path is made by walking

(Antonio Machado)

Chapter 4

Intuition in a spectral model of the mind

On caesuras, bridges, and other crossings

Renato Trachtenberg

> It is very important to be aware that you may never be satisfied with your analytic career if you feel that you are restricted to what is narrowly called a "scientific" approach. (. . .) It is so important to dare to think or feel whatever you do think or feel, never mind how unscientific it is.
>
> (Bion, 1978, 102)

Introduction

Intuition is the expression of an undecidability and an uncertainty. It is therefore part of a complexity which, since Bion, has included psychoanalysis in a dimension of uncertainty where formulating better questions becomes more important than answering them. Tolerating the absence, whether temporary or not, of these answers is just as important as avoiding precociously filling the void of our ignorance. Enduring paradoxes is our great challenge. Intuition (regardless of what it means to each of us) places us at the epicenter of this turbulence we call complex psychoanalysis. In order to view intuition from this perspective, I will include it in a spectral model of the mind while simultaneously addressing the topic of caesura, which is so closely linked to the spectral model that we cannot mention one without considering the other. At the end, I will try to build a bridge towards a linking theory, allowing me to develop a key point: viewing intuition as a linking concept, not only as a product of the link between analyst and analysand but also of the link or caesura between associative and connective logics (Moreno, 2014, 2016). In other words, a connection between what is produced by the conscious and/or unconscious observations made by analyst and analysand (associative) and the so-called novel, random facts that limit what belongs to the analytic couple – a limit established from the outside, from the effect of presence.

The analytical meeting can produce novelty, which in turn can *produce* (in) the analytical meeting. The effect of presence, *presentation*, produces something not previously represented that might never be again, remaining as an otherness, something unattainable, in each session.

DOI: 10.4324/9781003293392-8

The meaning of intuition?

Intuition conceived as a spectral model can be contrasted with different mental activities that follow other logics, which both articulate and clash with logics that allow intuitive moments. Regardless, a definitive concept of intuition is an impossibility in itself.

Much like psychoanalysis, beauty, truth, or love, intuition defies any attempt to trap it in a definition. Let me quote some of its Wikipedia (in)definitions: "its functioning, and even its existence, is an enigma to science. Although several theories on the subject do exist, none is considered definitive"; "anticipation, the ability of fore-seeing, guessing in advance: having an intuition of the future." In the words of Sandler (1997, 59): "Intuition is something that exists, but cannot be understood, only perceived, observed, trained, and used." In these (in)definitions of intuition, I emphasize the idea of intuition as something that connects us with the future, such as the notion of pre-conception, memory of the future, and imagination. As the mathematician Alan Kay once said, the best way to predict the future is *to invent it*. On several occasions Bion referred to imaginative conjectures as an important part of the psychoanalytical function in order to "see" or intuit dimensions not otherwise available to our senses. Intuiting is therefore also a means of connecting with something that has not yet occurred. A well-known example is maternal reverie, whereby a mother's bond with her baby allows her to sense and anticipate the infant's anxiety or distress before any sensory signal becomes apparent to others or even herself. This ability decreases with time, when the signals of the pre-natal mind give way to the development of the baby's postnatal mind, with components such as memory, desire, and need for understanding. Buber's words, quoted by Bion (1977a, 39), would apply here: "in his mother's womb man knows the universe, and forgets it at birth."

In his last session of analysis, Bion allegedly asked his analyst, Melanie Klein: "What is psychoanalysis, after all?" Her answer went something like this: "As you yourself said, Dr. Bion, it is a pre-conception in search of an embodiment." I think that had Bion asked the same question regarding intuition, he would have received the same answer. As Bion would later say, "psychoanalysis is a word in search of a meaning; a thought waiting for a thinker; a concept waiting for a content" (Bion, 1977b, 323).

"Q: What about the knowledge we don't know we have – what we sometimes call 'intuition'?"

"Bion: If you want to talk about it, you have to invent a word like 'intuition', hoping that it is about something and that in fact you have intuition. . . . It is rather like the poet who is able to express something in a way that draws the attention of the reader to what he might otherwise not be aware of. The person who uses a word like 'intuition' may not have enough knowledge to be convinced that there is such a thing, but he may feel there is, and he may express a term, but he has to take the risk of somebody saying, 'What do you mean by intuition?' All he can say is, 'If you hear me use it often enough, I hope you may get a rough idea of what I am talking about.' The pattern will emerge in which it would seem to be appropriate to say, 'Ah, that's what he means by "intuition".' . . . This seems to me to be part of the fascination of this kind of occupation" (Bion, 1976a, 42).

Intuition in Bion's work

Even before its full-fledged appearance in *Transformations* (1965), and particularly *Notes on Memory and Desire* (1967b) and "Commentary" of *Second Thoughts* (1967a), Bion had already presented notions that described intuition without naming it: alpha function and reverie, pre-conception, thoughts-without-a-thinker, selected fact between PS and D, binocular vision, reversible perspective, evolving in the movement O>K and invariants in the theory of transformations, among others. These antecedents are, almost without exception, the same as those used for the notion of caesura in Bion's work. There are therefore invariants between intuition and caesuras. They are the third element of a duality, a characteristic of the complexity at work in open, tertiary (non-dual), and non-stable systems. However, I acknowledge there is another antecedent underlying many of Bion's concepts (including his notions of intuition), a model of thinking that, among other benefits, frees us from causality, evolution, fanaticism, morality, and comparison between ideas or mental states: the spectral model. The first spectral model in Bion's work was narcissism ↔ socialism (Bion, 1948). Psychoanalysis as an expression of complexity requires a spectral modeling or configuration in order to be thought. Chuster[1] has retrieved and developed the notion of the spectral model and its connection to the open, non-linear systems at the heart of complex thinking. After several years of obscurity, the model reemerged in the idea of psychotic and non-psychotic parts of the personality (1957), oscillation between PS and D (1962b), transformations in/from "O" (1965), the movement between patience and security (1970), etc. The possibility of thinking without comparisons or morality and its derivatives (good/bad, superior/inferior, health/illness, etc.) – by introducing bi-directionality (↔) and multidimensionality, with the ends of the spectrum acting as references of proximity and distance rather than departure and arrival – anticipates the notion of complex thinking (Morin, 2003) and the corresponding substitution of dialogics (coexistence and tolerance to paradoxes) for dialectics (synthesis). The spectral model underlies the statement by Kant so often quoted by Bion: intuitions without concepts are blind, and concepts without intuition are empty.

In proposing an analytic work without memory, desire, or comprehension (Bion, 1967b, 1970) – combined with the negative capability described by Keats (Bion, 1970), the esthetic formulation of the same proposition – Bion provides the conditions required for intuition.

Much like the conditions for intuition, the introduction of the concept of caesura (1977a) expands the spectral model. I consider the advent of caesura in

Bion's work a fundamental step that gives new meaning to the idea of intuition and, at the same time, to the movement and notion of an *in-between* in the spectral model. In the *in-between* of a spectrum – the bridge between its margins – the possibilities of developing intuitions increase, and we move away from the major or minor fanaticisms of everyday life.

Spectral model and caesura

> I will resort to an expression that I consider useful, borrowing a term from mathematicians: 'absolute initiative.' By 'absolute,' I mean both directions – the initiative to return and the initiative to move forward. The key point is the initiative, not the destination . . . I say 'initiative' to express a neutral, intermediary area *between* the two directions. Who gives birth to a baby? The mother or the full-term fetus? Does the full-term fetus in any way indicate he no longer wants to be inside the mother? Or does the mother indicate she no longer wants to bear this burden?
>
> (Bion, 1978, 101)

This Bion quote incorporates the idea that every link contains a point, an *undecidability* of origin, where we do not know who originated an event or whom it belongs to, where we cannot decide what belongs to the mother or to the baby, to the analyst or to the analysand. In my opinion, this idea, used by Chuster as one of the ethical-esthetic principles of psychoanalysis, also involves the notion of complementary and heterogeneous symmetry. The spectral model can be applied to different poles, where a false relation of opposition and antagonism is replaced by a non-evolutionary form of thinking, therefore without the presence of morality, idealization, or fanaticism. Thus, the spectral model allows us to think of a virtual space, an *in-between*, a third dimension, caesura, which connects the poles of a spectrum. Only at the ends of the spectrum is concept without intuition empty and intuition without concept blind. The spectral model is closely related to the paradigm of complexity, present throughout Bion's work but developed further from his text "Caesura" onwards, where it is defined as a paradox. Historically, caesura appears as Freud's response to Otto Rank and his idea of birth trauma. Freud's remark about caesura includes a certain notion of continuity that is not present in Rank. However, Freud holds that continuity arises in spite of the "impressive caesura." Bion would later say that continuity is part of caesura and not something that occurs in spite of it.

As a spectral concept, caesura functions within the ethics of differences and singularities and not comparative and evolutionary morals – a feature that still prevails in the positivist remnants found in solid modernity. When caesura does not meet the criteria Bion used to define it (a paradox reconciling simultaneous separation and continuity), I feel we should no longer refer to it as such, since an impermeable caesura is not a caesura but a *shibboleth*,[2] which is how I refer to it in several papers (Trachtenberg, 2005, 2012, 2013a, 2013b, 2018, 2019). My reference here is the criticism Bion levels at the expression "impressive caesura" as used by Freud. Caesura is impressive only in its impossibility. In this sense, Strachey's footnote (Freud, 1926, 131) about the printing error in the 1926 German edition is very illustrative: "*censure*" was published in lieu of "caesura." In Bion's words (1976b, 271):

> I am impressed by the fact that the physical birth is so impressive. . . . The fact of birth certainly impresses the individual and the group. But it seems to me that it is too limiting to assume that physical birth is as impressive as many people suppose it is. . . . I think the lack of discussion of this point is a blind spot. Freud developed this idea of 'the impressive caesura of birth' of our being too impressed by it. He didn't investigate it deeply – a great mistake from our point of view.

When Bion unearths Freud's well-known statement (1926) – "There is much more continuity between intra-uterine life and earliest infancy than the impressive caesura of the act of birth would have us believe" – he transforms it into a spectral concept: "So . . .? Investigate the caesura; not the analyst; not the analysand; not the unconscious; not the conscious; not sanity; not insanity. But the caesura, the link, the synapse, the (counter-trans)-ference, the transitive-intransitive mood" (Bion, 1977a, 56). Caesura encompasses both the continuous and discontinuous, union and separation, contact and rupture. It is part of the very constitution of the mind (internal/external, unconscious/conscious, infinite/finite, etc.). There is no conscious and unconscious, finite and infinite before a caesura comes into being. On the other hand, Bion views this constitution as a continuously recurring process. The vertex created by caesura favors the difference between mental states without comparing them. Transience becomes visible. This position, centered on the selected fact "difference," works with the clinical practice of transformation in O – becoming – and avoids transformations in hallucinosis that create superiority/inferiority scales.

This laid the groundwork for abolishing, in psychoanalysis, the notion of causality and its counterpart, results, in favor of an *undecidability* of origin and an infinite universe of meaningful discourse. According to Bion, the causal theory is valid and omnipotent solely in the sphere of morality: only morality can cause something. Patience (Bion, 1970) includes the patience of not searching for causes, for when one seeks the *why*, one loses the *what*, the phenomena in transit, the coexistence models of the states of mind. Chains of relationships, meanings and functions cannot be obtained by a mind that thinks in terms of causes. The sense of causation and its moral implications prevent intuition from developing (Sandler, 2005).

In the analytic space, a *shibboleth* is observed when, for example, an analysand cannot perform the functions of an analyst and vice versa. According to Bion, the psychoanalytic function of personality does not establish rigid borders between one and the other (much like paternal and maternal functions do not establish borders between fathers and mothers). From the perspective of the psychoanalytic function, being the analyst or the analysand can serve as a defense against the impact of the human mind's complexity. The issue lies in the *or*. The *or* border is hard to cross, being both exclusive and excluding. Analysand and analyst imply a caesura, an *and*, heterogeneous symmetries. The symmetry between analyst and analysand should be maintained in every analysis, striving to support the link between the analysand in every analyst and the analyst in every analysand.

Caesuras allow us to live in at least two worlds simultaneously, even though one of them prevails as an object of observation. The caesura becomes the vertex through which analyst and analysand alike can observe the phenomena occurring during the psychoanalytic session. "The caesura is an endlessly plastic imaginary function that symbolically connects two distinct mediums so as to enable them to communicate" (Chuster & Trachtenberg, 2018).

The concept of caesura indicates that, during the session, the psychoanalyst is in a transient state of becoming a psychoanalyst. When we use a *shibboleth* in order to determine who is a psychoanalyst and who is not, we forget that the identity of a psychoanalyst is always in a state of "becoming." Through caesura, Bion describes the analyst during the session as a "becoming," being constantly born in spite of the "impressive" caesuras of institutionalized birth. In this sense, the mental state of becoming a psychoanalyst is an indicator that a caesura is at work – similarly to the caesura of birth, which prevents us from determining when a person is born or how much of a person still has not yet been born. Defining one-self as a psychoanalyst is important for sensorial (i.e., professional, institutional, social, theoretical, legal, etc.) purposes. In the analytical meeting is an endless path, as is truth.

Caesura implies the coexistence of multiple mental states with different levels of development in a situation of emotional turbulence. As such, mental growth broadens the possibilities of this coexistence, making new links between mental states possible. This coexistence and the way these fragile, infinite agreements move, link, and negotiate with each other is known as the singularity of the subject. Greater tolerance of this possibility, without an overwhelming need for exclusions/projections, is my concept of achievement analysis. When one dimension prevails for a certain amount of time, we tend to forget the remaining ones. This is when we say someone is an honest, deceitful, intuitive, or envious person and issue our *totalitarian* diagnoses, expressing the reductionist aspect of a pre-complex language (language of substitution) with the presence of memory, desire, and a need for understanding. As we have seen, complex language always implies a third element in the picture: the caesura, the link, the relation that allows us to come and go within a spectrum of possibilities. This is what indicates the presence of ever-complex ethics (Morin, 2005; Chuster et al., 2014; Trachtenberg, 2008, 2013b, 2018).

Buber, quoted by Bion, notes that "the basic words are not single words but word pairs. One basic word is the word pair I-You . . . . When one talks about

I-You the significant thing is not the two objects related, but the relationship – that is, an open-ended reality in which there is no termination" (Bion, 1992, 370–371). One cannot talk of omnipotence, said Bion, without thinking of helplessness; the basic word is omnipotence/helplessness. If we place the words *full-term baby* and *mother* (or *analyst* and *analysand*) at either end of a spectrum, the significant term is the *Relation*, the *and*, rather than the related objects. In the words of the Argentinian philosopher Alejandra Tortorelli (2009): "it is not the mother who receives the child, it is birth that receives both." Birth is the *Relation*, the caesura. In other words, there is no mother or child before the linking encounter. The classic (and very true) theory of the child's helplessness in relation to an adult capable of supporting, thinking, or dreaming him should not, on the grounds of common sense, exclude the idea that the mother is also helpless as a mother in this encounter. These are symmetrical, albeit *heterogeneous*, helplessness.

Oftentimes, surprise, disbelief, and dismay (Freud, 1919) regarding an intuition give rise to resistance against it by the analyst and/or analysand. The psychoanalyst's fear of disclosing his intuitions before carefully investigating whether his personal equation is present – as if it were possible to exclude it – often prevents it from being used. Undesirable exposure may include the psychotic part of personality. On the other hand, I feel that the differences between the psychotic and non-psychotic parts of personality should not prevent us from conjecturing on the presence of the former in intuition. If we manage to distance ourselves from the moral residues of diagnoses and place the psychotic and non-psychotic parts in a spectrum, we no longer think in terms of evolution. Bion did not posit that the psychotic part of personality evolves towards the non-psychotic. This development unfolds from (-) complexity to more (+) complexity, i.e., new and different forms of coexistence between both or other dimensions.

When caesura is active, the paranoid dimension of the psychotic part participates together with the elements of the non-psychotic part in the emergence of intuitions. The paranoid doubt about whether to share an intuition with the patient or not is an indicator that the time has come to state it (this often begins with an apology of sorts by the analyst for having thought or imagined such an odd thing). The psychotic ability of sensing what the other person is thinking or feeling is, in its spectral and *caesural* form, part of the interplay with the non-psychotic facet of the personality, a factor of the imaginative and intuitive function of the mind. Moving away from memory, desire, and the need for understanding is, according to Bion, a threatening situation in which the usual sensory instruments of orientation fail us and we risk coming close to a psychotic experience. In a spectral model of the mind, the greatest danger lies at the extremes – either the psychotic or non-psychotic part of personality, the "serious" illness Bion calls *normality*. I see the contribution of the psychotic part, for example, as a sort of instrumental paranoia that enables an awareness of something happening in the link, something that my sensorial experience fails to capture but my imagination or intuition can anticipate. I use the expression "instrumental paranoia" as a quality of the mind (as "instrumental splitting," Bion's expression for a moment of decision or choice), a wild thinking able to "sniff out danger" and anticipate an action or response. It differs from psychiatric paranoia by the presence of doubt and uncertainty, which are the expression of the non-psychotic part of personality when caesura is present. The persecution implicit in the psychotic part of personality is fundamental for the birth of an intuition, which also needs the non-psychotic part to sustain it. The psychotic and non-psychotic parts establish symmetrical and heterogeneous relationships.

Intuition may suffer from idealization, worship, and reverence. This involves a one-way evolutionary model, with intuition on the right-hand side and observation, concept, or rationality on the left. However, it may also suffer from depreciation, debasement, and fear and would then be placed on the left because of its undecidable historical connections with divination, occultism, and telepathy; idealized scientific thinking would be on the right. The origins of intuition lie far from the sources of enlightenment, modernity, or positivism. Its origins, its "manners", make it unworthy of sitting at the same table as the proud determinist classical sciences. The history of intuition in so-called scientific psychoanalysis is a history of curiosity, deep (and sometimes hidden) interest, and at the same time, an apology for being unable to avoid incorporating and using it. Freud's work and clinical practice provide good examples of the former.

Future or progression is no better or worse than past or regression, just as negative numbers are no better or worse than positive ones. The same is true for positive and negative transference (Trachtenberg, 2018). Progression can mean a worsening of an illness and regression an indicator of good health after a disease. The truth is that evolution – of either ideas or biological species – has no direction. Darwin himself said that "the variability of living beings and the action of natural selection seem to have no more of a design than a leaf does when it follows the wind that happens to blow" (Moreno, 2016, 73).

Intuition and the spectral model of associative/connective logics[3]

According to Morin (2003), complexity includes uncertainties, indetermination, random phenomena. It is not about proceeding from simplicity to complexity but rather from complexity to even greater complexity. The realities linked to chance, which classical science ignores, come back as the return of what the sciences repressed both in their condition of unpredictability and their quality as an event. We cannot fail to include a form of knowledge that could be called capture – as in a camera capable of capturing an accurate snapshot of reality outside the subject, without necessarily understanding it.

A moving border is set in motion – a caesura, a continuous back-and-forth movement between the associative coming from the past, from the unconscious ("cause of being," Leibniz), and the connective, whose origin is unknown and may as well not exist ("cause of itself," Spinoza). Association and connection make up an *in-between*, at times barely noticeable, from which we can free ourselves from binary "A/B" positions. Both activities share the analytical field and do not refer to one another; instead, they coexist and follow two different sets of logic (Moreno, 2014, 2016).

According to Moreno (2016), the concept of transference has existed for more than a hundred years and has been subject to extensive investigation. As such, we resist the idea of sharing it with the concept of interference, related to linking. Interference, initially understood as an obstacle to be suppressed, much like transference at its inception, became a key concept in this relation where radical novelty is produced. Interference aims at accounting for this novel meeting situation, in which transferences attempt to reduce it to something previously represented or occurred, albeit unknown, again including in the past what is presented in the link between presences. This is the difference between an object relation and linking.

Classical autism involves the prevalence (partial but exaggerated or absolute) of the connective procedure. This is why an autistic child cannot differentiate his *inside*, his thoughts, or even imagine that those around him have an interior space. It is the purest example of connective functioning, with no need to think about the causal linking between facts. In a spectral model, it is key to think that at the ends, at the poles, there is something preventing or inhibiting mental development (Moreno, 2016).

The associative procedure, with its notion of a causal determinant center (the unconscious), undoubtedly occupies pride of place throughout Freud's work. Yet his writings, clinical work, and life episodes bear witness to his belief in the existence of something conveyed outside the associative – in his words, "transmission of thoughts without communication signs" (Moreno, 2016, 146). This Freud capable of thinking outside the box (a common trait of geniuses) did not disappear: for him, the links between telepathy (Freud, 1921, 1922, 1923) and phenomena not explained by reason were contradictory but firm, and together with his daughter Anna and Ferenczi, as well as other private acquaintances, he repeatedly indulged in experiments with telepathy, such as the transmission of thoughts between blindfolded people sitting around a table holding hands (Moreno, 2016).

Freud had given up hypnotism and direct suggestion (which he thought was driven by "forces without justified cause") in order to build psychoanalysis on the foundation of free association, unconscious determinism, i.e., a conception in which the unconscious becomes the main (in some passages, the sole) determinant cause of psychic events. At the same time, he firmly believed in the existence of (as he called it) transmission of thoughts in the absence of communication signs.

The progress of physics at that time (early 20th century) showed that in several fields of investigation, such as radiation, relativity, and gravity, an effect could be transmitted from one body to another located elsewhere, without any mediating contact. This was a puzzling fact that defied explanation but was nonetheless evident and accepted as such.

In 1935, quantum physics first addressed a new phenomenon, called entanglement, and a "connectivity" contrary to the *separability principle* that reigned supreme over classical physics. Bohr eventually came up with the term "influence," arguing that there is a universal connectivity: every object is connected and inter-acts instantly (i.e., faster than the speed of light) with the whole universe. As the poet Francis Thompson wrote in his poem "From the Mistress of Vision" (quoted by N. Bohr) in the early 20th century: "When to the new eyes of thee/All things by immortal power,/Near or far,/Hiddenly/To each other linked are,/That thou canst not stir a flower/Without troubling of a star" (Moreno, 2016, 147).

In that same year, Schrödinger singled out an astonishing phenomenon of quantum mechanics: entangled particles do not behave as separate particles func-tioning alone but rather are united, behaving in a mirror-like fashion; what one particle does is always strictly related to what the other does, regardless of their distance from one another (be it atomic proximity or astronomic distance).

This has no explanation or equivalent in classical physics and defies the the-ory of inseparability. While the latter states that each object moves by itself according to the forces applied upon it – that is, the objects are conveniently separated, in the same way as the thoughts of one person are separated from those of another – entanglement involves two or more objects sharing unique states. One state decidedly influences the other without a mediating "commu-nication" between them and does so simultaneously. This affects all objects within a system, even when spatially separated and irrespective of the distance between them. For example, two particles can be entangled in such a way that when one of them rotates upwards, the other automatically rotates downwards, regardless of being a few angstroms or a million miles apart, in the same city or on different planets.

Thus, what happens in a system will immediately influence the particles (and maybe the objects) entangled with it; these influences spread instantaneously, even when the systems are separated.

Could thoughts be transmitted in a similar way? The influence of entanglement is transmitted faster than the speed of light, which apparently means that what is being transmitted is not information but something else. Perhaps the transmission of thoughts, or intuition, is also based on *something else*. It cannot be said that intuition has the same explanation as quantum entanglement, nor can it be refuted (Moreno, 2014, 2016).

A major portion of Freud's creative achievement lies in the *in-between* of the two positions – in its coming and going. The dispute that divides classical from quantum physics occurred and occurs in a manner remarkably akin to the dispute between the associative and the connective process in psychoanalysis. There are effects that do not stem from association and therefore appear to lack a cause.

As such, there are three options: to reduce what we consider "real" to that which results from known causes; to accept that there may be facts we cannot account for because we lack the knowledge and measures to allow us to predict them, which is the same as saying that they are facts temporarily without a cause; or to assume that these phenomena are strictly without a cause or, as stated by Spinoza, caused by themselves. In other words, there are no causes whose posi-tion transcends the effects.

In the early 18th century, Leibniz stated the principle of sufficient reason: there can be no fact real or existing, no statement true, unless there be a sufficient reason why it should be so and not otherwise (Moreno, 2000). This principle excludes from the outset anything unmotivated or devoid of reason. Therefore, anything that goes against the principle of sufficient reason (i.e., that there are unmotivated facts) is a true heresy for orthodox deterministic scientific thinking.

Basically, the issue can be summarized as follows: the general laws of classical science relating causes and effects in a linear way are based on what Bachelard called capability of neglecting the infinitesimal (Moreno, 2000) – the neglect of tiny variations not subject to laws or statistics (bear in mind that Freud, on the other hand, was able to conceive psychoanalysis precisely because he did not neglect the infinitesimal). In computing, these infinitesimal variations are called "noise," which is of no interest, as opposed to "signal," which is of interest. The key point is that what is signal or noise is determined by the interest of the observing subject and the theory supporting his observation. Bion himself described the moment someone starts to listen to noises (called interference in radio transmissions) as not noises but signals, which prompted the development of astrophysics.

Moreno's expression "radically novel" refers not only to the novel (such as a new combination of existing elements, better adapted but homogeneous with the existent combination; a rearrangement of things or the unfolding of existing but withheld potentialities, such as a seed waiting to sprout), but to acquiring a hitherto impossible new key different from existing keys.

What would it take to think outside determination? "To reason the indeterminate" sounds like an *aporia*, and in a way, it is. This could force us into a false choice between a determinism excluding radical novelty and a kind of absolute contingency. In a way, this is what Kant sought to avoid with his spectral model: intuitions without concepts are blind, and concepts without intuition are empty.

The time at which an occurrence included merely as a hole in the previously established knowledge acquires a place and a name is evanescent, unforeseeable, and elusive. Furthermore, the occurrence excludes the presence of a transcendent place where its events could be reported or understood "from the outside." Hence, when an occurrence takes place during the session, the analyst, in spite of his privileged position, is involved in "this" that the link produces and is not exempt from this generality. The occurrence allows what was not, *to be* (instead of *to be understood*). This time can be (and often is) used to build a more or less fictitious and unreal story to *understand* what happened previously, but *afterwards*: its effects make it undeniable that something took place (Moreno, 2000, 2014, 2016).

As psychoanalysts, we are part of the experience: the realist hypothesis (where observer, observed, and observation may not interfere with each other) is overturned not only in practice but also in science; it is essentially opposed to it. However, far from drowning us in impotence, this has become a fundamental instrument in the psychoanalytical arsenal.

As soon as a connective impact arises, the associative in the human being strives to capture the novelty, to devour it, to seize it and discover its rational causes; thus, everything is reduced to causal logics, to a rational fact. An associative logic is established that preserves the logos: the event believed to be some sort of "miracle" was generated by its antecedents.

The quantum (in physics) and the connective (in psychoanalysis) were dealt a similar blow: both were expelled from the accepted knowledge of their respective disciplines. According to Moreno (2000, 2016), a notion arises that the "toll" we might have to pay in order to belong to a scientific world consistent with Leibniz's principle of sufficient reason (everything that happens is a coherent expression of its causes) may ultimately suffocate us.

All of this resembles current conceptions in philosophy, anthropology, and even quantum physics. Reality, for example, is now considered a construct located in a space where there is always some virtuality *between* observer and observed, *between* at least two instances, instead of an unmovable and "truly true" object. Hence, the proposal of deviating if only slightly from the theories of causes in the past – determining what happens in the present – and admitting the existence of the single, the connective, the immanent, the becoming; that which happens without us knowing exactly what caused it: occurrences. In analysis this takes place in a space *between* the link, that is, not only that which was forged in the past and is now developing but also what is *produced* in the living link between patient and analysand, in the immanency of the analytical situation. Intuitions are born and develop *between* the associative and the connective (Moreno, 2014, 2016).

This *in-between* reminds me of bridges, invariants, non-abysmal borders, possibilities of coming and going. It reminds me of a spectral psychoanalysis without any "impressive" caesuras *between* its theories and its thinkers.

A development potential

Before Freud, psychoanalysis existed as a thing- in- itself, a thought without a thinker. A special mind, in a special time and place, thought what nobody else had thought before. He had an intuition of genius. As occurs with many men and women of genius, there is a delay, a shorter or longer lapse of time between an intuition and its acceptance by others. All geniuses of art and science had to endure it – including Bion. Like all ideas of intuitive geniuses, many of his ideas have development potential (achievement language) that drives us to keep working on/ with them and grasp new realizations. Just as they seem depleted, they gain a new lease on life, new meanings suddenly emerge, new roads open up by the very act of walking. Is there a limit to this development potential? Is it infinite? Does it depend on us too?

Notes

1 According to Chuster (1997, 2000, 2002, 2014, 2018, and personal communication in 2012), the spectral model is defined as the indefinite and indeterminate extension

of phenomena from which one can extract or construct an indefinite number of concepts but which can never be reconstructed by means of a composition of the latter; the spectrum is in permanent expansion and expresses the irreversibility of time. Spectral modeling involves renouncing to obtain answers and the need to constantly create interpretations; yet the purpose of explaining is never achieved. This would be an expression of the infinite unconscious. The spectral configuration allows no causes or results. It implies an idea of movement defined by its possibilities of oscillation, and its absence inhibits development. Hence my use of the see-saw metaphor – a child's game sustained by its instability, not by balance (Trachtenberg, 1998, 2005).

2 *Shibboleth*: "ear of wheat" in Hebrew. In the Bible (Judges, 12), this word is used as a password by the Gileadites in order to exterminate the members of another Hebrew tribe, the Ephraimites, who could not pronounce it the same way they did (they said *sibbolet)*. Due to this dialect difference, the Ephraimites were killed at each attempt they made to cross the Jordan River. It is often used to mark and identify those initiated in a certain field of study, theory, sect, political party, etc. According to some dictionaries, *shibboleth* is any word used as a test to detect people from another region or country; any word that is exceedingly difficult for a foreigner to pronounce. This is the model and word Freud utilizes to define and separate those who are psychoanalysts from those who are not. The unconscious, the theory of dreams, the infantile sexuality, and the Oedipus complex are thought to be the "*shibboleth*" concepts defining an identity – being a psychoanalyst. They establish clear, non-negotiable borders separating "supporters and adversaries of psychoanalysis" (Freud, 1905, 206), its followers from those who "must renounce forever to understand it" (Freud, 1933, 7).

3 This section is explicitly influenced by the ideas put forward in the last few years by the Argentinian psychoanalyst Julio Moreno (2000, 2014, 2016).

References

Bion, W. R. 1948. *Experiencias en Grupos*. Barcelona: Paidós.

Bion, W. R. 1957. "Differentiation of the Psychotic from the Non-Psychotic Personalities." In: *Second Thoughts* (1967). Northvale: Jason Aronson.

Bion, W. R. 1962b. *Learning from Experience*. Northvale: Jason Aronson.

Bion, W. R. 1965. *Transformations*. London: Heinemann.

Bion, W. R. 1967a. "Commentary." In: *Second Thoughts*. Northvale: Jason Aronson.

Bion, W. R. 1967b. "Notes on Memory and Desire." In: Spillius, E. B. (ed.). *Melanie Klein Today* (1990), vol. 2. Rio de Janeiro: Imago.

Bion, W. R. 1970. *Attention and Interpretation*. Northvale: Jason Aronson.

Bion, W. R. 1976a. "Penetrating Silence." In: Mawson, Chris. *The Complete Works of W. R. Bion*, vol. 15 (2014). London: Routledge.

Bion, W. R. 1976b. "Four Discussions." In: *Clinical Seminars and Other Works* (2000). London: Karnac.

Bion, W. R. 1977a. "Caesura." In: *Two Papers: The Grid and Caesura*. London: Karnac.

Bion, W. R. 1977b. *A Memoir of the Future (Book 2: The Past Presented)*. London: Karnac.

Bion, W. R. 1978. "Seminar Held in Paris." In: *Revista de Psicanálise (SPPA)*, 8 (1): 95–102.

Bion, W. R. 1992. *Cogitations*. London: Karnac.

Chuster, A. 1997. "O ensino de Bion." In: *Revista do Instituto Bion*, 1: 30–57.

Chuster, A. 2000. "Psicanálise e sociedade: a contribuição de Bion." Paper presented at the XXIII Congresso Psicanalítico da FEPAL, Gramado, Brasil. 3–9 September.

Chuster, A. 2003. *As Origens do Inconsciente* 1 Janelas da Mente (2003) W.R. Bion-Novas Leituras, vol.II, Co. de Freud, Rio de Janeiro.

Chuster, A., col. 2002. *A Psicanálise dos Princípios Ético-Estéticos à Clínica.* Vol. II of *W. R. Bion: Novas Leituras.* Rio de Janeiro: Companhia de Freud.

Chuster, A. 2014. *A Lonesome Road: Essays on the Complexity of W. R. Bion's Work.* Rio de Janeiro: Trio Studios/Karnac.

Chuster, A. 2018. *Simetria e objeto psicanalítico: desafiando paradigmas com W. R. Bion.* Rio de Janeiro: Trio Studio.

Chuster, A., Soares, G. and Trachtenberg, R. 2014. *W. R. Bion: a obra complexa.* Porto Alegre: Editora Sulina.

Chuster, A. and Trachtenberg, R. 2018. "Course on the Work of Bion Held at the 2018." Bion International Conference, in Ribeirão Preto, Brasil.

Freud, S. 1905. "Tres ensayos de teoría sexual." In: *Obras completas,* vol. 7. Buenos Aires: Amorrortu.

Freud, S. 1919. "Lo ominoso." In: *Obras completas,* vol. 17. Buenos Aires: Amorrortu.

Freud, S. 1922. "Sueño y telepatía." In: *Obras completas,* vol. 18. Buenos Aires: Amorrortu.

Freud, S. 1923 (1922). "Observaciones sobre la teoría y la práctica de la interpretación de los sueños." In: *Obras completas,* vol. 19. Buenos Aires: Amorrortu.

Freud, S. 1926. "Inhibición, síntoma y angustia." In: *Obras completas,* vol. 20. Buenos Aires: Amorrortu.

Freud, S. 1933. "Nuevas conferencias de introducción al psicoanálisis." In: *Obras completas,* vol. 22. Buenos Aires: Amorrortu.

Freud, S. 1941 (1921). "Psicoanálisis y telepatía." In: *Obras completas,* vol. 18. Buenos Aires: Amorrortu.

Moreno, J. 2000. "¿Hay lugar para lo indeterminado en psicoanálisis?" In: *Clínica familiar psicoanalítica.* Buenos Aires: Paidós.

Moreno, J. 2014. *Ser humano: la inconsistencia, los vínculos, la crianza.* Buenos Aires: Letra Viva.

Moreno, J. 2016. *El psicoanálisis interrogado: de las causas al devenir.* Buenos Aires: Editorial Lugar.

Morin, E. 2003. *Introdução ao pensamento complexo.* Lisboa: Stória.

Morin, E. 2005. *O Método 6: Ética.* Porto Alegre: Sulina.

Sandler, P. C. 1997. *A apreensão da realidade psíquica.* Rio de Janeiro: Imago.

Sandler, P. C. 2005. *The Language of Bion: A Dictionary of Concepts.* London: Karnac.

Tortorelli, M.A. 2009. "Entre." Conference held in Buenos Aires, July 4.

Trachtenberg, R. 1998. "A Gangorra". In: *Revista do CEPdePA*, 7: 137–154.

Trachtenberg, R. 2005. "El modelo ético-estético de Bion/Meltzer: de la pasión por el psicoanálisis ◇ por el psicoanálisis de la pasión." Paper presented at the 44th IPA Congress in the Panel "Un modelo ético-estético basado en Bion y Meltzer", Rio de Janeiro, July 28–31.

Trachtenberg, R. 2008. "As fronteiras: uma proposta para pensar diferenças entre ética e moral." In: *Revista do Instituto de Psicologia (Ipsi)*, 2: 26–32.

Trachtenberg, R. 2012. "Cesuras e des-cesuras: alguns pensamentos sobre o lado oculto da lua." In: *Berggasse 19 – Revista da Sociedade Brasileira de Psicanálise de Ribeirão Preto,* 3 (1): 97–121.

Trachtenberg, R. 2013a. "Caesura, Denial and Envy." In: Levine, H. & Brown, L. (eds.). *Growth and Turbulence in the Container/Contained: Bion's Continuing Legacy.* London: Routledge.

Trachtenberg, R. 2013b. "Cesuras e des-cesuras: as fronteiras da (na) complexidade." In: *Revista Brasileira de Psicanálise*, 47 (2): 55–66.

Trachtenberg, R. 2018. "Sem Título." In: *Berggasse 19 – Revista da Sociedade Brasileira de Psicanálise de Ribeirão Preto*, 9 (1): 74–94.

Trachtenberg, R. 2019. "The Impressive Caesuras: Some Thoughts about Complexity and Paradoxes." In: Alisobhani, A. K. & Corstorphine, G. J. (eds.). *Explorations in Bion's "O": Everything We Know Nothing About*. New York: Routledge.

Chapter 5

Apocalypse → revelation. The ways of intuition

Alessandro Bruni

In the *Dao-De-Jing*, *"Dao"* means the "way", the "flow", the "mysterious becoming of things". The ideogram *"Dao"* includes the sign of the foot.

(Lao Tzu. 6–5th century B.C.)

In Buddhist traditions, *"Mahā-yāna"*, *"Hina-yāna"* and *"Vajra-Yana"* mean *"the big vehicle", "the small vehicle"* and *"the diamond vehicle"*. Here there is no longer a *"road"*, a path, there is only *yana*, *"the vehicle"*, a way of travelling,

"Janua" was the Latin version of the original female divinity, present throughout the ancient world, governing passages, changes. Therefore, it also meant "door", also "door to the sea", hence the name of the city of Genoa. *Janua* then became *Janus*, the two-faced god of Italian origin, who governed the "passage through the door", the "change", the "renewal of nature" that begins on New Year's Eve with the month of Januarius, after the winter decline.

It is not by chance that the metaphor of the road was used by esoteric and mystic doctrines. Their aim is to achieve a more naïve vision of the hidden nature of things.

Furthermore, in ordinary language, we often say, "But it's obvious!" Paradoxically something becomes "obvious" that was not obvious a moment before. In Latin *"obvius"*, from *"ob"* and *"via"*, means "something that meets you on the road, something that presents itself spontaneously and easily to your thought or imagination". For these reasons, thousands of people all over the world love the experience of the wayfarer on paths like the one that leads to Santiago de Compostela.

There is no doubt that psychoanalysis too shares with esoteric doctrines the meaning of this travelling metaphor, in so far as the aim of every analysis is to meet and discover (*apokalyptein*) the unconscious and the unknown.

Now, if you will forgive me my passion for etymological archaeology, which I inherited from our mentor Francesco Corrao, I would like to begin by reflecting on the space of difference generated in ordinary language by the term "intuition". When we say, "to be intuitive", we refer to a precious attitude of the way of thinking. On the other hand, we say "I had an intuition!" On the

DOI: 10.4324/9781003293392-9

one hand, an attitude, a psychic quality, a potentiality; on the other hand, a concrete result of this attitude.

We soon discover that the quality of "space" between the two meanings is decidedly mysterious since it resists any easy definition and can be ascribed rather to a "psychic happening" that avoids predictability and conscious participation.

"Apocalypse" and "Revelation", from a strictly etymological point of view, can be considered synonymous. The term "*apo-kalypsis*", invented by the Jews who spoke Greek, comes from "*apò*", and "*kalypto*" (which means "cover" or "hide"). So originally *apo-kalypsis* meant the concrete act of discovering, in the primary sense of removing a cover. Similarly, "revelation" meant removing a veil. However, the term "revelation" in the religious tradition moves towards the more precise meaning of the apparition, in Greek "*phania*", of a new knowledge, obtained through divine intervention, which often takes the form of a sacred book written and handed down to the faithful. It thus comes close to the sense of an "*epiphany*", "*hierophany*" or "*theophany*". Although scholars of etymology exclude that revelation means "putting back on a veil", their clarification suggests that in current use the term "revelation" could presuppose the idea that after the discovery (*apokalypses*) that exposes us to something unknowable, the new knowledge has to do in any case with a new veil, a veil certainly less far from the "*Noumenos*", the "*itself unknowable Thing*" of Kant, or the "*O*" of Bion, but still inevitably a new veil of "*K*", knowledge. To lift or cross, even if only occasionally, the Veil of Maya, the illusional aspect of our knowledge, the ancient idea of the Vedas of India, taken up by Arthur Schopenhauer, lifting the veil of Maya puts us on the path along which we have the opportunity to witness the happening of intuition.

Freud named his discovery psychoanalysis only in 1896 after an intense experience of "*apocalypse*", when on some nights of torment, possibly intensified by his use of cocaine, he wrote the "Project of Psychology" (Freud, 1895a), in which he believed he had reached a general theory of the psyche, straddling a ridge illuminated by two epistemologically distinct vertexes, neurology and "neurotics" on the one hand and the clinical phenomenon of the "*talking cure*", the cure of words, on the other. Freud wrote to Fliess on October 20, 1985:

> During an industrious night last week, when I was suffering from that degree of pain which brings about the optimal condition for my mental activities, the barriers suddenly lifted, the veils dropped, and everything became transparent, from the details of neurosis to the determinants of consciousness. Everything seemed to fall into place, the cogs meshed, I had the impression that the things now really was a machine that shortly would function on its own. The three systems of neurons, the free and bound states of quantity, the primary and secondary processes, the main tendency and the compromise tendency of the nervous system, the two biological rules of attention and defense, the characteristics of quality, reality, and thought, the state of the psychosexual group, the sexual determination of

repression, finally, the factors determining consciousness, as a function of perception – all that was correct and still is today! Naturally, I can scarcely manage to contain my delight.

(Freud, 1895b)

Freud then had to endure depression after this "vision". The "*apocalypse*" was not followed by a satisfactory "*revelation*". Freud realized that despite his consider-able knowledge of neurology, he would not be able to build a unified field theory of the psyche. Then he decided to abandon the "neurotics" in order to build a theory aimed solely at the new discipline, "psychoanalysis". The Project of Psy-chology risked being lost. Fortunately, it was found at Fliess's house. It shows us all the intensity of Freud's vision. The neuroscientist Karl Pribram and the psy-choanalyst Merton Gill together produced an accurate interpretation of Freud's text, noting the many intuitions contained in it, intuitions that would become the fertile environment of all the subsequent developments of psychoanalytic theory. (Pribram, Gill, 1976)

"Psycho-analysis", therefore, and not "Psycho-synthesis". Analysis in Greek means "dissolution", "decomposition", literally "*lysis upwards*". I would say, archaeological decomposition of meaning until the emergence of the significant elements present in what follows.

The fundamental rule proposed by Freud, the analytical settings and the mental attitude that derives from them, all together promote in the patient, in the analyst or in the group the conditions that make the occurrence of intuition possible. The patient's free associations and the analyst's fluctuating attention already configure a decidedly heretical relational order with respect to ordinary communication. If a layman listened from the outside to an analytical exchange, he would probably say that it is the madness of two people, and indeed he would not be mistaken. The difference lies in the not-so-easy task of the analyst, who must be aware of this and must observe from a third vertex the "*crazy*" interaction between himself and his patient or his group. The situation is a bit like what shamans call "*controlled madness*".

Bion, in his work with the psychotic part of the personality, proposes the need to expand fluctuating attention to all the boxes of the grid, that is to say, to more extensive fields of reference for analytical work than those that Freud himself had explored and mapped in his topics. In general, he basically proposes two types of exercises for the analyst to stretch his "*mental muscles*".

The first type concerns the mental structure inside the session and suggests "opacifying" memory and desire and practicing "hallucinosis" (Bion, 1965, 1970).

The second type of exercise is a theoretical one, dedicated to working outside the session. It is about the need to assimilate and dispose of a suitcase of abstract theoretical elements that are as light as possible, extracted through an alchemical distillation from those psychoanalytic theories that he considered most essential and of general proven validity. These are the "Elements of Psychoanalysis" pro-posed in analogy to the "Elements of Geometry" (Bion, 1963).

The combination of the two exercises, *intra moenia* and *extra moenia*, makes it possible to overcome the mental flooding produced by theories that are too "difficult" because they are redundant, epistemologically confusing and not very formalized.

These "exercises for mental muscles" make it possible, on the one hand, to preserve some empty space for consciousness engaged in the empathic and mysterious interaction with the patient or with the group, while on the other hand, in extra-analytical work, they facilitate theoretical modelling "upwards" of the new experience acquired during the session.

"*Opacifying*" memory and desire implicitly establishes the bridge between the two working settings, inside and outside the session. Bion is mistakenly quoted as saying "*without*" memory and desire. "*Opacifying*" does not mean "*eliminating*"; it means rather putting aside, in the shadows, diminishing its presence in the field of consciousness. Memory and desire continue to be available, in the shadow of the pre-conscious, as potential functions of thought ready to bring events of intuition out of the analysis room and to allow them to evolve into new "*revelations*" expressed in the form of models congruent with the abstract elements of contingent related theories.

The exercise of "*hallucinosis*" becomes necessary in the expansion of the analytical work towards the psychotic dimension of personality. To appreciate its value best, I suggest you reflect on the new model of the psyche that derives from the meta-psychological distillation carried out by Bion on Freudian and Kleinian thought. The theory of the alpha function declares that a single process determines two dislocations of the psychic field, one of which is embedded within the other.

The first is the non-psychotic←→psychotic dislocation. Within the non-psychotic side there opens a second conscious←→unconscious dislocation (Bion, 1960). The graph you see summarizes the question.

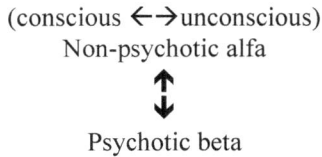

(conscious ←→unconscious)
Non-psychotic alfa

↑
↓

Psychotic beta

Bion's transformations into hallucinosis indicate the deformations suffered by perception and ordinary thought when alfa function fails in its task of dealing with particularly virulent primitive engrams and materials, stored in the psyche slums because of traumas and original deficits. Bion denotes these materials as "beta conglomerates" and considers them similar, if not identical, to aspects of "O", the unknowable truth.

A common example of a partial failure of the alfa function is given by a nightmare that plummets to an anguished awakening. During sleep the alfa function tries to transform a heavy beta conglomerate into alfa elements, but the emotional virulence that spreads out from it strongly increases the arousal of the system to such a point that it triggers the alarm and causes awakening.

The seriously psychotic patient, who cannot bear the frustration of the impact with "O", can only use the transformations into hallucinosis to replace "O" with a "pseudo reality".

From his side, the analyst, using his own properly governed hallucinosis, can reach and ride the patient's divergent hallucinations, trace back to their original connections with "O" and allow different outcomes towards alfa thought epiphany.

To return to our theme, this theoretical parenthesis is useful to point out that the events of intuition can acquire different dynamics depending on whether they occur within the unconscious←→conscious polarity, characteristic of the neurotic dimension, or rather within the non-psychotic←→ psychotic, where you have to deal with the hallucinosis.

At this point, since I fear that I have flooded your mind with an excess of abstractions, I will try to re-present my idea through a clinical description, which for Bion should always be considered as a theory expressed in more concrete terms.

The patient, whom I will call Francis, was the third of five children. He came because of a serious form of agoraphobia that was now preventing him from continuing a normal life, which, moreover, thanks to his remarkable qualities of intelligence and curiosity, could have been very satisfactory. The patient had a difficult relationship with a very religious and depressed mother. He had a peculiar way of opening his eyes that seemed almost hyperthyroid: when an intense emotion or fear attacked his attention, he seemed to really want to come out of his eyes to merge with the other, communicating an unconscious impulse of attachment and adherence, like a child in urgent need of emptying the sack and *"returning to the womb"*. In the particularly intense moments of the analytical work, this state of visual *"tension"* was often a sign of the emergence of very powerful states of anxiety that sometimes resulted in real productions characterized by a mixture of fragmented and hallucinated memories.

What happened in one session was that at a certain point I had perceived the warning of one of those states of *"fibrillation"* that I had learned to recognize. The patient was still and rigid on the couch, his eyes had a strange look, and he began to breathe more intensely, perhaps in a state of hyperventilation. I suspected a state of increasing hallucinotic stupor, and at some point, I felt the need to say something. I do not remember exactly what, but it was something that reconfirmed my presence near him. After a few seconds he seemed to recover from that state of collapse and said to me,

> Doctor, thank God you spoke to me! It was terrible! The space was expanding and the distance between things was increasing more and more; in the end you moved away as if towards infinity and I was about to lose you.

We had just breathed a sigh of relief when a little later, a similar, but so to speak opposite, phenomenon began to occur. Again, he was paralyzed on the couch, but the feeling this time was as if he was crouching inside himself. Again, he was able to talk to me and tell me that he had sunk into the couch as if he had been sucked into it by a force that pulled him from the inside downwards. He mentioned, to describe his anguish, the famous case in Italy of the child, Alfredino, who had died stuck in a well, despite attempts to save him. Then at the end of the session the patient calmed down. During the following days after the session, we noticed immediately with great mutual surprise the almost total disappearance of his agoraphobic symptom. He also became able to travel by plane for his work.

In my post-session *"speculative imagination"*, the patient had to deal with a very persecutory oral primitive object that had made its first appearance in the dreams of the first years of analysis. He used to make original dreams of anguished sucking, lack of air and a *"suction-type"* attachment to slippery surfaces. Particularly in one nightmare he realized that attached to his mouth's gums there were growing some particular shellfish which are able, by sucking the air, to strongly fix their only valve on submerged rocks. In this way, he became terrified that he would be unable to eat.

I visualized this persecutory object as a sort of *"high vacuum"*, a *"realization"* of Bion's concept of *"envious force that takes existence away from objects"*, denoted by the graph ⇐⇑, which represents a movement of retrocession on the grid towards box A1, the door of emergence of *"O"*, the ultimate unknowable reality (Bion, 1962, 1965).

During growth, this state of mind must have somehow been expelled and cemented in the perceptual structure of the external space and as such could account for the reactive defense of the agoraphobic symptom. When the patient was out of doors, he actually felt as if he was *"sucked"* from space, as if the air was pulling him from all sides to the point that he feared he would be dismembered in all directions. The agoraphobic symptom was in fact an attempt to counteract this persecutory object as much as possible, with the consequence, however, of expanding the space around him in a hallucinotic way.

In the hallucinotic transformation present in that session, the possibility of letting the phenomenon evolve up to a certain point had actually led to a visionary perceptual experience of the explosion of space, to the point that the distance between us was perceived as extending to infinity. With my *"affective"* intervention of reassurance and closeness, the phenomenon seemed to have reached an optimal stage that could allow a first representation.

At that point there was a change of direction in the next phase, where the object in question, the *"high vacuum"*, could be re-introjected, reincorporated, and finally dethroned, having transformed its emotional charge in the acquired verbal representations.

I feel today that the process can be considered a *"Transformation in O"* (Bion, 1965), since immediately after the session the patient's agoraphobia had disappeared altogether.

In the sequence described I hypothesize two moments of intuition. The first one was inside the session, simply the spontaneous choice of *timing* of my affective intervention. If I had spoken sooner, perhaps the hallucinosis would not have developed sufficiently, and if I had spoken later, probably it would have been exhausted into nothing, without possibility of representation.

The second moment of intuition concerns the speculative elaboration that I have just shared with you. Here, the availability of an abstract graph of Bion has allowed me an agile theoretical modelization.

References

BION W.R. (1963) – *"Elements of Psychoanalysis"*, reprinted by Karnac Books, London, 1984.

BION W.R. (1965) – *"Transformations: Change from Learning to Growth"*, reprinted by Karnac Books, London, 1984.

BION W.R. (1970) – *"Attention and Interpretation: A Scientific Approach to Insight in Psychoanalysis and Groups"*, Tavistock Publications, London, 1970.

FREUD S. (1895a) – *"Project for a Scientific Psychology"*, *Standard Edition, Vol. 1:* p. 283–387, Hogarth Press, 1950.

FREUD S. (1895b) – *"The Complete Letters of Sigmund Freud to Wilhelm Fliess: 1887– 1904"* (Jeffrey Moussaieff Masson, Ed. and Trans.), Belknap Press, Cambridge, MA, and London.

PRIBRAM K.H., GILL M. (1976) – *"Freud's 'Project' Reassessed"*, London: Hutchinson.

Chapter 6

Psychoanalytical intuition in dream and waking life. Their relations to caesura, imagination and language of achievement

Arnaldo Chuster

Intuition is a function of ±
W.R. Bion, *Transformations* (1965)

This chapter is about a crucial difference in the psychoanalytical work: the difference of vertex between the state of mind of the psychoanalyst and the state of mind of the analysand and its relations to *intuition* in apparently opposed states of mind, *dreaming* and *awake*, and the *caesura* between those states.

It is also about the search for a well-succeeded psychoanalytical language, that is, a language derived from the use of *intuition* to describe the *emotional turbulence* and the *transformations* caused by the meeting of different vertices. Bion (1970) named this language the *Language of Achievement*.

As a psychoanalyst, I attempt to create such language that could be the language of my work. In order to do it I use my *intuition*, trying to put what it informs through my *imagination*. *It means* to allow myself to develop *imaginative conjectures* and *rational conjectures*.

Bion (1970) transformed the expression *Man of Achievement* used by the poet John Keats in a letter to his brother George. Bion sustains that a *Man of Achievement* like Shakespeare and Freud is an example of *Language of Achievement*, which is a *prelude to action* and *at the same time a kind of action in itself*.

In this same letter, Keats coined the expression *negative capability* as the condition to become a *Man of Achievement*: *when a man is capable of being in uncertainties, mysteries, doubts, without any irritable reaching after fact and reason*. Bion (1970) introduced the expression to think of the creative aspects of the psychoanalytic technique.

In order to develop a little further, the subjects mentioned earlier, I started my chapter investigating the links between the *psychoanalytic act* and the *poetic act*, having Keats on one side and Bion on the other side.

Such investigation inevitably led me to a confluence of many questions linking intuition, imagination, poetry, ethics and psychoanalysis. Therefore, I had to face a *complexity*, which made me deal with many of Bion's subjects such as a *theory of thinking*, the *psychoanalytical object*, *psychoanalytical function of personality*,

DOI: 10.4324/9781003293392-10

elements of psychoanalysis, the *Grid, Transformations, Caesura, Language of Achievement* and *Language of Substitution.*

My first feelings in the core of the confluence I could describe in a poem by a famous Brazilian poet, Carlos Drummond de Andrade:

A stone in the middle of the road

In the middle of the road
There was a stone.
A simple stone
However, it turns out to be impossible.
To forget such stone
No matter how simple it was to my tired retinas.

This is not a mobile phone, neither a stone.

The Brazilian philosopher Prof. Carneiro Leão[1] used to quote such poem to signify that the stone is not a simple stone but the *ineffable* and *unknowable reality.* One must face such unavoidable fact involved in the process of thinking. Therefore, the use of the word "stone" is not an ordinary repetition but the relentless *mystery* existent in all things. Such *mystery* forces us to think more and to creation; thus, it moves us to search for realizations.

I associate the aforementioned poetical-philosophical question with one component of Bion's *psychoanalytical object* (1962b), which is the letter Greek (μ), as in *mystery*, which I think it also, represents *complexity* (Chuster, 1999, 2002, 2011, 2014, 2018) of our object of work.

The *psychoanalytical object* (Bion, 1962b) *formula:* φ ($\Im$) ($\pm Y$) μ

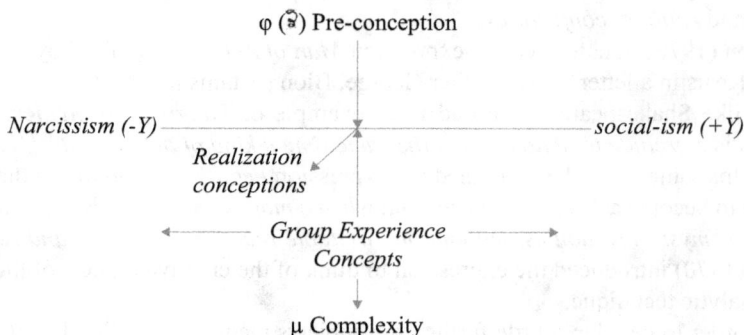

$$\varphi\ (\Im)\ \text{Pre-conception}$$

Narcissism (-Y) ———————————————————— social-ism (+Y)
*Realization
conceptions*

*Group Experience
Concepts*

$$\mu\ \text{Complexity}$$

I use the term *complexity* not in the popular sense but as an intuitive contemporary theory based on the ideas of Edgar Morin.[2]

Complexity means that it is necessary to expand the subject of our investigation in many directions. For instance, it is the case when I try to expand apparently unrelated vertices, as it is the *poetic act* and the *psychoanalytical act.*

Complexity means to investigate if both acts should be capable of dealing with the same subjects such as infinite tensions and contradictions, inspiration and critique, life and death, inside and outside, container and contained, all of them *symmetries* that create a universe in constant emotional turbulence and expansion.

While thinking on my chapter, before my decision for a specific vertex, I found myself stuck in developing a universal history of intuition. This was a task, obviously immense, structured in a huge report of the countless moments of discoveries and creations in all areas of knowledge. Therefore, as soon as I fell into myself doing such a job I realized it was at least wise and prudent to let this job for another occasion.

Therefore, my next step was to reduce the field of investigation, focusing in what could be the main advantage of this project: to build a *history of psychoanalytical intuition*. I imagined for it two axes. The first axe is a historical longitudinal axis that goes from Freud to our days. The second axe is a vertical axis that goes from the beginning to the end of a single session.[3]

Beginning of a session

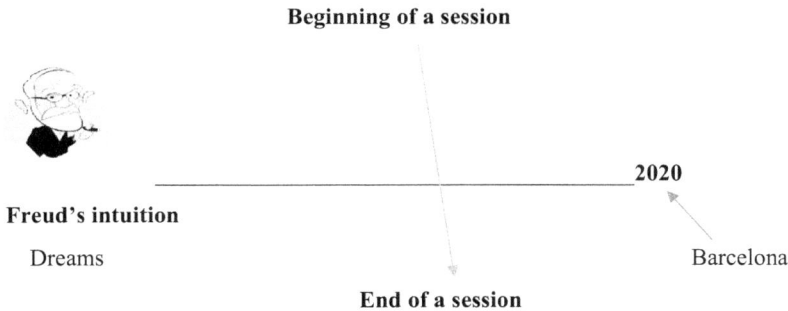

Freud's intuition

Dreams

2020

Barcelona

End of a session

For a dialogue in the vertical history, I suggest changing in Bion's Grid (1975) the rows so far destined to *Scientific Deductive System* (G) and *Algebraic Calculus* (H) to *history of imaginative conjectures* (G) and *history of rational conjectures (H)*.

	Definitory Hypothesis	ψ	Notation	Attention	Inquiry	Action
β	A1	A2				A6
.α	B1	B2	B3	B4	B5	B6
C	C1	C2	C3	C4	C5	C6
Pre-conception	D1	D2	D3	D4	D5	D6
Conception	E1	E2	E3	E4	E5	E6
Concept	F1	F2	F3	F4	F5	F6
Imaginative conjectures	G1	G2	G3	G4	G5	G6
Rational conjectures	H1	H2	H3	H4	H5	H6

I suppose that such perspective would allow us some possibilities to further examine the uses of our intuition through the uses of imagination during the analytical work. I could do it if I consider the link *intuition-imagination* as a quality of *dreaming* (which means *C row of the Grid*). The second step is to consider *intuition-imagination* being transformed in psychoanalytical conceptions and concepts by means of rational conjectures (awake state of mind).

I can rephrase the previous paragraph in a simplistic way: In order to navigate in the dark, deep waters of psychoanalytic work I use my intuition as my *"northern star"* and principles of *ethics* as my *"guardian angel"*. Both should guide and protect my intuition-imagination-in-progress to reach an interpretation.

Of course, this means that I created a *Grid* of my own, which I suppose could make me able to verify *a posteriori* whether I had my *"guardian angel"* at work, which I call *ethical-aesthetical principles* (Chuster, 1999, 2002, 2014, 2018) coherent to the psychoanalytical field and psychoanalytical language.

Those principles I can use as a base to construct instruments of observation in the psychoanalytical field. I described six, all of them a consequence of thinking in terms of complexity. The first one is uncertainty, which implies incompleteness, undecidability of origin, infinity, singularity, negative capability.

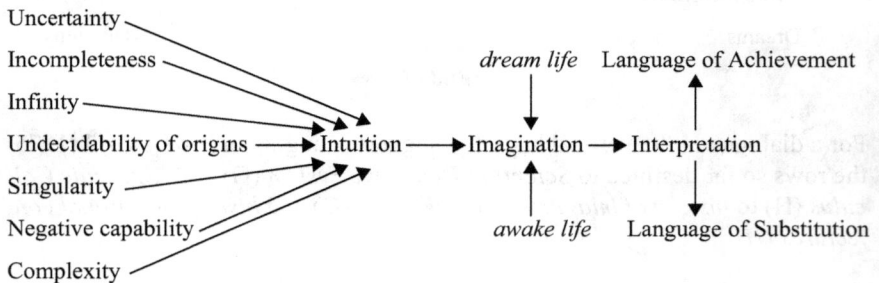

I must apologize for skipping the unavoidable epistemological discussion between using models or principles, resuming this approach as such: *Powerful literature and poetry are created by negative capability*, but *negative capability defined as an ethical-aesthetical principle* could belong to many areas like psychoanalysis, mathematics, art in general.

I will get here a little help from Proust[4] in order to make a question. He said that the poet speaks two languages; he speaks a foreign language inside his own language to create a meaningful language. Do we psychoanalysts have the same experience? Do we speak two languages in our interpretations? Alternatively, do we just create a third language in order to create a communication between those two? Could those be languages of dreaming and awake states of mind?

I will try to develop the idea of speaking the language of dreams and the language of waking life by means of a link created by intuition.

According to Agamben (2018),[5] poets can perform their creative experience because they plunge body and soul into the opacity and mists of philological inquiry. They can intuitively move to an inner debate many archives of desires, illegible manuscripts of complex annotations.

However, what does the psychoanalyst do? What are those archives and complex annotations?

Should a psychoanalyst work as poets do?

I am sure we should not worry about being poets or writers. However, we have common issues, which I think are the *negative capability* and the *Language of Achievement* that produces a *constant conjunction*[6] (Bion, 1962b, 1963, 1970).

I think *Language of Achievement* is the one that breaks up with daily language and becomes a source of semantic improvement. It opens a new world instigating understanding, imagination and the act of becoming oneself (*transformation in O*) instead of just knowing about. It is a language at the service of K→O.

Therefore, I can consider "*poetic*" not just as a literature branch but the place inside us of a semantic innovation, a proposition of a world that brings a new understanding of oneself. This new understanding may move us to a path toward who we really are (*transformation in O*).

I resume this proposition with a quote from Paul Valery[7]: "*Poems are never finished – just abandoned*".

Now, I will quote another famous Brazilian poet, Manoel Bandera, to illustrate the incompleteness of links between the dreaming state of mind and awake state of mind.

I will take his account of how he created the poem "Dreamed Sonnet". I will use it as an analogy to the psychoanalytic work. He wrote that he had dreamed the whole poem, but when he woke up, he could not remember all the words. Therefore, he had to request his **intuition** to fill in the blind spots or lapses of his memory.

Bandera, as a good example of Proust aphorism, speaks two languages in his poem, the one of his dream and the one of waking life. As they communicate, we have the creation of a third text.

I emphasize with the poet's account the use of *dream-memories* in opposition to those *desired memories* that Bion (1967) propose we should get rid of in the psychoanalytic process.

Dream-memories come out while intuition is at work, whereas the other kind goes in an opposite direction, which is the direction of empty concepts that hinder psychoanalytical observations. Those kind of *desired memories*, instead of illuminating the experience, turn them blind.

The poem

The parts of the dream remembered by Manoel Bandera[8]:
My everything, my lover, my friend
Here I portrait you in a sonnet
With my profession of faith and sentiment
. . . . oblige
I like not love . . . .
. . . . do not like my dear friend
. . . .
Nevertheless, in every moment I will be sincere as the day light

Bandera said that in his awake mind remained only vague impressions of the other words. However, he kept a kind of *strong blind feeling* about the general meaning of the poem. This was his guide to rebuild the poem fulfilling the gaps.

After working on his emotional experience, he presented the following text:

My everything, my lover, my friend
Here I portrait you in a sonnet
With my profession of faith and sentiment
I confess I am obliged **to kneel on your feet.**
What in my soul I kept from ancient times
Such experience of a restless desire
I like not love that **ideal object**
Only carnal love *I also do not like* my friend.
What love has as its best it is irradiance
How poor we are! That come not from us.
Where from then? Heaven? Far away?
I promise with passion, and joy, to arise.
Nevertheless, in every moment I will be sincere as the day light

Notice that we have a **third** text fulfilling the memory gaps:

I confess knelled on your feet, I am.
What in my soul I kept from ancient times
Such experience of a restless desire
Ideal object and only carnal love
What love has as its best it is irradiance
How poor we are! That come not from us
Where from then? Heaven? Far away?
I promise with passion, and joy, to arise.

I will expand now the links between dream intuition and waking-life intuition, formulating some questions: Do they differ from each other? How is it a transience between them? How is that in analysis?

I am not able to analyze the poet Bandera (or any other), but it seems a hunch that the words of his dream described an open loving state, but when he woke up, while fulfilling the gaps there is a kind of defense against this feeling.

If something similar happens in analysis, I will try to examine it as a *complexity* and not as a simple contradiction. I will not try to solve what seems a problem or make rush decisions. That requires what Bion (1962b) named as a search for *K* link. I understand *K* not as what one knows but what one would know because one does not know. *K link* is our connection with the future. That is, I hope that between not knowing and knowing can arise a future of knowledge, which requires raising questions in order to open new areas and creating some "rules" of language to express them.

I cannot use the common meaning of words to do that. I need to change my vertex no matter how difficult it is to do this. One can say I am avoiding the trap of supposing to know what the patient is saying with simple colloquial words. I try not to be blind by knowing too much.

A dive into philology sometimes could create a useful rule. I could cope with words keeping my transitive humor, face to face to the intransitive humor of the seriousness of the situation.

I could also resort to Bion's *theory of Transformations* (1965) to look for new areas of investigation and language. I also could say it is a good procedure if a question is unanswered. An unanswered question could raise many others that have possibilities of never having an answer.

This is again an inference of my *ethical-aesthetical principles* applied to the psychoanalytical field (Chuster, 1999, 2002, 2014, 2018).

The poet transformed his words by virtue of his mental work. When I am dealing with a patient, I must try to have a different vertex about what caused the forgetting of the words.

If a link is missing between the words, I could imagine something that may produce a link. In order to do this I can resort at the same time to *rational conjectures* and *imaginative conjectures*.

I can rephrase it in a more sophisticated and complex form: I am looking for a vertex that could translate what sank under the proximity of "O".

For instance, in analysis there are some occasions in which it is adequate to say that the patient's feelings are connected to pauses like weekends, vacations or even a pause between the last session and the current session. Nevertheless, I should assume that psychoanalysts might recognize that they do not know the answers for all breaks, because it involves the issue of time. Some patients may lose a common sense of time. They can act like the anxious rabbit of *Alice in Wonderland* that is always late, but his clock does not have hands.

On the other hand, scientific observation shows one cannot deal with time without space. Therefore, I will assume that intuition is a function of preconception meaning time, space and existence, the latter as a resultant of time and space. I will expand my first quote of Bion in this chapter.

Intuition is a function of   ±   Existence

Time

Space

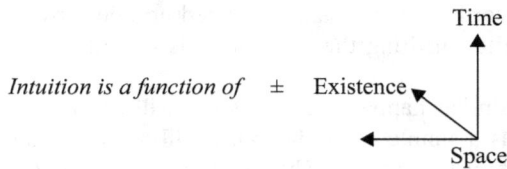

The reason to give a "name" to the patient's feelings is part of observation, but it also could be to set aside the commonsense meanings or even the un-common-sense meanings. I try to reach a language more precise and less saturated. Psychoanalytical trained intuition may allow one to say something about the patient changes in a container/contained relationship or time/space between objects and to make associations in the process of reaching many diverse meanings of an understanding of what is happening in the process of existence.

Understanding involves what is happening in both sides. If we can find a symmetric interpretation between two different mental states, one can find a psychoanalytical link.

Sometimes a patient is reporting a fact, but he forgets a very common word to describe it. If I am observing correctly and I have the option to say something, which would fulfill the gap_ and the patient could say I am right or I am wrong. Where was the word? In which state of mind?

A woman patient started the session reporting very angrily that her husband made a bad comment about her gain of weight. Then she made a brief pause and said she could not find the word she was looking for to express her feelings.

In sequence she explained that her husband use to criticize her for the gain of weight, and at the same time, he used to bring home very fatty foods. Then she said her husband was being *lenient* to her suffering for not being able to react against the need to eat.

I understood her vertex. However, I moved to a different vertex: I said that the word *lenient* is very common in our present times as a synonym of an agreement between the justice system and a criminal person that decided to speak. The result of the agreement is a softening of the condemnation or a kind of agreement.

The patient, who happens to be a lawyer, got angry about my interpretation. Turbulence came out, bringing her outside angry state of mind to our link. She accused me *of being too much a psychoanalyst* and of trying to prove that I had a better point of view than hers.

A simple word contains a vast world.

Since I read *Making the Best of a Bad Job* (Bion, 1979), I always said to myself that the simple existence of the psychoanalyst bothers patients because there is a Not-Me in the session. I know I can have many troubles if, besides being a Not-Me, I dare to say something, because if I say it, it is a double Not-Me.

I made at the session a supposition that a hidden, deepest story was scaring the patient, something very primitive like the search for an omnipotent mind, a perfect mind in danger of destruction if she dares to think. The better alternative could be to keep a hate link (H), which is a false premise: the basic food for *Transformations in hallucinosis* (Bion, 1965).

So far, I relate all the questions to expressing the links between two different mental states. In think the ideas exposed in the paper *Caesura* (1975) embrace those questions.

Some questions concerning caesura between states of mind

Imagine that between analyst and patient there is a screen, infinitely plastic, capable of appearing anywhere, at the same time creating a boundary and a connection.

Such a screen requires pure imagination; it entails a symbolic element to give it a name of a transient quality. The symbolic element is a product of intuitive capacity translated as imaginative capacity.

I think this description is an extremely important feature of the analytic work. One needs imagination to translate intuition. Patients and analysts have varying imaginative capacities. The difference is not quantitative, because many patients, like many analysts, have a flexible imagination that can move and change quickly. The difference is a difference of vertices.

Nevertheless, there are patients who do not have a flexible imagination. They become more superficial and demand a lot from the analyst.

A woman patient was very curious – in an invasive sense – to know whom I would vote for in the presidential election. In her view, I could not refrain from answering this question. She said in a very hostile manner, *you do not dare to avoid answering my question.*

I thought that the patient was trying to bring me to a dangerous area, the area of equivalent vertex.

As I did not answer because my "guardian angel" always says not to answer questions related to the ongoing session, I returned the question to her, allowing her imagination to work.

As I refused to answer, she instantaneously concluded that *I was voting for the candidate opposite to her own* (a fascist in her view) and threatened to "*denounce me to colleagues of the psychoanalytic society who most surely would harm my career for my decision in electing a fascist*".

This reaction is a good example of a *transformation in hallucinosis*. All the elements as rivalry to O, violence, lies, cruelty of the superego, a moral logic based on false premises, intolerance to frustration, hate, minus K, are present.

I told her that *she excluded from her mind all other options besides those two opposite vertices: against or the same. Nevertheless, she imagined that my psychoanalytic group has the same vertex as her, but they are intolerant to my supposed different choice.*

She said, *this is a classical psychoanalytical interpretation in order to avoid showing your position.*

I said, *I do not know if it is classical interpretation. It should not be, as we are supposed to be in analysis, but I can observe that somebody here is being intolerant. Is it you, me or somebody else as the group of psychoanalysts, which happens to be a very familiar group incapable of dealing with political differences amongst people? However, I have an idea about this. You are angry for many other reasons, which I suppose are haunting you all the time.*

She kept silent for some moments, and then she told me a dream. In the dream, *she saw me running away from her, but it was not me, it was her father,* who had abandoned home when she was four years old. She never saw her father again.

A ghost from the past could be used as a personal myth of the patient's seldom terror and unsafety about possible disasters in many areas of her life.

However, there is a hidden story, which is the inner place her violence came from; one may call it the *assassin superego*, the superego that attacks and kills links.

Usually, such a superego is emotionally much more intolerant to the analyst's possible flaws and expresses a huge contempt for the meaning of things. The criticisms are biased and usually intensely cruel.[9]

Most certainly, *transformations in hallucinosis* (Bion, 1965) overload the analyst's imaginative ability, when confronted with thoughts rigidly justified by ideological discourses which are very productive in false premises.

In order to deal with those transformations, *negative capability* is required to the analyst's work. That is, in analysis, it is necessary to tolerate the expression of these feelings and to follow the field of (both sides of the link) responses, relying on the intuitive/imaginative link with the patient – seen as a developing mind that was stuck by virtue of deep psychic pains interfering in the creation of conceptions and concepts about his/her world.

It is important to find a language capable of translating the failure caused by those psychic pains that took the path of interpreting the psychotic part of the personality. Thus, the problem is not the intensity of the pain but the psychoanalytic vertex toward this pain. Such a vertex depends on the ability to think not of the pain itself but of the *meaning* of the pain – that is a fundamental ethical issue.

Bion's ideas make fully evident that the function of psychoanalysis is to preserve human thinking and thereby to preserve human and social autonomy. For this, we must take care of the history of psychoanalytic intuition, which is our basis for constructing imaginative and rational conjectures for our interpretations.

As psychoanalysts, we are neither doctors nor psychologists. We are involved in a unique practice, seeking and investigating the deep meaning of things to favor and preserve thought and the ability to think by means of a long-time[10] trained intuition.

Notes

1   Carneiro Leão, E. *Aprendendo a Pensar*, Vozes ed., Petrópolis, 1977.
2   Morin, E. *Introdução ao Pensamento Complexo*, Sulina, Porto Alegre, 2005.

3 At this point, a question came out that I can use as a future title for a paper: *Are we losing or are we keeping the intuitions Freud bequeathed to us?*
4 *Les Oeuvres completes*, de Marcel Proust, 2016, p. 234, Kindle edition.
5 Agamben, G. *O fogo e o relato*, Boitempo, São Paulo, 2018.
6 A function of the consciousness of the observer. For instance, an observer can select five facts while another can select seven.
7 Lawler, James R. *The Poet as Analyst: Essays on Paul Valéry*, University of California Press, 1974. pp. 230.
8 Bandeira, M. *Meus Poemas Favoritos*, Ediouro, Rio de Janeiro, 1996.
9 One may ask using one of Money-Kyrle's expressions: *what kind of world this person inhabits.*
10 This is an example of an inner world full of generalizations and discrepancies. (*Man's Picture of his world*. Karnac Books, ed. Revised by Meg Harris Williams, London, 2015).

References

Bion, W.R. (1956) *Differentiation of the psychotic and non-psychotic personalities*. In: *Second Thoughts* (pp. 43–64). London: Heinemann, 1967.
——— (1957) *On arrogance*. In: *Second Thoughts*. Northvale: Jason Aronson Inc., 1967.
——— (1962b) *O Aprender da Experiência*. Rio de Janeiro: Zahar.
——— (1963) *Elementos de Psicanálise*. Rio de Janeiro: Zahar.
——— (1965) *Transformações*. Rio de Janeiro: Imago.
——— (1967b) Notes on memory and desire. In W. Bion (1992). *Cogitations*. London: Karnac books (extended 1994 version).
——— (1970) *Atenção e Interpretação*. Rio de Janeiro: Imago.
——— (1975) *The grid and caesura*. Rio de Janeiro: Imago.
——— (1979) *Making the best of a bad job*. In: *W.R. Bion: Clinical seminars and other works*. London: Karnac, 1994.
Chuster (2018b) *Simetria e Objeto Psicanalítico; desafiando paradigmas com W.R. Bion*. Rio de Janeiro: Trio Studio.
Chuster, A. (2014) *A lonesome road: Essays on the complexity of W.R. Bion's work*. Rio de Janeiro: TrioStudios/Karnac.
Chuster, A.; Trachtenberg, R. (2009) *As sete invejas capitais*. Porto Alegre: Artmed.

Part 3

Intuition . . . a matter of two

Chapter 7

Intuition and science

Robert Caper

Psychoanalytic knowledge

I would like to begin by recalling that Bion held that all knowledge is ultimately scientific and referred many times in his writing to psychoanalysis as a science. In this, he joins Freud, who asked, "what else [but a science] can it be?" (1938, p. 282). In asserting that it is a science, however, Bion was not suggesting, as do many contemporary psychoanalysts, that we should try to establish the "scientific" nature of psychoanalysis by grounding it in something such as neurology or "neuropsychoanalysis". He argued instead that psychoanalysis, being a quest for knowledge, simply *is* scientific, and if it does not fit at present within the confines of established scientific disciplines, that is a problem for established science, not for psychoanalysis. His project is to expand our concept of science until it can encompass what psychoanalysis knows, not to reduce psychoanalysis until it fits within the limits of any other science.

Today, I would like to follow Bion's lead by addressing the question of knowledge – how we know what we claim to know – in psychoanalysis, using knowledge in natural science not as a standard into which psychoanalysis must fit if it is to be respectable but only as a different sort of knowledge, to which psychoanalytic knowledge (which, incidentally, is already as respectable as it needs to be) may be compared.

The natural scientist, as Bion points out, relies for his knowledge on the evidence of his physical senses, which operate in a mechanical way: the activity of our physical sense organs can be understood in purely physical terms. The "sense" that the psychoanalyst uses to detect the object of *his* study – another mind or personality – is not mechanical. It is his own personality, acting as "a sensory organ for the perception of psychic qualities", in Freud's words.[1] The analyst "reads" communications from the patient's unconscious by using his personality as a non-mechanical sensor. To what is this non-mechanical sense organ directed?

Bion distinguishes between what natural science studies, which he calls the inanimate world, and what psychoanalysis studies, which he calls the animate world. He "conjectures phenomenologically" that underlying all of our perceptions – whether of the inanimate or animate world – is an objective reality that is itself

DOI: 10.4324/9781003293392-12

not directly perceivable.[2] For the "inanimate" world, we use our sense organs to detect, say, light reflected from a table as it falls on our eyes, and we conjecture the existence of something of which the light is reflected. We do not see the table; we see the reflective effect the table has on the light that falls on it. This something corresponds roughly to Kant's *ding-an-sich*, the thing-in-itself. Bion calls the domain of these things, unknown because unknowable and not perceivable, "O". Although unknown, unknowable and imperceptible, these creatures of O may evolve, to use Bion's term, until they "intersect" with our limited ability to perceive and grasp things – what he calls our "K-capacity".

In contrast, the O – the unknowable ultimate reality – of the "animate" world is not some conjectured Kantian table made up of atoms and molecules, reflecting light into our eyes, but unconscious psychic reality. The "sense" for detecting this animate unconscious psychic reality is not our mechanical sense organs but what Bion calls the *analyst's* O – his own unconscious psychic reality, acting as a receptor for the patient's projective identifications. The potential of the analyst's capacity to know – what Bion called his K-capacity – is his closeness to his own animate O – his own unconscious psychic reality. Bion refers to this closeness as the analyst being "real".

Just as the natural scientist must interpret the evidence of his senses in order to acquire knowledge of the inanimate world, the psychoanalyst must interpret his psychic reality if he is to gain knowledge about the object of his observation – the patient's psychic reality. We cannot simply take our countertransference and assume that the patient causes it by projective identification, because our countertransference is not simply the patient's virgin projection, it is the product of our unconscious *transformation* of that projection.

Scientists who study the inanimate world have been able to refine the instruments they use for observation in marvelous ways. Think of the spectacular images from the Hubble space telescope or the fascinating electron microscope images of the very fine structure of our world. Is there a comparable way to refine the sensitivity of our O as an instrument for the observation of the patient's O – his psychic reality? The task would involve the analyst becoming more "real" – more present in the moment with the patient. Bion suggests two ways to do this: one is to rid ourselves of memory and the other is to rid ourselves of desire. He is clearly not suggesting that we rid ourselves of *unconscious* memory and desire, which is, of course, not possible, but that we recognize our *conscious* tendency to remember – referring to things in the past – and desire – referring to things in the future – and try not to let these distract us from what is transpiring in the present. This is part of the analyst's "being O". The ability to tolerate this state, he says, is the single most important result of the analyst's own analysis.

While events in the inanimate worlds can be detected through the senses, events in the animate world can only be intuited. Bion stresses the need to keep both memory and desire at bay because of their effects on intuition: "For any who have been used to remembering what patients say and to desiring their welfare, it will be hard to entertain the harm to analytic intuition that is inseparable from *any* memories and *any* desires." Take a moment to reflect on how radical this proposal is, and then reflect on how necessary it is.

Intuition – meaning, in this context, the analyst's use of his unconscious psychic reality to sense the unconscious psychic reality of his patient – corresponds to what Freud attributed to consciousness as the "sense organ for the detection of psychical qualities". I would like now to discuss some research from outside the analytic consulting room that seems to bear on the operation of our sense organ for intuition.

Song and dance

In 1966, William Condon, working at the University of Pittsburgh, devised a technique for observing conversations between adults using high-speed cinematography followed by a close, frame-by-frame analysis of the words and motions of the speaker and listener. Using this technique, Condon was able to detect body movements too ephemeral to be visible to the naked eye. These films revealed what he described in retrospect as "two sets of interesting and consistent findings" that he called self-synchrony and interactional synchrony. In the formal language of academic science, he wrote,

> Self-synchrony" refers to the integrated behavior of the individual in which correspondence can be demonstrated, for example, between the film frame of occurrence of a change in sound elements of his own speech and the film frame of occurrence of a change in his own body movements. "Interactional synchrony" designates a similar correspondence between change in sound elements in the speech of a speaker and points of change in movement configurations shown by the listener. These synchronies are not readily detectable at normal communication speed, appear to occur primarily in relation to speech, and are usually totally out of awareness of the individuals so engaged.
>
> (Condon and Sander, 1974, p. 456)

In other words, speakers, without being aware of it, dance in subtle ways to the rhythms of their speech, and their listeners do the same. This duet of song and dance is deficient or absent in individuals with impaired capacity to communicate, such as those suffering from aphasia, autism or schizophrenia.[3]

> What was most surprising about this work was the observation that infants as young as two days also danced in response to adult speech: [One] 2-day-old neonate sustained equally synchronous segments of change of movement [that is, as synchronous as those of adult listeners] with the adult's speech across full 89-word sequence. In other words, this Is in no way accidental but a sustained and precise concurrence. Another 2-day-old sustained movement synchronous throughout, with a series of 125 words of female speech presented by tape recorder. . . . [This] precision of synchronization . . . was

found to characterize the correspondence between adult speech and infant movement in all 16 infants [studied]. Fourteen of these infants were from 12 hours to 2 days old and two others were at 14 days after birth. The correspondence occurred whether the adult speaker was actually present and talking to the neonate, or whether the voice came from a tape recorder. An audiotape containing American English, isolated vowel sounds, tapping sounds, and Chinese language excerpts was used as a stimulus, as well as a living adult speaker. Two of the infants were held, and the rest were supine in their cribs. Chinese, presented to American neonates, was associated with as clear a correspondence as was American English. Disconnected vowel sounds, however, failed to show the degree of correspondence which was associated with natural rhythmic speech. Tapping sounds also failed to show correspondence except at times when occurring in proximity to speech.

(Condon and Sander, 1974, p. 461)

These observations lead Condon to a perspective on human communication from which one sees infants pre-programmed to respond to the rhythms and tones of adult speech. He suggests an inquiry into human communication as "an expression of participation within shared organizational forms rather than isolated entities sending discrete messages." The responsivity of infants to human speech rhythms literally recruits them bodily into what Condon calls the "shared organization" of human vocal communication long before they are able to understand the semantic content of words.[4]

Infants seem to have the ability to distinguish meaningless voice sounds ("isolated vowel sounds") from meaningful speech. In other words, they are able to detect the presence of meaning in human speech long before they understand its semantic content. A significant portion of the meaning conveyed by speech must therefore be non-semantic. This may seem surprising until we recall the direct emotional impact of music. Human speech consists of strings of words that have meaning and syntax. Whatever their meaning, these words are normally uttered with rhythm, variations in loudness, and variations in pitch. These fundamental elements of human speech are also fundamental elements of music.[5] What Condon discovered was that people dance to the music of speech – their own and that of others. This dance begins at least as early as the day of birth, when there is no question of the semantic content of speech having any impact. The music of speech "entrains" dance-like movement, and the infant is first recruited into the linguistic community by being given music it can dance to. Language is not simply something learned by children from adults. It is also a vehicle through which what Condon calls innate human organizational forms may be shared and joined.

Donald Meltzer has proposed that the genesis of language is

essentially two-tiered, having a primitive song-and-dance level (the most primitive form of symbol-formation) for the communication of emotional states of mind . . . upon this foundation of deep grammar there is subsequently superimposed the lexical level of words for denoting objects, actions and qualities of the external world, that is, information.

(1986, p. 181)

What we might ordinarily regard as language is only a part of language and not its most fundamental part. Meltzer distinguishes between a deep musical language, used for communicating about the internal world (that is, states of mind), upon which is built a more superficial, lexical language useful for communicating about the external, material world.[6]

I suggest that our intuitions about others operate largely in the register of song and dance. We resonate unconsciously with the vibes sent out equally unconsciously by others, and our intuition rests largely on sensitivity to these vibes.

Memory, desire and intuition

Bion describes memory and desire as intrusions into the analyst's state of mind that cover up, disguise and blind him to

> the point at issue: that aspect of O that is currently presenting the unknown and unknowable though it is manifested to the two people present in its evolved character.[7] This is the "dark spot" that must be illuminated by "blindness". Memory and desire are "illuminations" that destroy the value of the analyst's capacity for observation as a leakage of light into a camera might destroy the value of the film being exposed . . . I wish to reserve the term "memory" for experience related to conscious attempts at recall. These are expressions of a fear that some element, "uncertainties, mysteries, doubts" will obtrude.
>
> Bion, *Attention and Interpretation* (1971) p. 94

If the analyst succeeds in minimizing memory and desire, he will find himself in a dream-like state. The point of avoiding conscious attempts to remember something about the patient is that it allows a "dark spot" to form in his mind so that something else – an involuntary recollection that Bion calls "dream-like memory", may fill it: "the sacrifice of memory and desire is conducive to the growth of dream-like "memory" which is a part of the experience of psycho-analytical reality" W. R. Bion (1967b).

The dreams that patients have outside the session are relevant; but they are not transformative like the dreams that the patient has *in* the session (his live unconscious psychic reality), which give the O (unconscious psychic reality) of the patient a chance to intersect with the O (unconscious psychic reality) of the analyst via an intuition that is dream-like, ephemeral and, like the contents of a dream, difficult to remember precisely. The fate of this intuition is to contribute not to memory (which is part of knowledge), but to mental growth (which is an evolution of O). What contributes to psychological growth in psychoanalysis is not an interpretation that is remembered and contributes to something called "insight" but an experience that is assimilated into one's dream life.

The unique relationship in psychoanalysis between our knowledge (K) and the thing we have knowledge about (O) means that if the acquisition of knowledge is always scientific, as Bion maintains, then a science of psychoanalysis must have a logical structure – a "geometry", as Bion put it – radically different from anything that has gone before. If the work of building such a structure from the ground up seems daunting or discouraging, it is only because we have complacently forgotten that Freud's discovery of the unconscious imposed on us the burden of developing a radically new way of thinking about the mind. But not to worry; whenever we forget that, Bion is here to remind us.

Notes

1 "What part now remains in our description of the once all-powerful and all-overshadowing consciousness? None other than that of a sensory organ for the perception of psychic qualities" (1900, p. 488).
2 "I shall use the sign O to denote that which is the ultimate reality represented by terms such as ultimate reality, absolute truth, the godhead, the infinite, the thing-in-itself. O does not fall in the domain of knowledge or learning save incidentally; it can be become, but it cannot be known. It is darkness and formlessness but it enters the domain K when it has evolved to a point where it can be known, through knowledge gained by experience, and formulated in terms derived from sensuous experience; its existence is conjectured phenomenologically" (Bion, 1971).
3 "Microanalyses of pathological behavior have revealed marked self-dyssynchronies, in which correspondence between linguistic elements and kinesic elements is reduced or absent: for example, these are encountered in subjects with aphasic, autistic, and schizophrenic conditions" (Condon and Sander, 1974, p. 458).
4 "The sustained synchrony of organized correspondences between adult speech and neonate body movement at this microkinesic level, within periods lasting less than a second, raises issues about the nature of communication across many levels. It would suggest that infant motor organization, entrained by the organized pattern of adult speech over many months from birth, may be preparing operational formats emerging toward a later, and also developmental, implanting of speech. It thus suggests inquiry into the 'bond' between human beings as an expression of participation within shared organizational forms rather than isolated entities sending discrete messages" (Condon and Sander, 1974, p. 462).
5 Early versions of computer-generated voices produced words strung together in syntactically correct sentences, but they sounded like machines trying to talk. Only after programmers learned to incorporate musical elements into their artificial voices did they begin to resemble human speech.
6 See also Meltzer (1975, p. 193).
7 If the analyst is occupied with desiring the patient's welfare, she will be thinking of whether the patient is communicating something "good" (conducive to his welfare) or "bad" (detrimental to his welfare). This will distract the analyst from simply hearing, without prejudice, what the patient is saying – RC.

References

Bion W.R. (1967b). *Notes on memory and desire*. In W.R. Bion (1992). *Cogitations*. London Karnac books (extended 1994 version).

Wilfred Bion. *Attention and Interpretation*. Tavistock, London, 1971. (also, in: Seven Servants, Jason Aronson, New York, 1977).

William S. Condon and Louis W. Sander. Synchrony demonstrated between movements of the neonate and adult speech. *Child Development*, 45(2):456–462, 1974. ISSN 00093920, 14678624. URL www.jstor.org/stable/1127968.

Sigmund Freud. The interpretation of dreams. *The Standard Edition of the Complete Psychological Works of Sigmund Freud*, 4–5, 1900.

Sigmund Freud. Some elementary lessons in psychoanalysis. In James Strachey, editor, *The Standard Edition of the Complete Psychological Works of Sigmund Freud*, volume 23, pages 279–286. Hogarth Press, 1938.

Donald Meltzer. *Explorations in Autism*. Clunie Press, Perthshire, Scotland, 1975.

Donald Meltzer. *Studies in Extended Metapsychology: Clinical Application of Bion's Ideas*. Clunie Press, 1986.

Chapter 8

Mystic intuition and the language of dreams

Annie Reiner[1]

[One] source of distortion is the tendency to link F [Faith] with the supernatural because of lack of experience of the "natural" to which it relates.

(Bion, 1970, p. 48)

One has to look down from a far distance in space in order to see the shape of the Earth. Likewise, we need a kind of overview of a session in order to see the whole picture. Not the *whole* whole picture, for as Bion makes clear, the apprehension of O – the thing in itself, absolute truth – is not possible with our egocentric mental apparatus. We can, however, get a somewhat more comprehensive "view," one that does not require eyes, of course, or other sense organs – ears, nose, etc. – but is instead sensed or dreamt with a blind third eye. Suspending our ego functions and becoming one with the object of our perceptions affords us a broader perspective beyond our usual perceptions.

However, just as NASA would not send astronauts into outer space without a careful return strategy, one should not traverse this mental outer/inner space without some idea of how to return to one's familiar earthly self.

Nothing is more clear than the lack of clarity generated by "O" – Bion's most controversial concept. He did, however, consider it central to clinical work. It is also central to the topic of this book, for it involves a deep intuition in tandem with dream states. The most controversial aspect of O is surely its association with the mystic, which has generated worldwide heated discussions about whether Bion meant it to represent a mystical state. I will nonetheless dive right into this hot debate that I think is situated at the heart of his legacy.

The mystic and the analytic group

The question of whether or not Bion meant O to represent a mystical state is perplexing to me, since he stated this so directly. Even some admirers of Bion's earlier contributions see this mystical O as an unfortunate chapter of his work. Perhaps it is a problem of language, for I think what is essentially at issue is not whether Bion meant O to represent a mystical state but rather what *he* meant by the word "mystical."

DOI: 10.4324/9781003293392-13

One common argument views mysticism as antithetical to science. I agree that traditional religious beliefs usually associated with mystics are often antithetical to a scientific or psychoanalytic perspective, but this does not make it antithetical to how *Bion* defines it.

> Mystics appear in any religion, science, time, or place. Such persons "contain" the "messianic idea" or the "messianic idea" may "contain" the person.
>
> (Bion, 1970, p. 110)

The following statement makes it even more clear.

> I shall use the term, "mystic" to describe these exceptional individuals. I include scientists, and Newton is the outstanding example of such a man: his mystical and religious preoccupations have been dismissed as an aberration when they should be considered as the matrix from which his mathematical formulations evolved.
>
> (ibid., p. 64)

To expunge Bion's idea of the mystic from his work seems to miss this point, that these "crazy" mystical ideas are the *basis* and/or *fulfilment* of his work rather than an aberration. The messianic idea is a new idea, theretofore unseen, that naturally may seem odd and threatening, like the concept of O. But I view Bion's earlier, more universally admired theories of thinking as a foundation to understanding the mystical meaning of O in psychoanalysis. What I hope to add today is the idea of a *relationship* between two very different states of mind: the intuitive mystical state *conjoined with* a capacity to think, as Bion defined it. It is not a continuum; these are different mental functions, but using these intuitions in an analytic way does require a foundation of thinking, which for Bion (1962a, 1963, 1962b) includes a *relationship* between thinking and feeling, thoughts as containers for feelings.

Bion (1970) uses the word "mystic" as synonymous with "genius" or "exceptional individual," replacing strictly religious implications with any transcendent mental experience. These are visions into a realm, unknowable except through metaphysical channels of becoming one with an experience, much as infants do. However, it is not enough to be an infant. One's mind must also be capable of *processing* these dream-like states.

These distinctions may become clearer with reference to some clinical vignettes. In analyzing several extraordinarily intuitive people with capacities for telepathic awareness and prescient views into future events (cf. Reiner, 2004, 2012, 2017), I noticed that each had suffered severe early emotional traumas that led to breakdowns of mental boundaries of time and space, making development of boundaries between self and other impossible. Ferenczi (1932) noted something similar, when traumatized infants of mentally ill mothers sought relief for their lack of real attachment in an escape to a realm he called "the astra." He called them "wise babies." Like my patients, they developed capacities for knowledge unavailable to others (ibid., p. 81), capacities similar to the over-view of O and yet vastly different, for these dream-like retreats into distant "stars" are essentially states of dissociation and fragmentation.

How then does Bion's view of the mystic differ from the heightened intuition in some religious mystics and/or the often-pathological states of traumatized "wise babies" we see in treatment? Bion's theories of thinking help us to navigate this distinction between mental health and pathology. One thing I learned from my "extraordinary" patients was that their uncanny intuitive "knowledge" *was often not useful in thinking*. Their escapes from grief and loss were in fact primitive *substitutes for thinking before a real capacity to think had developed* (cf. Reiner, 2004, 2006, 2012, 2017). They could not, therefore, trust their remarkable intuitions. It was "knowledge" that could not be known, for these mystical states were driven by an escape from painful emotions that could not be thought about or integrated.

Bion's O redefines the use of mystic states in psychoanalysis by including the idea of a healthy mind/self as a feeling-dreaming-thinking entity. O, then, is *a transcendent view in conjunction with a mind able to digest primitive feelings, i.e., to think*. The analyst's intuitive access into waking dream states akin to the mystic's must be accompanied by a mind able to think about visions gleaned through a non-rational, *dis*organized mind.

I am not suggesting that all mystics lack this capacity. I would not know. But I am pointing to the analyst's need for dual capacities of deep feeling and deep thinking. And yet openness to such intuitive visions reflects a breakdown or suspension of the known ego, enabling break *throughs* into those waking dreams, but often, for those traumatized "wise babies," these are breakdowns that never healed. My patients first had to be helped to develop a self/mind capable of holding their own *feeling*s. One must walk a fine line with such patients, honoring their unique gifts but helping them to process disturbing mental detritus of early deprivations.

In the absence of a capacity to think, as Bion described it, these visions are often viewed concretely as messages from a reified God rather than knowledge gained through intuition. It is the difference between Christian dogma – Christ as the Son of a reified external God – and Christian Gnostics who viewed Christ as a teacher of metaphysical mysteries. The latter is a scientific model of learning through internal experience, while the former, requiring allegiance to an omniscient external God, is anti-science.

If this intuitive capacity of O is essential to psychoanalytic work, do we all have to be mystics? I hope not, but it does mean we have to put up with the awareness that we are not omniscient and so must continue to break down our own mental barriers to learning if we are to help our patients do the same. And yet as we know, people do not like change. Many prophets are mocked or destroyed for their unfamiliar ideas, as changes are felt as catastrophic threats to all one knows. What greater stimulus for fear is there than an infinite unknown that is infinitely out of reach? And what greater stimulus for envy of those for whom this realm is even nominally more within reach? We can destroy the idea and the envy by killing the messenger – the mystic, genius or exceptional person. As one of those "extraordinary individuals," Bion brought significant change to psychoanalysis, not in spite of his enigmatic vision but *because* of it. One wonders whether this most arcane truth he attempted to unveil is also being killed.

By all accounts, Bion felt he had failed adequately to explain these elusive aspects of his work despite diverse attempts to express them. He tried "mathematizing" psychoanalysis in *Transformations and* using evocative stream of *un*consciousness in *Memoir of The Future*. I raised this issue in a conversation with Francesca Bion, decades after her husband's death, saying that it must have been frustrating for him to feel that his ideas were not understood. She replied, "Yes, it's always hard for a genius to be understood" (Bion, F., 2012).

Truth and beauty – a clinical vignette

One young woman with this kind of intuitive/spiritual gift had been traumatized by emotionally unreceptive parents. Although like a damaged, confused baby or fetus, an essential purity and curiosity had survived.

I presented this case in a conference for a visiting analyst, and a large number of participants saw only the patient's pathology. I was disturbed to see her gift overlooked and distorted in the group's mind. One intuitive audience member aptly commented that the group seemed to be doing to the patient what her parents had done to her. She had not developed a way to think about the enormous storm of mental energy still available to her but was still clearly hungry to learn. The group's inability to see the vital potential of this person's mind caused me to wonder whether we as analysts are trained to see that extraordinary person or hidden genius in a patient's mind. Unfortunately, we see a lot of ugliness that often obscures it, but dealing with pathology without an eye to the still-living potential for truth and health is not enough.

> Beauty is truth, truth, beauty – that is all
> Ye know on earth, and all ye need to know.
> (Keats, 1819, pp. 825–827)

Although truth does not always feel beautiful to the patient, we analysts need to see the beauty in even the most painful truths if we are to help lift someone out of the deadness of a mind built on lies.

The life and death of the self

The death of the self is an idea central to Eastern and Western religions. Christ says:

> Lay down your life and follow me.
> Anyone who wants to save his life will lose it;
> Anyone who loses his life for my sake will find it.
> (Matthew 16: 24–26)

What "life" does one need to renounce? I think, like Winnicott's (1960) "False Self," it is a self deprived of the natural truth of a deeper self. By giving up that truncated false self, one may find the more expansive intuition of O. This is done, Bion says, by suspending memory, desire and understanding – a temporary death of the self with which one is generally identified. It arouses threats of ego regression, the boundarylessness of one's infant mind.

Bion (1991) wrote, "Most people experience mental death if they live long enough. You don't have to live long . . . all you have to do is be mentally alive" (p. 178). Writing of his traumatic experiences as a young tank commander in World War I, he wrote, "I died at Amiens on August 8, 1918" (Bion, 1982, p. 265). His later success in gathering up the pieces of this mental explosion probably helped fuel his impressive creativity. Although I never went to war, I also experienced the death of a self I had previously thought myself to be. How is it that we can walk around thinking we are one person, only to find out we are someone else? We can call it the "return of the repressed" or the return of that which was *never* repressed, felt or mentally represented. But I learned that sanity is not the absence of *in*sanity but the capacity to process great floods of feeling that *feel* insane but generate creativity and growth.

Until then I had known nothing about the wall protecting the imposter baby that grew into a facsimile of myself. Like all babies, my imposter baby was adorable. Everyone loved her – parents, friends, teachers, lovers, etc. Even her first two analysts loved her, for they couldn't distinguish mental life from mental death.

People avoid pain, not knowing they then also have to avoid pleasure. The imposter babies we see in treatment must give up their false lives to make room for real pain and joy and to facilitate access to O. These two brief clinical examples may help illustrate the complexity of these mental states of life or death.

Clinical example #1 – "Lola"

"Lola" began treatment three years ago feeling anxious and lost, with intense feelings of self- hatred. She is, however, extremely loveable and very bright, though strikingly unaware of her feelings. She was weaned at two months when her mother's milk dried up. While she described her parents as "loving," they saw her as "too sensitive," a child they could not understand. I found Lola's dreams peculiarly opaque at first. Images evoked no feelings, no meaning. This had begun changing by this session.

> I was in the yard of my childhood home playing with my dog, "Roo-coo."
> I went into the kitchen, my parents gave me some kind of special artifact, which I took to my bedroom. . . . Later I wondered, 'Was my mother sad when Roo-coo died?'"

Lola and her mother loved Roo-coo, who was put to sleep when Lola was away at college. I asked about the dog's name and she laughed, "It doesn't mean anything!" Lola did not know what the artifact was but felt it was "important."

I thought that Roo-coo represented Lola, who felt she had "died," put herself to sleep (perhaps when she was weaned), and didn't know whether her mother had felt sad or even noticed she was gone. I said she treasured the special "artifact" her parents gave her (love? life?) but had no idea what it meant. Lola looked at me sadly. "I always felt I had to fix my parents . . . I knew things they didn't know." Like the wise babies, Lola seemed to possess unknown knowledge of the beautiful but unknown artifact of her real self. She had felt loved by her mother, but like a dog perhaps, slavish and unconscious. It was this dead imposter self who hated her real self, while her real self hated the imposter that had usurped her life.

Lola's dreams became increasingly more meaningful. They had begun to help her to think, and in that dreaming self her true story was slowly being born.

Clinical example #2 – "Erin"

Adopted at four months, "Erin" knew nothing of her early months in foster care, but she arrived at her new home with a painful rash and unable to cry – emotionally dead, one might surmise. Her adoptive mother, well-intentioned but unstable, became clinically depressed, and Erin, only twelve, often served as her caregiver.

For several years, Erin's analysis felt like I was holding that infant silently on my chest, a particularly loving infant that words were impotent to reach. By the time we terminated, seventeen years later, Erin had changed a great deal. She had a creative life and was CEO of a large company. While we felt she had more work to do, we both sensed it was time for her to go live her life. She did well, but stressed by toxic company politics, she found herself feeling lost, and three years later she returned to treatment for a "tune-up." After months of once weekly sessions, she felt whole again, and quit her job to follow her own creative dream. In this session she happily reported having received interest in her novel.

> I dreamt I was in a fetal position; I could not move. Something in me said, "You have to remain still." I said, "That's not true! Stillness is death!" It was like a debate between two parts of myself. I am suddenly a baby in a crib. My Mom walks in and says, "Come on, you can move. Time to get up!" I knew I could move but I was afraid to . . . or I did not want to get up.

"Weird dream," Erin said, "because I *am* moving, enjoying my work, and things are happening." She paused. "I think I didn't *want* to get up and interact with my mother. I adored her . . . she was always active, always doing things, but when I was little, I never wanted her to touch me."

I was confused by this dream. Changes often stimulated Erin's terror of abandonment, so I wondered if her creative re-birth had aroused a desire to stay in a safe womb with me, to avoid this scary change. However, this did not fit with today's sense of lightness, hope. I then imagined this dream as the "birth" of Erin's *imposter* self. Her job as a CEO was in part an identification with her active, busy, idealized mother. She has here gone back to her fetal self, but this time, I thought, to get up *as herself*, to live *her* story, not her mother's. Although she *can* get up, she doesn't *want* to if it means having to be or care for that needy mother. That job, like the one she recently quit, left no room for her inner self.

I agreed that stillness *can* be death. However, it can also be a nodal point from which to begin anew, moved by her own energy, not her mother's anxiety or *her* anxiety *about* her mother. The latter is movement that *looked* like life but was driven by her imposter self. She is struggling with these meanings of life and death, for what feels like death may be the death knell for the imposter that has lived *her* life, while her real infant self was frozen in the fetal position. T.S. Eliot's poem in *Four Quartets*, came to mind.

> At the still point of the turning world. Neither flesh nor fleshless;
> . . . at the still point, there the dance is,
> But neither arrest nor movement. And do not call it fixity . . .
> Except for the point, the still point,
> There would be no dance, and there is only the dance . . .
>   (Eliot 1943, pp. 15–16).

Familiarity with both kinds of stillness is needed to determine if it is the static "fixity" of emotional deadness or a stillness underlying a sense of being that gives rise to real movement. These wise babies, or little mystics, who at some point mentally died cannot develop their authentic selves, but I saw here something like the *generative* stillness of Eliot's "still point," from which authentic movement of the self can emerge. It is like a singularity from which one's mental universe is born.

Bion called dreams "unconscious thinking." Erin's dream deftly expresses complex matters of her metaphysical life and death, the distinction between a vital self and the imposter that acts *just like* a person while relegating that vital self to deadly stillness. It helped me to think about that frightening "still point of the turning world" at which the *imposter* baby must die, leaving what seems like terrifying nothingness that may instead be the beginning of everything real. If we pose the question – "To be or not to be?" – we must first cultivate the intuition to determine which is which, to help patients to die so they can live.

Note

1 A version of this chapter titled "Intuição mística: verdade e beleza" was originally published in the *Revista Brasileira de Psicanálise*, 55(2), 27–38, 2021.

References

Bion, F. (2012). *Private Phone Conversation*. London/Los Angeles.

Bion, W. R. (1962a). *Learning from Experience*. New York: Basic Books.

Bion, W. R. (1962b). A theory of thinking. *International Journal of Psycho-Analysis*. Vol. 43, Parts 4–5, 1962.

Bion, W. R. (1963). *Elements of Psychoanalysis*. New York: Basic Books.

Bion, W. R. (1970). *Attention and Interpretation*. London: Karnac.

Bion, W. R. (1974). *Brazilian Lectures I*. Rio: Imago Editora Ltda.

Bion, W. R. (1975). The dream. In: Bion, W. R. (1991). *A Memoir of the Future*. London: Karnac, pp. 1–216.

Bion, W. R. (1982). *The Long Week-End*. In: Bion, F. (Ed.). London: Karnac.

Elliot, T. S. (1943). Burnt Norton. In: *Four Quartets* (1971). New York: Harcourt Brace Jovanovich.

Ferenczi, S. (1932). *The Clinical Diary of Sandor Ferenczi*. In: Dupont, J. (Trans.) (1985). Cambridge, MA: Harvard University Press.

Keats, J. (1819). Ode on a Grecian Urn. In: *The Norton Anthology of English Literature* (1979). New York: W.W. Norton & Co., pp. 825–827.

Reiner, A. (2004). Psychic phenomena and early emotional states. *Journal of Analytical Psychology*. Vol. 49, 2004, 313–336.

Reiner, A. (2006). Synchronicity and the capacity to think. *Journal of Analytical Psychology*. Vol. 51, 2006, 555–575.

Reiner, A. (2012). *Bion and Being: Passion and the Creative Mind*. London: Karnac.

Reiner, A. (2017). Bion's 'O' and Ferenzci's 'astra.' In: Reiner, A. (Ed.). *Of Things Invisible to Mortal Sight: Celebrating the Work of James S. Grotstein*. London: Karnac.

Winnicott, D. (1960). Ego distortion in terms of true and false self. In: *The Maturational Process and the Facilitating Environment* (1990). London: Karnac.

Chapter 9

A thought without a thinker: intuition, negative capability, and psychoanalytic function of the personality

Intuition: a memoir of the future?

Lia Pistiner de Cortiñas

at once it struck me what quality went to form a man of Achievement, especially in Literature. and which Shakespeare possessed so enormously – I mean Negative Capability, that is when a man is capable of being in uncertainties, mysteries, doubts, without any irritable reaching after facts and reason.

(Keats)

If psychoanalytic intuition does not provide a stamping ground for wild asses, where is the zoo to be found to preserve the species? Conversely, if the environment is tolerant, what is to happen to the "great hunters" who lie unrevealed or reburied?

(Bion, 1991)

Julio Cortazar described "Negative Capability" as the gift of being loyal to an intuitive certainty that reason casts aside and common sense does not accept; it is a "thinking" that might seem unwise and illogical from the point of view of reason and of logic, but from a deeper perspective it could reveal as superior and transcend the logic of conceptual thought. I start this chapter with a quotation from Keats on "*Negative Capability*", a mental state essential for the analyst: it means being open to apprehend what intuition reveals in a psychoanalytic treatment, when he is in at-one-ment with his patient. In what follows I will speak about "intuition in the psychoanalytic treatment", so I will relate intuition with some psychoanalytic concepts.

Intuition and reverie

At the beginning of life, the most significant function for the human being's mental and emotional development was named Reverie by Bion. *Reverie implies the first object relationship with a special empathic quality of the mother* that later, if everything goes well, is extended towards other relationships. The term "reverie" emphasizes the *dreamlike quality* of this function; it implies an opening towards intuition as a *dreamlike representation* of emotional states, which can be a first step towards understanding the meaning of the patient's material and then to formulate

DOI: 10.4324/9781003293392-14

the interpretation. The mother, when taking care of her infant, needs to "dream" her baby, and this "dreaming" – an intuition which implies the containing, detoxifying capability of her mind – also gives the infant the possibility to internalize this function. In this extension of the meaning of "dreaming" – and considering reverie as a function – intuition is one of the factors. Anxiety can become for the baby a "*nameless terror*" – but when transformed through reverie, it is detoxified and now can be assimilated by the infant's personality. *Reverie implies a capability of capturing the intuitive dimension through the mother's "dreaming": receiving the infant's needs and giving them a meaning. Meaning nourishes mental life. Reverie enables the infant to internalize and develop this function. Reverie also is a communication channel, where – if everything goes well – intuitive communications circulate.*

Projective identification is a means of the infant's primitive communication. Freud wrote that the infant's cry is a communication when the child is in contact with a fellow human being. With the increase of social complexity, this detoxifying function can be performed also by the father and other people. The mother's reverie needs the father's containment. The environment can facilitate the development of this function or make it more difficult. In *Attention and Interpretation* (1970), Bion investigates the creative mind of the mystic and seems to name the pre-conception – a kind of expectation that contains an intuition – with the mysterious name of "thought without a thinker". *Is intuition a thought without a thinker or a thought that has not yet a thinker?* Is it a capability that acquires different values if complemented with thinking, as a process of working through what was first an intuition? Can we consider intuition a *memoir of the future*? Bion refers to the sensorial world: the sense organs apprehend the sensory world; how do we apprehend the emotional world? His answer is: through intuition. *With this formulation of "thoughts without a thinker" Bion extends the creative aspects of his theory of thinking, which encompasses the movement of the human mind towards the future and towards emotions and object relations. These "thoughts without a thinker" are opening towards the future, waiting to be thought.* From this perspective we can consider the relationship of this formulation with Nietzsche's idea that what humanity needs is to produce a 'Super-man', what Bion calls genius or mystic: the individual with intuition capable of illuminating a truth that changes the direction of humanity. These intuitions revealed by a "genius or mystic" that appear in certain historical times develop ideas that establish a *historical caesura*, which implies a "*catastrophic change*" (*Bion, 1970*) that means that something is becoming different from what it was before, as in the case of Socrates, Leonardo, Shakespeare, Freud, Picasso, etc. These intuitions reveal a truth that implies significant changes for humanity. But intuitions of common people can become a stimulus as well for the development of an apparatus for thinking.

Intuition and prenatal aspects of the mind

We can conjecture that the Kleinian notion that internal objects are prior to external ones is a precedent of Bion's ideas about innate pre-conceptions: the pre-conception (is it also an intuition?) of the breast stimulates the infant towards his first fundamental experience, the emotional relation with the breast, the basis of learning from experience. The "breast" here means an emotional experience. "Breast" is an emotional experience which implies the parents (pre-oedipal conception) and the society that guaranties that they come together to feed the baby, a creative mind, generating new solutions and so in an evolution, from the creative mind comes a new intuitive pre-conception.

I will now refer to intuition and caesura between prenatal and postnatal aspects of the mind. Infants are conscious of what they feel, but this is a rudimentary consciousness: they can feel their emotions but cannot name them and are not aware of their meaning. At the beginning of life, they can only differentiate between pain and pleasure. When naming the emotions, with the development of an evolved consciousness, sometimes we cannot relate the name with the emotion, because of dissociations; there is a caesura between what we call prenatal and what is postnatal: I am referring to the *psychic birth of the emotional experience*.

Intuition and O

When Bion developed the theoretical change from Learning from Experience, the K link, towards mental growth as becoming oneself (*at-one-ment*) *that is* mental growth of the personality as *becoming one with oneself*, without the critical intervention of the Super- superego, he makes a significant change in his theory. If we keep in mind his conceptualization of the Super-superego as usurping the Ego functions of contact with internal and external reality, we understand that what he postulates is an evolution towards Mental Growth, which he describes as becoming one with oneself, becoming authentic, a conceptualization close to Winnicott and his description of maturing as *finding in oneself a place inside where to exist and feel real*. Super-superego and reverie mutually exclude: if the place of reverie is occupied by this Super-superego who usurps the Ego functions, no intuition is possible, because Superego's criticism does not allow it. The postulation of evolution towards Mental Growth has consequences for the aims of psychoanalysis: it implies not only getting to know about our feelings, about our mental life, but Bion refers as well to a deep connection with the internal world, where one is becoming oneself through intuitions in a profound relation with internal and external reality. This development implies that through psychoanalysis, the emotional experiences can be embodied in images and words, which find their best expression in dreams and the work of artists, who express in their art images of emotional experiences. The acceptance of incompleteness, uncertainty, doubts and of the relation finite–infinite are factors of the mental state that stimulates the development of intuition at the service of mental growth.

Innate preconceptions and "memoirs of the future"

Through speculative imagination we can conjecture that the embryonic mind has a rudimentary capability of registering sensations and giving answers to these sensuous stimulus – which as β elements have not yet become metaphorical: the infant "knows" he is hungry, but he doesn't know how to name it. Early in life a mother (the maternal function) can link the infant's feelings and sensations with their mental equivalent: the innate preconceptions of the infant allow it to form primitive proto-conceptions, which as sensuous patterns are awaiting a birth and a postnatal development: the infant's mouth has a pre-conception of the breast but needs the maternal *reverie* to continue developing. These pre-conceptions can remain "asleep" as β – elements. These elements, when not transformed in alpha – in conscious or unconscious thoughts – can be projected towards the body as *somato-psychic* aspects or be transformed in hallucinosis.

Intuition and dreaming

Bion extends the meaning of "dreaming": it is a process that happens while sleeping and also in wakefulness: it is a transformation that through images represents and gives *meaning* to stimuli from the internal or external world. For the analyst "dreaming" means intuition, but it has a quality related to the fact that it is a psychoanalytic trained intuition, trained to be part of his observational technique, which has the aim to apprehend emotional qualities, in himself and in the patient. So we can consider the psychoanalytic treatment as a process of "*dreamlike transformation*". Bion extends the technical rule of "free-floating attention" towards the discipline of: "without memory, without desire, without understanding", a discipline for the analyst who needs to extend the field of his intuitive apprehension. The ultimate reality is unknowable, Bion names it *O (the infinite void without form)*:

"*Dreaming*" *is a mediator and integrates the two principal directions of O and their convergence with experience: O→K and K→O;* a direction that goes from O towards K: the transformation in a disposition to know, which implies being open towards intuition resigning certitude. K never can apprehend the ultimate reality: a disposition to know implies tolerance of uncertainties. This implies a possibility to reopen again constant conjunctions already achieved, towards new possibilities that can be apprehended by intuition. The sensuous stimuli that go along with the emotional experience "call" their innate equivalents – the inherent pre-conceptions (that we could call "memoirs of the future") being incarnated in them. I consider Memoir of the Future the mysterious name of Bion's last book as referring to these intuitions that can later be transformed in conceptions or concepts.

Intuition and psychic reality

How do we apprehend psychic reality, which does not have sensuous elements? Bion answers this question: with *intuition* that is the equivalent of seeing, hearing, smelling . . . for the sensuous.

"I am supposing that there is a psychoanalytic domain with its own reality – unquestionable, constant, subject to changes only in accordance to its own rules although these rules are not known." (Bion, 1970) These realities can be apprehended by intuition, if the adequate apparatus is available in the conditions appropriate for its functioning. The conditions in which intuition operates are pellucid and opaque. These opacities are expressed by Bion's technical rule: without *memories, desire and understanding. Such freedom from opacities cannot be achieved in psychoanalysis if intuition has been already damaged* by indiscipline, in any time. As closer the psychoanalyst can come to get rid of these opacities – and no doubt of other opacities not yet identified – more he will be able to trust that the sources of his observations are not his "personal equation".

Bion Cogitations (1992, p. 365)

The analysis of the analyst is fundamental to discipline our counter-resistances as much as keeping in mind the emotional turbulence in which a psychoanalytic session develops. The *psychoanalytic trained intuition* needs a discipline; the discipline of "no memory, no desire, no understanding" because resistances of the analyst interfere and turn intuition opaque. This discipline has to be long-lasting, permanent and continuous.

Bion asks what the distinctive aspect of the objects of the psychoanalytic investigations is: the links. *What makes them psychoanalytic more than psychiatric, social or cognitive*? To answer this question, we must have in mind the use psychoanalysts make of *intuition* to select clues, as to be able to speak of what is *incipient* more than of what is obvious. *Incipient can be* defined as "the condition to be open to an early state of existence", as when we say that we are "smelling" something and as it is obvious, we are not referring to a concrete odor. Bion uses the term *pre-monition* to describe anticipations of emotions, intuitions that will appear later in a more developed way.

Could we define *intuition* as the mind's immediate apprehension without the intervention of a process of reasoning? In this definition intuition seems to be similar to *negative capacity*. *Intuition* took a technical philosophical meaning as the English name of the term used by Kant[1] of *a priori*, a first kind of registration of the experience. Bion, very much influenced by Kant, considers intuition an observational *empiric sensitivity*. We can think psychoanalytic intuition as a kind of *registration, apparently immediate, which, depends on a preconscious or unconscious apprehension of tiny, early signs of emotional data*. This kind of registration provides the raw material for interpretations and constructions, which require a more explicit process of observation and reasoning. The analyst's intuitive apprehension is an exploratory anticipation of attention (free-floating attention), as a kind of anticipation of future developments. These *psychoanalytic* capacities are part of the *psychoanalytic equipment and of the psychoanalytic function of the personality necessary for any treatment* but even more when dealing with difficult patients. The potential inherent to those anticipatory movements depends on the analyst's sensitivity to apprehend the *emotional turbulence* (Bion, 1976). The analyst has to apprehend, first, perhaps more through intuition, and then think of their meaning; that is why we speak of an *intuition psychoanalytically trained.* *Free-floating attention and "without memories, desires and understanding" are the technical conditions in psychoanalysis to open the door for intuition.* We could consider this question with a double arrow: intuition ↔ thought.

Intuition and systems in transit, subjacent and unstable

From Newton on, scientists studied systems that show stability, periodicity and equilibrium. But since Poincaré's writings, it was clarified that the systems in equilibrium are idealized systems and not the real world in which we live, which is unstable and multidimensional. The human mind is a changing, unstable system: which is the model of the mind that can include, in a meaningful way, unstable systems? Could we consider *a theory of linking as a first step in that* direction? The notion of link that Bion introduces is a concept that opens the possibility of investigating phenomena in transit and unstable along the time. Bion (1979) put this in words, saying:

> When two personalities meet, an emotional storm is created. If they make sufficient contact to be aware of each other, or even sufficient to be unaware of each other, an emotional state is produced by the conjunction of these two individuals, and the resulting disturbance is hardly to be regarded as necessarily an improvement on the state of affairs had they never met at all.
>
> (Bion, 1979, p. 321)

Psychoanalysis produces different meetings of an individual, not only with the analyst but also with himself. We need a model that can represent the complexity of the mind and provide a picture of its psychic dimensions. Some fundamental principles to build and think about this model are: (1) the principle of uncertainty, which in Bion is the negative capacity and (2) the principle of incompleteness. Both models have as a background quantum physics.

To these principles we have to add the *principle of expansion:* thoughts expand and dissipate in different dimensions, between which are the time and spatial dimensions. What is most obvious is the transit from conscious to unconscious and to pre-conscious. This model allows the investigation of the pre-verbal subjective parts of the infant and those infant aspects that dwell in the internal world of the adult. The mind is a universe in expansion, expansion which goes on throughout all our life if there exist the adequate conditions. The mind can become crystallized; the freshness of intuition can be a factor that contributes to maintain its vitality. There are also many mysterious phenomena that we cannot yet understand about *intuition* from the psychoanalytic vertex, as what we could call the *anticipatory* intuition: *for example we are thinking of a person and then we meet him/her* in the street, without anything to suggest this meeting; or having an idea in the very precise moment of meeting the patient before he/she starts speaking and the patient speaks about something related to the idea we had had at the beginning. I remember a vivid clinical illustration of this: going upstairs to my consulting room with a patient, I thought that the coat she was wearing reminded me of her brother, who was a "*desaparecido*" of our Argentinean dictatorship called "el Proceso". When on the couch, she starts speaking of her brother for the first time.

As a way of ending this chapter I suggest trying to relate intuition with some concepts that Bion developed:

Can we relate intuition with the notion of catastrophic change?

Bion defined catastrophic change as sudden, timeless and catastrophic: in this way he was introducing a different conceptualization than from the vertex of genetic continuity. We can consider an insight, appearing through an intuition that produces a sudden innovative change in the personality. This appearance is not the consequence of gradual changes in time but of an intuition as a sudden eruption.

Container-contained transformed

Let us think of the Evolution K→O from *knowing to being* (Bion, 1962). An insightful discovery in analysis transforms the relationship with our own personality and also implies the acceptance of new transformations that might come later. We need to be open towards what is new, towards uncertainty, and accept doubts, mysteries, without stubbornly appealing to reason, which implies having tolerance towards the *negative capacity* and through this tolerance to contribute to the development of psychoanalytic intuition.

Psychoanalysis as well as the personality can be considered a container. Transformations can be seen as the contained but also as a container.

Psychoanalysis as a new story

While with Freud and M. Klein, the analyst was looking for elements that have their reality in a remote past and/or in childhood experiences that go back to the infant, an imaginable story that departs from a forgotten and archaic logic, with Bion the analyst is also dealing with fragments of situations – facts – words that still don't have existence, because these fragments have not had yet any mental place in which to exist. Bion accepted treating patients in which predominated the psychotic part of the personality. The task of the analyst became therefore especially difficult and disturbing. Psychoanalysis conceives – from Freud on – that the analyst can and must put a limit to his omnipotence, and this is the best guarantee for the development of the patient's mental growth: the analyst must stimulate the patient's mental growth but follow his/her own way of development. Having discovered the unconscious and repression, Freud thought that the patient only could recover what he had lost of his repressed memories but not all of it, because what he had lost was in the unconscious. Bion thinks that the analyst needs to recombine, in a mixed kaleidoscope of time and space, facts that never existed, or to put it in another way, to build something for those events that were until now unthinkable so that they may be given a name and be thought, and also that the patient can develop some of his potentialities, a development that without the psychic birth of the emotional experience would be impossible.

Starting from Bion's postulation of psychoanalysis aiming towards the patient's at-one-ment, what he described as the "transformations in O", the analytic task can now be considered as the *structuring of a new story – for and with the patient.* But also the analyst will himself need transformations, directed towards O – his O – which can also be harmonized with the parallel transformations of the patient, modifying his own way of interpreting in accordance with the needs and the capacity of insight of the patient.

All of this introduces us to technical questions such as timing, discernment: dream, phantasy and narration, acquire a new indirect valorization. A good enough intuitive mother, and even an analyst can promote their child's/patient's mental growth, evaluating and regulating how much stimulation and how much experience they can tolerate, avoiding the risk of an excessive exposition. The interpretation has to keep in mind the story – up to that moment – of the psychoanalytic relation, and so the analyst's verbalization can go into the mental myth-poiesis-proto-symbolic dimension of the relationship and acquire this kind of narration, and so it will be not so much "a told story" – told by the patient – but a story built together between analyst and patient. This conceptualization takes us back to Meltzer's idea of modulation of mental pain as a quality of the alpha function of the analyst.

Interpretative language

So we arrive at a change of the interpretative language, which has lost progressively the trait of explanation of the unconscious phantasy in body images and of part objects: the kind of interpretation M. Klein used in her work with children and that she thought was the language of the unconscious phantasy when elaborating her theory in her clinical practice. She had no doubts about the permanent existence of an unconscious phantasy, although they wrote with Hanna Segal about symbolization disturbances. It is with Bion that we can also consider the psychic birth of the emotional experience. The language we use nowadays to communicate with the patient does not use body images to refer to mental objects (as breast, penis) – it proceeds in another direction, it is a language used to describe and indicate the meaning of the "emotional elements" that often are "discharged" in the body. Ann Alvarez says that it is important to use this kind of language with very disturbed children, who seem very sure to have a body but need to discover that they have a mind and emotions, emotions that have to be named to be able to think about them and undergo a process of working through. In using an interpretative language, the analyst's intervention has to be non-saturated; he/she needs to use metaphor and narration that should have the characteristic of a *dreamlike container*, constructed when the analyst is in the session with the patient and with his contribution. Meltzer said that the accuracy of the interpretation is not so important as the attention and the reciprocal attitude of the analyst's adaptation and the patient's cooperation to create and establish a container (giving it flexibility and firmness). Metaphor and narration are proposed instead of explanation.

Psychoanalysis in this way becomes a development of meanings that have not yet been contained, that have to be named, and with a direction open to new meanings. This implies a process of development and growth of an equipment to produce thoughts that can stimulate the evolution of the emotional elements towards an area where it is possible to think. The development of the capability to think emotions is proportional to the transformation of the language to communicate them. Bion called it the transformation of the *language of substitution* for a *language of achievement*, which, at the same time, gives the possibility to be open to new and unpredictable meanings. The language of achievement *par excellence* is that of poetry and other kinds of literature, but it is also the language of dreams and their "furniture". Bion, quoting Keats, proposes *"negative" capability:* "at once it struck me what quality went to form a man of Achievement, especially in Literature. And which Shakespeare possessed so enormously – I mean Negative Capability, that is when a man is capable of being in uncertainties, mysteries, doubts, without any irritable reaching after facts and reason".

Intuition and psychoanalytic function of the personality

I don't have much to add to this theme. I think it is obvious that intuition is a very significant factor of the psychoanalytic function of the personality.

Intuition – faith – at-one-ment

Bion makes a different formulation from the traditional concept of countertransference. He puts forward an original way of considering intuition (K→O) by transforming it in an operative factor. Only keeping in mind his effort to go deeper into the operations intrinsic to the intuitive process in the psychoanalytic field, it is possible to understand his considerations about the "act of faith" and of the "personality" of the genius or the mystic. The "act of faith" does not belong to K (the disposition to know) but to O (the infinite formless void). An "act of faith" implies having patience and has as a background something unconscious and not known because it has not happened yet. In this sense, the "act of faith" (the prototype of the mystic's personality) seems to be at the background of the intuitive factor that has tolerance and patience to wait until a pattern appears in what is the empty space and time that precedes the insight and having security when the selected fact appears.

The actor Joaquin Furiel (who was playing Hamlet in Buenos Aires) speaks about intuition

> Intuition is part of the work. There is no work without intuition. It is not that one prepares the character as if one had a recipe. Intuition is everything. I read many essays about Hamlet and saw many versions. I even saw Buster Keaton. . . . From all that you keep a gesture, an idea, an impression and you transform it in intuition, but you have to work a lot so the intuition can have a guide. In my case, intuition alone never worked. It is intuition in a methodological context.

I think that psychoanalytic trained intuition has the same characteristic.

Note

1 It is a known hypothesis of Kant that concepts without intuitions are empty and intuitions without concepts are blind.

References

1962: Aprendiendo de la Experiencia.-1ra. edición William Heinemann Medical Books. Ltd.

1ra.edición en castellano: 1966. Paidós. Buenos Aires.

Bion, W.R. (1970) *Attention and Interpretation*. Tavistock Publications Ltd., London.

Bion, W.R. (1975) *A Memoir of the Future*. Imago Editora, Rio de Janeiro. Reprinted 1991, Karnac, London.

Bion, W.R. (1976) *Emotional Turbulence*. New York International Universities Press. Also in "Clinical Seminars and Four Papers" Oxford:Fleetwood Press (1987).

Bion, W.R. (1979) *"Una Memoria del Futuro"*. "A Memoir of the Future. Book Three: The Dawn of Oblivion" Strathclyde: Clunie Press. London.

Bion, W.R. (1979) *Making the best of a bad Job*. IN Clinical seminars and other works. London Karnac books 1994. pp. 321–331.

Bion, W.R. (1992) *Cogitations*. London Karnac. (extended 1994 version).

Keats, J. (1817) *Letter to His Brothers Tom and George*.

Second Part

Second Part

Chapter 10

Intuition, construction and representation

Howard B. Levine

Bion's work remains generative for psychoanalysis, because it expands upon the radical epistemological position implicit in Freud that the domains of psychic reality and the phenomena of emotional experience exist but are infinitely complex and not fully representable beyond summation or complete description in everyday language. Freud (1937) had perhaps his clearest intimation of the problems that this presents for psychoanalysis in his Constructions paper. His clinical experience had forced him to acknowledge that constructions may function dynamically in the analytic process and the cure in the same way that the recovery of a once repressed traumatic childhood memory did. This realization exposed a deep epistemological divide concerning the truth-value of interpretations and the nature of evidence in psychoanalysis.

The key terms in Freud's reformulation are 'construction' and 'conviction.' As nouns, they refer to beliefs; that is, to ideas (constructions) and feelings (convictions) that appear as end products of psychic processes that seem to arise spontaneously and appear unbidden; processes not of *de*duction but of *in*duction. Their arrival in consciousness without awareness of the intermediate steps involved is usually surprising and unexpected.

A construction is a presumptive formulation or understanding, an 'imaginative conjecture',[1] that comes to the analyst's mind unbidden in the midst of the analyst's reverie. It conforms closely to Bergstein's (2019) description of intuition: "an unmediated knowledge or understanding of truth, not supported by any information derived from a familiar sensual source . . . [one that] cannot be communicated to another and cannot be corroborated by a rational method of scientific knowledge" (p. 30).[2] *Constructions are the ideational outcomes of intuition*, and *conviction is the affect associated with the sense of rightness, relief and fit that a useful construction may produce.*

Constructions are not intended to be statements of historical fact – the latter are what Freud (1937) termed '*re*constructions' – and should not be evaluated in regard to the factuality of their content. They are, instead, something broader and more open-ended: statements of beliefs or possibilities offered as possible instruments for mental growth (Bianchedi 1991). Their "merit lies in their *capacity* for *generating psychic movement*, transforming psychic barriers into caesuras,

DOI: 10.4324/9781003293392-16

affording a multidimensional view, and enabling the patient to move from a pre-occupation with [concrete and actual aspects of] external reality to an observation of his internal reality" (Bergstein 2019, p. 178).

Like any intuition, constructions can serve as containers for what otherwise may be "experience [that] remains non-mental, as an overwhelming frenzy of stimuli inside the mind and body" (Bergstein 2019, p. 13). In the clinical situation, this 'non-mental experience' can reflect pre-verbal, perhaps even pre-natal events and sensations, the consequence of trauma and the surging, unbound and not yet represented drive derivatives and excitations of the id. In addition to providing containers for that which is unrepresented, constructions can help produce a space for emergence of the not yet knowable and stimulate a reorganization of already represented and known elements that can modulate excitation by naming it and making it an object of thought, producing openings to new possible meanings or understandings through metaphor, polysemy and implication.

As is any intuition, a construction is an extension in the domain of myth, some-thing that Bion (1963, p. 12) deemed a "necessary dimension" of the analyst's interpretation.[3] Its necessity follows in part from the fact that a *major task of the human psyche is representation of the previously unrepresentable* (Levine 2012). This is an endless task in which the inherently traumatic sensations of being alive and suffering Existence[4] are contained, ameliorated and made somewhat more toler-able. Following the lessons painfully learned in his experience during the First World War, Bion named the struggle to transform and represent the previously unrepresented and unrepresentable – i.e., to preserve the capacity to think by con-taining catastrophic anxiety in order to manage in life and make it less traumatic and therefore bearable – as a central goal of psychic functioning.[5]

In *Memory and Desire*, he addressed this process from a clinical vertex when he posed the problem of how we are to know and speak about emotional experience:

> I have always been skeptical about what are called 'clinical accounts.' I have felt that they are, after all, only versions of what took place: they are transfor-mations of what was a real experience . . . this reality that we all know about, which we feel is unmistakably borne-in on us in the course of psychoanalytic work, is then something which cannot really be properly expressed.
>
> (Bion 1965, p. 4)

While *some part* of this 'reality borne in on us' could be sensed or experienced – the psyche is capable of sensing inner psychic and emotional experience – Bion felt that it could never be fully put into and expressed by words:

> we are dealing with things that are real enough, which are absolutely real, even from earliest infancy on, but which cannot be expressed except in the kind of vocabulary which is quite unfitted for it by its derivation and characteristics.
>
> (p. 7)

Words were deemed 'unfit' for describing the 'truth' and essence of psychic reality, because language was a product of the human mind. Following in the tradition of Plato, Hume, Kant and the Mystics, Bion believed that while the domain of psychic reality and emotional experience was multi-dimensional, the human mind was restricted to a three-dimensional world limited to what can be apprehended by the senses.[6] Thus, Bion disqualified the semantic dimension of words as being able to fully describe and convey one's Experience, because he saw language as embedded in and derived from sensuous reality.

Emotional Experience and the unconscious, which he insisted were the proper objects of analytic inquiry, were not 'of the senses' and therefore are not accessible to being known by direct empirical observation in the same way as are 'facts' of the physical universe (Bion 1970, p. 7). They can only come to be known by direct Experience (by *becoming* and *at-one-ment*) and an element or aspect of this Experience may be grasped and spoken about by intuition. Similarly, in the domain of psychic reality, 'truth', whatever that might be, which Bion saw as essential for psychic growth, development and well-being, is emergent, continually evolving and constantly in flux. As Pirandello (1998) said, "Truth is a blur in motion." No sooner is a presumed truth apprehended or spoken than the moment has passed, the situation changed, and it is no longer current.

This discrepancy between what is Experienced and how it can be described – the difference between O and K – presents a serious challenge for us as practitioners of the 'talking cure.' We must find a suitable means (a 'language of achievement') for naming and expressing ('publication') what we believe is going on within the session and in the mind of the patient. And we must find reassurance in the face of the recurring doubt that psychoanalysis is an elaborate, unacknowledged form of suggestion and compliance.[7]

In *Attention and Interpretation*, Bion (1970) expressed the dilemma this way:

> The central phenomena of psycho-analysis have no background in sense data . . . . "How, then, are we to 'observe' and 'record' the patient's state of mind?"
>
> (p. 57)

Not knowing how to answer this question, he invoked Faith: "Since I wish to discuss this but do not know the answer, I will say 'by F'" (p. 57), implying that if a space was held open and the question explored, then perhaps an answer might someday achieve further realization.[8] Earlier, he had proposed "the term 'intuit' as a placeholder for the answer, suggesting that it was parallel in the psychoanalyst's domain to the physician's use of 'see', 'touch', 'smell' and 'hear'" (p. 7).

The setting in which we are to explore this question is the analytic situation, from the vertex of attempting to listen without memory, desire, and pre-conceived understanding (Bion 1965).

> The instrument of choice for contact with and observation of psychic reality in the linkage situation during the session is, for the analyst, compliance with

Bion's disturbing and cryptic injunction to remain '*without memory, without desire, without understanding . . . to allow and aid the intuition . . . of the dream-like psychical reality . . . in evolution.*

(Bianchedi 1991, p. 11, original italics)

Thus, patient and analyst must operate between two seemingly impossible extremes. On the one hand there is the epistemological impossibility of ever fully knowing or expressing one's psychic reality: "mental space as a thing-in-itself that is unknowable" (Bion 1970, p. 11). The one saving grace is that mental space "can be represented by thoughts" (p. 11). However, "thought is restrictive and can be directly experienced as such as soon as an intuition demands representation for private communication" (p. 11). The problem that ensues is the following: "Since thought liberates the intuition there is conflict between the impulse to leave the intuition unexpressed and the impulse to express it." (p. 11).

What is at stake in this conflict is the mind's need to try to make comprehensible sense out of the flux of overwhelming chaotic Experience by creating and ascribing meaning to experience and emotion. This psychic work and activity are what I have described as the Representational Imperative (Levine 2012). Our psyches are:

governed by an inherent pressure to form representations and link them into meaningful, affect laden, coherent narratives. This pressure, . . . originates in internal (e.g., drives) or external (e.g., perceptions) sources, exerts a 'demand upon the mind' for psychic work and ranges from catalytic to traumatic. If kept within optimal bounds, it has the potential to activate capacities for representation, which serve a vital protective role as they create, structure and organize the mind. It is the creation and linking of representations that will in part determine whether or not any given pressure can be contained within the bounds of what is 'optimal' or will exceed those bounds to become 'traumatic.'

(Levine 2012, p. 609, original italics)

While the Representational Imperative is a relatively recent evolutionary adaptation that helps us withstand the overwhelming force of being in the world, its adaptive potential may be co-opted by a desperate need to create and cling to false meanings in an attempt to cover over the anxiety and the dangers posed by our ignorance. At such moments, an Overvalued Idea may be mistaken for a Selected Fact, as truth is sacrificed to the illusory comfort of seeming omniscience.

As psychological products and states, both intuition and conviction remain subject to the distorting vagaries of unconscious psychological need.

[Th]e closest one can get to a fact in psychoanalysis is a feeling. A feeling could achieve a sense of evidence, because it gives a sense of certainty. But a feeling could also be connected to some unknown fact. This unknown may be a kind of amnesia or someone may try to fill the lack of knowledge with a paramnesia. The human mind may find countenance through both.

(Chuster 2016, p. 373)

Indeterminacy and uncertainty are the very stuff of human mental existence. And yet, there seems to be something to this impossible profession of ours. In his Tavistock Seminar of 28 June 1976, Bion (2005) put it this way:

in a situation where you feel completely lost; you are thankful to clutch hold of any system, anything whatever that is available on which to build a kind of structure. So from this point of view it seems to me that we could argue that the whole of psychoanalysis fills a long-felt want by being a vast Dionysiac system; since we don't know what is there, we invent these theories and build this glorious structure that has no foundation in fact – or the only fact in which it has any foundation is our complete ignorance, our lack of capacity.

However, we hope that it isn't completely unrelated to fact that psychoanalytic theories would remind you of real life at some point in the same way as a good novel or a good play would remind you how human beings behave.

(p. 2)

The latter is also true of a good construction borne of conjecture and intuition, the value of which can only be ascertained by what happens subsequently in the analytic process and the life of the patient. This explains why even detailed examples serve a rather dubious role in demonstrating the value of psychoanalytic clinical propositions. It is impossible to convey the *Experience* of a psychoanalytic exchange or moment to another person. One might talk *about psychoanalysis* but can almost never convey what it meant to be *in* psychoanalysis at the moment in question. The experience of psychoanalysis is highly personal, subjective and contingent moment to moment. Andre Green (2005) once said that for an audience of psychoanalysts, writing that reflects clinical thinking may allow the listener's analytic experience to crawl out between the lines of conceptual description.[9] I hope that I have been successful in being able to evoke that today.

Notes

1 "We do not pretend that an individual construction is anything more than a conjecture which awaits examination, confirmation, or rejection" (Freud 1937, p. 265).
2 See also Bianchedi (1991).
3 See Levine (2016).
4 I use the capitalized E, Experience, to refer to raw existential experience in the domain of O. That part of Experience which can be known (that can enter the domain of K) is what we commonly refer to as 'experience' in everyday speech and is written here with a small letter e.
5 See Szykierski (2010), Brown (2012), Tarantelli (2016).
6 See Bergstein (2019).
7 To my mind, (Levine 2011) Freud never satisfactorily resolved this question.

8 This last sentence might also serve as a description of his view of the analytic process and a summary of his *oeuvre*: "you start with the unknown, . . . you note a constant conjunction, that you bind it by a term which is virtually meaningless, and then proceed to investigate what you mean by that term, for the rest of your life if you are so inclined" (Bion 1965, p. 1).

9 "clinical thinking can be recognized beyond doubt when the theoretical elaboration raises associations for the reader that refer to this or that aspect of psychoanalytic experience. . . . [E]ven when clinical thinking does not speak expressly about clinical work, it awakens the memory of a patient or group of patients and brings to mind this or that moment of an analysis. These associations are an integral part of the way in which clinical thinking is articulated" (Green 2005, p. 10).

References

Bergstein, A. (2019). *Bion and Meltzers' Expedition Into Unmapped Mental Life*. London and New York: Routledge.

Bianchedi, E.T. (1991). Psychic Change: The 'Becoming' of an Inquiry. *IJPA*, 72: 6–15.

Bion, W.R. (1963). *Elements of Psychoanalysis*. London: Karnac.

Bion, W.R. (1965). Memory and Desire. In: *Three Papers of W.R. Bion*, Chris Mawson, ed. London and New York: Routledge, 2018.

Bion, W.R. (1970). *Attention and Interpretation*. New York: Basic Books.

Bion, W.R. (2005). *Tavistock Seminars*. London: Karnac.

Brown, L.J. (2012). Bion's Discovery of Alpha Function: Thinking under Fire on the Battlefield and in the Consulting Room. *IJPA*, 93: 1191–1214.

Chuster, A. (2016). Evidence. In: *The WR Bion Tradition*, Levine, H.B. and Civitarese, G., eds. London: Karnac, 2016, pp. 369–376.

Freud, S. (1937). Constructions in analysis. *S.E.*, 23.

Green, A. (2005). *Psychoanalysis: A Paradigm for Clinical Thinking*. London: Free Association Books.

Levine, H.B. (2011). Construction Then and Now. In: *On Freud's "Constructions in Analysis"*, Lewkowicz, S. and Bokanowski, T. with Pragier, G., eds. London: Karnac, pp. 87–100.

Levine, H.B. (2012). The Colourless Canvas: Representation, Therapeutic Action and the Creation of Mind. *The International Journal of Psychoanalysis*, 93: 607–629.

Levine, H.B. (2016). Myth, Dream and Meaning: Reflections on a Comment by Bion. In: *The WR Bion Tradition*, Levine, H.B. and Civitarese, G., eds. London: Karnac, pp. 307–314.

Pirandello, L. (1998). *Six Characters in Search of an Author*. Translated and Introduction by Eric Bentley. New York: Signet Classics.

Szykierski, D. (2010). The Traumatic Roots of Containment: The Evolution of Bion's Metapsychology. *Psychoan. Quart.*, 79: 935–968.

Tarantelli, C.B. (2016). I Shall Be Blown to Bits: Towards Bion's Theory of Catastrophic Trauma. In: *The WR Bion Tradition*, Levine, H.B. and Civitarese, G., eds. London: Karnac, 2016, pp. 47–63.

Chapter 11

Intuition in Bion. Between search for invariants and creative emergence

Goriano Rugi

Introduction

Psychoanalysis has never appreciated the concept of intuition and has kept it in an ambiguous position, generally assimilating it into that of insight. Intuition derives from the Latin *tueri*, "to look", which combined with *in* becomes "to look inside". But while the insight implies an awareness of the logical relationships between a problem and an answer, in intuition there is only a rapid, sudden feeling of coherence, without any logical, rational connection. It is a presentiment that is felt in the body, a flash of consciousness, which reveals the unknown and maintains the link with the invisible and the infinite. Intuition can therefore precede the insight, but it does not coincide with it. Freud (1932) placed intuition among illusions, together with divination, as the fulfillment of desires linked to emotional needs, a position that derives directly from his choice to keep psychoanalysis within the dominant scientific framework, which in spite of everything remained the positivist one. Paradoxically, the desire to bring determinism into the study of the unconscious makes Freudian psychoanalysis a science characterized in a rationalistic sense and very far from the canons of current science, increasingly involved with probability, irrationality, indeterminacy, and impossibility. Einstein (1954) uses intuition, which Freud eliminated from his method: "There is no logical way to discover these elementary laws. The only way is intuition, which is aided by the feeling you have for the order behind appearance".

Unlike Freud, Wilfred Bion (1970, p. 7) thinks that the psychic qualities psychoanalysis deals with remain ineffable and cannot be grasped by the senses but by "intuit", as an equivalent term for the physician's use of "see", "touch", "smell", and "hear". He thinks that intuitive ability must be exercised with a permanent, lasting, and continuous discipline, because it is hindered by memory, desire, and understanding, which remain routed on the senses. To grasp the patient's reality in analysis, Bion also puts aside the consciousness, which Freud indicated as the psychic counterpart of the sensory organs, and introduces a general postulate, which he denotes by the sign "O", that "It can be represented by terms such as ultimate reality or truth" (Bion, 1965, pp. 139–140). Being reality, O is not good or evil, it cannot be known, loved or hated, "Reality has to be 'been'", and because

DOI: 10.4324/9781003293392-17

"phenomena are known but reality is 'become' the interpretation must do more than increase knowledge" (*ibid*, p. 148). But how? Bion (1970, p. 28) assumes that "the more 'real' the psychoanalyst is, the more he can be at one with the reality of the patient. Conversely, the more he depends on actual events the more he relies on thinking that depends on a background of sense impression". Generally, the introduction of intuition and O refers to the "mystical" (Grotstein, 2007) or "less disciplined" period of Bion, (O'Shaughnessy, 2005). This has created profound misunderstandings, impeding a full comprehension of the new paradigm that Bion introduced in psychoanalysis.

In this chapter, I intend to rethink the epistemological meaning of the concept of intuition in Bion in order to resolve some misunderstandings and put forward some hypotheses:

1   Bion did not introduce the concept of intuition in the mystical period but from the beginning.
2   The concept of intuition has nothing to do with Bion's so-called "mysticism" but rather with his rejection of the positivist paradigm and the introduction of a new epistemology linked to Bergson, Poincaré, Husserl, and Whitehead.
3   The analysis of the functions that Bion attributes to intuition offers unexpected connections with neuroscience and helps to place the analytical process itself within the wider process of knowledge development.
4   In particular, my principal hypothesis is that the intuitive process in Bion presents two aspects. One turned to the past, to "unconscious" knowledge, in the Bionian sense, and therefore to the search for invariance. The other turned to the future, as a creative moment that through dreaming leads to transformation in O, to growth. This double movement of intuition is precisely what current neuroscience highlights.

Origins of the concepts of intuition and O

Bion uses unusual terminology to describe the analytic process including intuition, binocular vision, observation, facts, transformations, invariants, catastrophic change, at-one-ment, incarnation, which do not belong to the classical language of psychoanalysis. Torres and Hinshelwood (2013) show that some of these terms and concepts come from the environment of the Tavistock Clinic, where Bion worked from 1933 to 1948. Tavistock was not just any other clinic. For decades it had been a powerhouse of new ideas regarding integrated and socially oriented medicine. Bion fed on this dynamic, eclectic atmosphere and came into contact with the ideas of Crichton-Miller, Trotter, Bergson, Poincaré, and Whitehead. Since his first works Bion (1952, p. 165) therefore declares his intention to investigate "the group through psycho-analytically developed intuitions". Then, in *Elements*, Bion (1963) affirms the intention to sharpen and develop intuition, and in *Transformations* he differentiates an "intuitive psychoanalysis" from an "axiomatic psychoanalysis", considering the former more suitable for representing genetic stages and the latter to represent the use made out of them (Bion, 1965, p. 122). So Bion refers to the Grid as a method for developing and using intuitive decisions, where attention can be paid to the development of the patient's thinking (vertical axis) or to the patient's use of his communication (horizontal axis), warning that the metaphorical quality of a term can be lost by changing the context, making a metaphor come close to a β element.

P.C. Sandler (2005) links Bionian intuition with Kantian intuition, but Bion more likely derived this concept from Henry Bergson (1896), who distinguishes two ways of knowing. First, the *intellectual-analytic method*, which serves to describe physical objects and is always relative knowledge because it depends on one's point of view. Second, the *intuitive method*, which is a form of global, immediate knowledge, more useful for grasping the continuous flow of life, an absolute knowledge that with "an effort of imagination and in harmony with the object is inserted into the state of mind of the object so as to coincide with it and what is unique in it". For the philosopher, intuition can therefore reach the "ultimate reality", the absolute and the infinite, but on condition of a great effort and a procedure capable of eliminating the previous thoughts and perception. Bion therefore looks to Bergson but also to Poincaré, Husserl, and Carnap, who refute the positivist position that truth is reached through empirical testing. Therefore, Bion embraces contemporary epistemology to face the new problems that the clinic presents, starting from the studies of groups and psychoses. Bion thinks that only intuition is capable of facing the problem of grasping the psychic reality that is devoid of known sensory realization. He conceives intuition as a holistic cognitive modality, which belongs to the whole system and allows us to get in touch with O, with what happens in the session and the "ultimate reality" of the patient's mind. Intuition and O are therefore closely linked, and the ability to understand the transformations passes through the effective understanding of the nature of O, which, however, is an elusive concept, in which we feel the presence of many meanings: the idea of origin and zero; of an abstract sign that refers to infinity, divinity, and the Platonic form. Therefore, it takes on different meanings according to its contexts and levels, passing from reality itself, the absolute facts, to the godhead, the noumenon, the infinite, and the absolute truth.

Where does this concept originate? Torres and Hinshelwood (2013) notes that Bion was familiar with the ideas of Alfred N. Whitehead. In particular Bion appreciated *An Introduction to Mathematics*, where the importance of the symbol 0 (zero) is described due to its abstract connotation. Whitehead was a follower of Bergson, from whom he had taken the idea that matter and mind are not different substances but that they have the same basic properties, since there is already virtual intentionality and memory in the simplest components of matter itself. In his evolutionary vision, Whitehead conjugated Bergson's ideas and the Heraclitean doctrine of "everything flows", with a mathematical fervor that sees notation and formalization as possible means of freeing the mind for higher tasks. Together with Bertrand Russel, Whitehead wrote the *Principia Mathematica*, an ambitious, coherent, and complete work, which claimed that every true statement of arithmetic could be derived within it.

Bion's program of formalizing the various psychoanalytic theories to visualize the functioning of the system in the Grid and follow its transformations (conforming to the rules) in clinical reality presents many points of agreement with Whitehead's ideas and Hilbert's program.[1] In both cases it is a question of observing the coherence of an abstract system within a real system. The set of theories of Freud and Klein had the same presumptions of consistency and systematicity as the *Principia*. Therefore, Bion's initial plan was to discover a logical and dynamic system of mental functioning without questioning contents or validity of axiomatic psychoanalytic theories.

The union of these concepts – Bergson's intuition and Whitehead's ideas about zero and notation – provided Bion with a suggestive epistemological background, which may have led him to represent the "ultimate reality" of the patient's mind with the sign "O". This, therefore, was not only a reference to a mystical and unattainable reality but also a logical sign, a notation, which can take on various meanings.

Bion, however, was too refined an epistemologist not to understand that the coherence of psychoanalytic axioms clashes with the problem of extrapolation from a finite to an infinite set of data. The observations are based on models with a finite number of cases, while the axioms should hold for an infinite number of them. This calls into question the truth of the axioms themselves. The fact is that deductive systems lose value as they are used for vaster situations: "The dilemma can be stated thus: the system, if consistent within itself, is limited; if not limited, then it cannot be regarded as self-consistent because its self-consistency is contingent" (Bion, 1970, pp. 24–25). In this observation we recognize the echoes of Gödel's incompleteness theorem, which shows that given any set of arithmetic axioms, there are true propositions which cannot be deduced from the set. Russel and Whitehead's axiomatic systems, therefore, had faults, because no axiomatic system is able to produce all the arithmetic truths unless the system is inconsistent. Bion's solution to the problem of the coherence of the axiomatic systems of psychoanalysis therefore converges with the incompleteness theorem, which affirms an inherent limitation in the axiomatic method.

Bion's formal rigor seems to leave nothing out, but paradoxically, he lands on something that keeps the door open to *intuition*. The Grid not only does not eliminate paradoxes, as the *Principia* claimed, but it is founded on the paradox, like that beta elements are placed before alpha elements. Although Bion does not worry about contents in the Grid, his operation opens to creativity. Unlike Hilbert's program, which neglected dynamics and thought of transposing the abstract into the finite real, Bion works on dynamics and a binocular vision between abstract and real. In other words, Bion seeks formalization but always maintains contact with the real world, creating a movement that provides the possibility of transcending caesuras through binocular vision. In this sense, the Grid maintains a tension between concrete and abstract, between formalization and experience.

This tension is also the clearest proof that regardless of the original ecumenical intentions of the Grid and its meta-psychoanalytic character, it maintains a constant reference to clinical experience, to which it continuously returns and within which it finds its realization.

Introduction of O, transformations, and invariants

In the first instance, O is introduced to indicate the "absolute facts" that take place in the session; therefore the Kantian thing-in-itself remains unknowable. Bion uses the concept of thing-in-itself to overcome the paradigm of classical psychoanalysis, centered on representation as a correspondence between idea and reality. Kant thought that things in themselves were known only through the sensations we have of them, which we perceive as phenomena. Bion equates the phenomena with the transformations that each one produces of facts in itself. He distinguishes between "the patient's experience O and the analyst's experience O" (Bion, 1965, p. 24). He follows Kant, shifting attention from the object to the subject of knowledge and considering the facts in themselves as unknowable, but he is forced to abandon the Kantian model, because his real problem is the intuition of mental reality, which does not belong to the domain of the sensible world. In Kant, pure intuitions of space and time are *a priori* conditions of knowledge, but every intuition is always sense based, so that thinking can only become knowledge insofar as it is related to objects of sensation (experience).

Bion introduces the concept of transformation to grasp what happens between analyst and analysand, and above all to grasp what in the relationship with the other would lead to the development of thinking ability. All Bion's work (1965, p. 39) on transformations is a cyclopean attempt "to illuminate and solve the problems that lie unsolved at the heart of certain forms of mental disturbance", and these problems always revolve around the fate of beta elements, or the emotional reality that the patient cannot metabolize. Bion puts the relationship, the so-called patient/analyst emotional experience, at the center of the analytical work, revolutionizing the very foundations of psychoanalysis as a method of treatment. In fact, without a totally relational concept of mind, namely the idea that to make one mind you need another mind, and without the idea of care as growth, without the idea that meaning arises in the hard work of mutual recognition, psychoanalysis would remain an explanatory therapy that explains nothing, a therapy of words as its detractors suggest.

Bion therefore tries to make us understand how our manners of behaving, of experiencing emotions, and of thinking can change through relationships and words. In analysis, the interpretations that matter are therefore those that promote the genesis of the mind and nourish its growth, indicated as transformations in O. The interpretation must favor the transition from being aware of O to becoming O, from knowing reality to becoming real.

Bion then shifts our attention from contents to containers, or rather to their relationship and therefore to the analytical process, which coincides with the way in which the ability to think develops as an intersubjective experience, starting from the patient-analyst relationship, which repeats that of the mother-child relationship. The transformation must however lead to something shared, something on which the patient and his or her analyst can find an accord and showing how relationship and speech produce change and growth. For this reason, Bion introduces the concept of *invariant* which always accompanies that of transformation and without which transformations would remain an infinite series of closed and incommunicable variations. The interpretation is therefore a transformation that serves to show the invariants of the emotional facts that take place in the session. We know the invariants that Bion attributes to the three main types of transformations: *transfert* in the neurotic ones; *moral component* in the psychotic ones; *rivalry, envy, greed, thieving* in the hallucinosis.

These invariants have to do with psychopathology and are useful for the diagnosis of pathological transformations of sense and meaning. For Bion (1965, p. 148), "The point at issue is how to pass from 'knowing' 'phenomena' to 'being' that which is 'real'", and this is the question of how interpretation functions. The theory of transformations therefore would not be complete without the transformations that lead to growth. The problem is that there is a gap between phenomena, which can be known, and reality in itself, which remains unknowable. Reality can only become. This is the reason why "the interpretation must do more than increase knowledge" (*ibid*, p. 148). In this sense, psychoanalysis can be understood as a process of subjectivization through links that imply mutual recognition (Wainrib, 2012). It is therefore necessary to hypothesize that there is a zero point of the invariant in the normal development of growth, a point from which the rudimentary consciousness of the newborn begins to emerge from chaos due to the encounter with the mother. At its zero degree, the invariant corresponds to the emotional unison, I → EU, as it occurs in the mother–child union, which in its repeated encounters initiates the creation of meaning, in a comparison–recognition game that allows the child to get out of the primordial chaos.[2] It is in this meeting that for Winnicott (1971) the *experience of being* is created, the child and the object are one, "the breast is the self and the self is the breast".

The unison theory therefore represents the true basis of Bion's aesthetic paradigm, understood as a form of aesthetic knowledge, as it establishes the meaning in the area of the senses, even before the area of contents (semantics) (Civitarese, 2016). This going in time, this harmony of rhythm between mother and baby, is a process that Tronik and Boston (1998) calls "dyadic expansion of consciousness", in which the shared co-creation of meaning reduces chaos and entropy, promoting growth and development. And this process is a continuous state of significance that implies various forms of awareness and unconsciousness, but in the beginning the child has only a rudimentary consciousness, which "is not associated with an unconscious. All impressions of the self are of equal value; all are conscious. The mother's capacity for reverie is the receptor organ for the infant's harvest of self-sensation gained by its conscious" (Bion, 1967, p. 116). The mother is consequently the infant's unconscious, and it is her reverie that allows the baby to tolerate anxieties and to form his own alpha function and then the ability to dream, to think, and to develop the unconscious. Placing the zero degree of the invariant in the mother–infant unison thus allows us to identify the truth factor of the transformation in the *quality* of the intersubjective relationship itself, which passes through rhythm, warm reception, involvement, and thousands of shades of attention, tenderness, and compassion that achieve mutual recognition. This process is repeated every time in the analytic rapport.

At-one-ment and atonement

Therefore, what does "the process of at-one-ment with O" mean? (Bion, 1970, p. 33). O must evolve in order to be made an object of apprehension, to become a thought, and to be represented by an element of the Grid. About this, it is important to exercise the suppression of memory, desire, and understanding that favors the act of faith, which does not belong to the K system but to the O system, to faith in the reality of psychoanalytic experience, which remains ineffable. The analyst must be interested in grasping the *evolution* of this reality in the session when it emerges from the dark and from the formless with the evanescent characters of dreams. This O is the analyst's real goal, which the interpretation must be able to correctly grasp and express in words. But which O? Not just any O but an O which "in any analytic situation is available for transformation by analyst and analysand equally" (Bion, 1965, p. 48). Bion uses the term *reverie* to indicate the analyst's constant emotional monitoring of the analysand's emotions, but he speaks of *at-one-ment*, of unison, when the analyst gets in contact with the patient, he intuits his true emotional experience, which he captures in its evolution. Bion's concepts of "dreaming" the analytic session and "'becoming' the analysand" refer to this process. In the analytic work the analyst must therefore wait until a pattern emerges, and then he intuits the psychic reality. He must chase the patient in the paths of his associations, silences, and repetitions until he finds the invariant and intuits what the patient is really feeling, his true emotional experience. For Grotstein (2009) the process of at-one-ment is an act of "definitive empathy", in which analyst and patient enter a symmetrical state of resonance, whereby "dreaming of the session" or "becoming" the patient means retrieving inside the analyst virtually identical emotions to those of the analysand. However, Bion differentiates the at-one-ment from the process of knowledge and identification of empathy, which implies the relationship between two separate objects and cannot be reduced to a primordial model of mother–child, analyst–patient communication. The resonance process to which Grotstein alludes is perhaps only the first part of the process of at-one-ment with O, what Bion describes as "a step in the process of at-one-ment (the transformation O→K). In practice this means not that the analyst recalls some relevant memory but that a relevant constellation will be evoked during the process of at-one-ment" (Bion, 1970, p. 33). This first step therefore corresponds to the unconscious and intuitive search for the invariant, which preludes and stops with the occurrence of a constant conjunction. The whole at-one-ment process is something more primitive, which only mysticism, art, and Zen have been able to describe.

In *Zen and Archery*, Eugen Herrigel (1948) says that "bow, arrow, target and I" must become one, and this implies the suppression of desire, will, and ego. Modern poetry for Fernando Pessoa is a *look without opinion*, in which the perception of reality avoids any *a priori* vision; it is like looking through a dissociation of forms and perspectives (Pimenta, 1978). There is a break between the conceptualized way of seeing and the consciousness of the ego. Dieter Roth (1973) writes, "The bird that is an eye, the eye that is a bird", so if there is a bird inside the eye, then the eye at that moment is a bird. Consciousness therefore takes place only in the concrete and modifying experience of each passing moment. In other words, there is a "becoming" of the learned object every single time, a sort of union, a metaphor that becomes reality. It is the at-one-ment of Bion. Hence, Bergson's intuitive method and Bion's at-one-ment imply "becoming" the object, an exchange of identity, as in modern poetry, mysticism, and Zen.

Thus, what happens when the subject becomes the object, the analyst becomes the patient, and the container becomes the content? Bion uses the term at-one-ment, which with the dashes indicates union, but without dashes atonement means to make amends for sins committed, sacrifice, reconciliation between God and man. Atonement derives from the Jewish mystical tradition and connotes the Yom Kippur, the day of atonement, the most sacred festivity for the Jews. It refers to the day when Moses came down from Mount Sinai and the repentance of the Jewish people was accepted. Bion (1967) refers precisely to this meaning in the *Commentary*, when he says that the interpretation must clarify the manifestation related to the atonement, which has an essential role in a balanced mind development, because it is linked to the fear of "megalomania", the fear of taking a creative position, that is not evidence only of the persistent operation of immature relationship with a father.

In the interpretative process that leads to growth and the transition from knowing O to becoming O, Bion therefore postulates various steps: *intuition* → *at-one-ment* → *incarnation*. In these passages, through the word, the progression from the idea to the body is felt. In this process a difficult epistemic leap takes place, the transition from "apprehension of the object" to "becoming"; from "form" to "incarnation" (Rugi, 2015).

This is because a psychoanalytic process resembles more a cosmogenesis, a process of birth and growth, than a verifiable process. Rugi (2019) described this process in a previous work, but here it is essential to understand that Bion borrows the term *incarnation* from religion to indicate a very concrete phenomenon, such as a structural change, assuming the risk of possible misunderstandings, but aware that to draw from the mysterious background of the work of the word, the religious metaphor remains the most adequate one. Transformation in O is therefore compared to incarnation in the Roman Catholic religion's sacrament, to becoming the "godhead" that is in us. Bion uses Meister Eckhart's distinction between "Godhead" and "God". For Eckhart it is necessary to free oneself from

"God" and reach the "godhead" that is in us to become creators of oneself. The analyst can expand knowledge, but the necessary step to bridge the gap between knowing the phenomena and being real must come from a special part of the analysand, "from a particular part of the analysand, namely his 'godhead', which must consent to incarnation in the person of the analysand" (Bion, 1965, p. 148). Bion consequently compares the process of introjection of interpretation to "impingement on the individual of an object containing in itself the potentiality of all distinctions as yet undeveloped, a group, a conjunction and the need to bind the 'groupishness' of the group by a name, a column I element" (Bion, 1970, p. 150). What results is a sort of meshing in which the object and the individual seek their mutual adaptation, the harmonious relationship between container and content, up to the point the need for a link or "complementarity" arises. The interpretation therefore cannot come from above, neither from theory, nor from the subject supposed to know, but must come from a painful experience of the analyst. A correct interpretation therefore passes through a sense of depression, and the oscillation between patience and security is assumed by Bion as an indication of a good job. This deontological path of the Bionian method is therefore an extraordinary guarantee of the ethical and epistemological coherence of his thought.

The two sides of intuition

Intuition has two aspects: one turned to the past, the other to the future. The first is a kind of intuitive or unconscious reading of the unconscious; the second is directed to growth, to becoming the real Self, through the process of dreaming the session, where the patient dreams with the analyst what he was afraid of not being able to do on his own. Of course, this hypothesis implies the Bionian theories of the unconscious and dreaming that overturn Freud's theories. In Bion, only what has been transformed by alpha-function can become unconscious, so it is not the unconscious that produces the dream but the dream that produces the unconscious. The unconscious becomes a psychoanalytic function of the personality, and the ability to dream by day and by night becomes the way of thinking and making sense of the experience, of making painful emotions "unconscioused" and of creating the unconscious. There is therefore a continuity between conscious and unconscious experience, which Bion conceives as two dimensions of the psyche, produced continuously by the alpha function, which "by proliferating alpha elements, is producing the contact-barrier" (Bion, 1962, p. 54). This semipermeable film, which marks the point of separation between conscious and unconscious, is an area of functional articulation, which allows an interchange, a continuous visual accommodation, that makes it possible to see from both sides of the caesura, in a *binocular* vision. This aspect of continuity, for which the conscious is also an expression of unconscious thought, makes us understand that our way of perceiving reality is always conditioned by an unconscious vision, which roots out not only in our past but also in the proto-mental system. The individual is rooted into a group of archaic and even mythical dimension, which at certain moments can break into our actions and behaviors (Rugi, 2020). It is Merleau-Ponty's extraordinary lesson for which "perception is unconscious" and the unconscious is "to look for, not in the depths of us, behind our 'conscience', but in front of us, as articulations of our field" (Merleau-Ponty, 1964, p. 197). This "transcending the caesura", this possibility of "penetrating the barrier", remains one of Bion's most enduring teachings. It is the idea that there are various caesuras and that it is possible to cross them, that an interpretation is like an idea *in transit* capable of penetrating barriers, reaching fears "buried in the future that has not happened, or buried in the past that is forgotten" (Bion, 1975, p. 84). Interpretation must therefore use the "Language of Achievement", where words are a "prelude" to and not a "substitute" for action, a language that makes action and its choice thinkable (Bion, 1970), capable of transforming pain, to upset "defensive jargons and empty shells" (Pistiner de Cortiñas, 2005), to subvert the "rigid framework of meaning" (Riolo, 1993), to reach archaic residues, prenatal emotions, thoughts without thinker, wild intuitions, which remain split, until the ability to cross the caesuras can penetrate the barrier. This world often inhabits the spaces of poetic creation.

The analyst therefore pursues the analysand in search of what he really feels, and the essential thing is not to inhibit the evolution of the session, waiting for the emergence of emotional truth, and yet when this emerges, it bursts omnipotently, threatening, like a truth, which we knew but which frightens us and which we think we cannot tolerate. Interpretation cannot therefore be limited to grasping the anguish, but must "contain" the patient, dreaming about his emotional experiences, helping him or her to dream and tolerate the truth he or her thinks they are unable to tolerate and think. "The interpretation is an actual event in an evolution of O that is common to the analyst and analysand" (Bion, 1970, p. 27). More than a hermeneutic of the symptom, Bionian psychoanalysis is therefore a continuous process of signification, in which the analyst must be able to create the conditions of "thinkability" in the direction of the dream, which develops the ability to symbolize what has never become a symbol. This can only happen within a relationship that focuses on mutual recognition and tension towards truth. Psychoanalytic treatment therefore promotes a learning process through intersubjective experiences, and the tension towards truth is food for the mind, which enriches the unconscious-conscious level of symbolization of the subject and promotes a structural change, an incarnation, an embodiment, when the subject agrees to identify with his or her creative side.

Intuition and neuroscience

Is this also valid in science? Not exactly. Poincaré (1908) says that "It is demonstrated through science, but it is discovered through intuition". Logic is therefore sterile without intuition, but intuition must be subjected to rigorous experimental verification. When the analyst works on the mind, the burden of criteria and means of right thinking collapses entirely on the mind, which becomes hyper-responsible in its precariousness. The suppression of desire, memory, and understanding thus becomes an expression of an exasperated search for ethics that accompanies Bion in the construction of his method. Bion avoids trapping the analysand in the analyst's desire for care and knows that change can only belong to the patient's creativity. Therefore, Bion never forgets that he is working with a real person and not on a physical object, and yet we discover unexpected similarities between the functions that Bion attributes to intuition and those which neuroscience highlights.

De Wolf and Lumer (2017) propose an effective synthesis of the current interests of neuroscience in intuition. According to the authors, intuition could be triggered at the level of basal ganglia, the head of the caudate nucleus, areas of the brain strongly connected with the body and emotions. But then intuitions require the intervention of the insular and frontal orbit cortex, the most cognitive part of the brain, which connects memory with all higher cognitive functions. Consequently, intuition emerges from the work of the whole brain, the visual, cognitive, perceptual, emotional, motor part, and the unconscious memory. It rests on background neuronal processes, which work unconsciously, when we try to consistently assemble internal or external stimuli starting from our previous experiences. This activation occurs before the trigger of the occipital-temporal lobes' cortex, where the recognition of the objects takes place. Intuition therefore occurs when we still do not perceive the object, but we see and try to make sense of reality, it is a sort of "preliminary perception of coherence". Summing up, neuroscience conceives intuition as unconscious knowledge, which occurs by assembling stored information that has not yet entered consciousness. We realize this unconscious knowledge only later, when synchronization is complete and entry into consciousness is no longer barred. The brain is in fact an organ predisposed to extract meaning from reality. We are bombarded with stimuli of all kinds, and we are constantly called to extract meaning from chaos. This ability is acquired, just like the alpha function.

Therefore, to make sense of the world we need both perception and unconscious memory, not the conscious one but Bion's dream-like-memory! In fact, our brain has a great ability to extract invariants, to recognize patterns. Intuition therefore works unconsciously on the stream of previous experiences, looking for clues of coherence on an immense memory network. In other words, there is a sounding of information in long-term memory, in neuronal networks, that makes all sorts of pattern recognition. This ability is essential and cannot occur through a rational process, but what is necessary is an unconscious, automatic, and intuitive process, because the amount of information that must be computed is beyond our imagination.

Gerald M. Edelman (1992) states that there is no "filtering" with respect to stimuli, so that all information, internal and external, is processed even when it does not become conscious, and this is in harmony with Bion's ideas of alpha function, which works on the whole sensory and emotional reality, on dreaming day and night, and with the conception of the unconscious, formed by previously dreamed elements. This pattern-recognition ability is essential and cannot occur through a rational process. De Wolf and Lumer remind us that our brain has the ability to store around 1 million gigabytes! That is 300 years of uninterrupted programming of a digital video recorder. Each of our brain's 80–100 billion neurons has about 1,000 connections combined so that each one stores many memories simultaneously. This increases the storage capacity of the brain exponentially, but it would still be too little to store the reality of our experience, to recognize a face in its thousand changes of light, movement, time . . . and then there are emotions that modify memories and facilitate or hinder memory. Intuition therefore has an essential role, it is a preliminary recognition of patterns, in the infinite and formless sea of our unconscious, from which we extract "constancy", or as Bion says, "invariants", in an automatic and intuitive comparison between what we see and what has been stored. Then, intuition is defined as a subjective experience, generated by an unconscious process, capable of extracting probabilistic contingencies from acquired experiences and knowledge. Otherwise, in the words of Stanislas Dehaene (2009), intuition is a rapid, automatic knowledge inaccessible to introspection, which relies on neuronal background processes, starting from a stream of previous experiences. Yet all this is not enough, because we have to go beyond the patterns, think of new images, and this is the creative process. De Wolf and Lumer (2017) think that here dream comes into play, with its ability to create new images that escape an overall and coherent synchronization. In other words, only after the unconscious recognition of a pattern has occurred can we be open to the new, and this brings creativity into play. Here it is necessary to bypass the controlling part of the brain, to abandon ourselves to the continuous flow of stimuli from the unconscious brain, with the ability to dream and to stand in front of chaos and ambiguity.

In fact, intuition is necessary when information is insufficient and we stand in chaos, but if the information is sufficient, then the pattern is explicit. Creativity, instead, implies ambiguity and metaphorical use of the object, as occurs in art. Giacometti explained that in creating a face the difficulty lies in rendering the expression and the look of the eyes. To paint the glance well, a little uncertainty is needed. A sculpture works if it's not too perfect, just like an unsaturated interpretation. The artist also provides us with the most beautiful metaphorical image of intuition in a self-portrait from 1935. It is a drawing that represents the author's face frontally, slightly asymmetrical and the nose a little in profile. The right eye has a resolute look towards the outside, but the left eye is closed, or rather it seems turned towards the inside. This is intuition, a double vision; a look inwards, a rummage within ourselves, through self-perception, which consists of memories and unconscious experiences; a look outward, through perception, and imagination, in the incessant search for the new.

Notes

1   Hilbert's program was to demonstrate the coherence of abstract mathematics within real mathematics, that is natural integers. His problem was to defend the axiomatic method,

represented by the *Principia Mathematica*, which risked being put into crisis by the theory of paradoxes and finite/infinite conflict. On this topic see: Russel B., Whitehead A. N. (1910–13). *Principia Mathematica*, Cambridge: Cambridge University Press; Nagel E., Newman J. R. (1958). *Gödel's Proof*, New York: University Press; Hofstadter D. (1979). *Gödel, Escher, Bach: An Eternal Golden Braid*, Basic Books, Inc.

2 I→EU, where I stands for Invariant, E for Emotional and U for Unison.

References

Bergson H. (1896). *Matière et Mémoire*, Félix Alcan, Paris. *Matter and Memory*. George Allen and Unwin, London, 1911. Republisced by Zone Books, New York, 1991.

Bion W.R. (1952). Group dynamics: A review. *International Journal of Psychoanalysis*, 33, 235–247.

Bion W.R. (1962). *Learning from Experience*. Jason Aronson, Oxford, UK.

Bion W.R. (1963). *Elements of Psychoanalysis*. Karnac, Ltd, London.

Bion W.R. (1965). *Transformations*. Heinemann, London.

Bion W.R. (1967). *Second Thoughts*. Karnac, Ltd, London.

Bion W.R. (1970). *Attention and Interpretation*. Tavistock Publications, London.

Bion W.R. (1975). Caesura, in *The Complete Works of W.R. Bion*, edited by Chris Mawson, V. 10, Karnac Books Ltd. 2014.

Bion W.R. (1992). *Cogitations*. Karnac, London.

Civitarese G. (2016). On sublimation. *International Journal of Psychoanalysis*, 97, 1369–1392.

Dehaene S. (2009). Origins of mathematical intuitions: The year of cognitive neuroscience. *Annals of the New York Academy of Sciences*, 1156, 232–259.

De Wolf E., Lumer L. (2017). *Intuition*. Palazzo Fortuny.

Edelman G.M. (1992). *Bright Air, Brilliant Fire*. Basic Books, Inc, New York.

Einstein A. (1954). *Ideas and Opinions*. Crown Publishers.

Freud S. (1932). New introduction lectures on psycho-analysis. *S.E.*, 22.

Grotstein J.S. (2007). *A Beam of Intense Darkness*. Karnac Books, London.

Grotstein J.S. (2009). . . . *But at the Same Time and on Another Level* . . . Karnac Books Ltd, London.

Herrigel E. (1948). *Zen in der Kunst des Bogenschießens*. Weller, Konstanz.

Merleau-Ponty M. (1964). *Le Visible et l'Invisible*. Édition Gallimard, Paris.

O'Shaughnessy E. (2005). Whose Bion? *International Journal of Psychoanalysis*, 86, 1523–1528.

Pimenta A. (1978). *Il silenzio dei poeti*. Feltrinelli, Milano.

Pistiner de Cortiñas L. (2005). Scienza e finzione nel gioco psicoanalitico. *Koinos Gruppo e Funzione Analitica*, 26, 2, 9–36.

Poincaré H. (1908). *Science et méthode*. Flammarion, Paris. *Science and Method*, London, Thomas Nelson and Sons (1914).

Riolo F. (1993). *Ermeneutica e interpretazione*. Di Chiara G., Neri C. (cura di), Psicoanalisi Futura, Borla, Roma.

Roth D. (1973). *Typische Scheisse*. Neuwied.

Rugi G. (2015). *Trasformazioni del dolore. Tra psicoanalisi e arte. Freud, Bion, Grotstein, Munch, Bacon, Viola*. FrancoAngeli, Milano.

Rugi G. (2019). Intuizione e incarnazione. *Koinos, Gruppo e Funzione Analitica*, 7, 2, 67–84.

Rugi G. (2020). Group Oedipus and primary scene: Insertions and contaminations between virtual and archaic. *Funzione Gamma, Site and Journal of Group Psychology*, N.44.

Sandler P.C. (2005). *The Language of Bion: A Dictionary of Concepts*. Karnac, London.

Torres N., Hinshelwood R.D. (2013). *Bion's Sources*. Routledge, London.

Tronik E.Z., Boston C.P.S.G. (1998). Dyadically expanded states of consciousness and the process of therapeutic change. *Infant Mental Health Journal*, 19, 33, 290–299.

Wainrib S. (2012). Is psychoanalysis a matter of subjectivation? *International Journal of Psychoanalysis*, 93, 1115–1135.

Winnicott D.W. (1971). *Playing and Reality*. Tavistock Publications, London.

Chapter 12

Bion and the infinite unconscious – an intuitive science

Ignacio Gerber

> To everyone the problem of the infinite has seemed very difficult, if not insoluble, precisely because they have not distinguished between [. . .] that which can only be understood but not imagined, and that which can also be imagined. Had they paid attention to these distinctions; they would never have been overwhelmed by such a huge multitude of difficulties. For then they would have clearly understood what kind of infinity cannot be divided into any parts, i.e. cannot have any parts; and what kind can be so divided without contradiction. Again, they would have understood what kind of infinity can be conceived to be greater than another infinity without implying any contradiction, and what kind cannot be so conceived.
>
> Spinoza's Letter on the Infinite to Lodevjic Meijer, 1663

> I prefer the dichotomy Finite–Infinite than Conscious–Unconscious.
>
> W.R. Bion

Unconscious – the infinite "in act"

Is there a common ground, a consensual fundamental concept, accepted unreservedly by all the psychoanalytical schools and even by the dissident schools that started to emerge from Freud's? Here is a question that is always there and which has been a driving force behind so many controversies throughout the history of psychoanalysis.

It seems evident, almost obvious, that the Freud postulation of an Unconscious creates and defines Psychoanalysis and becomes its fundamental concept. The Unconscious is the common ground shared by all the post-Freudian schools. Of course, there are different visions in detailing this notion of a strange Unconscious that escapes our conscious control, but the certainty of its ineffable but essential existence runs through all the aforementioned trends and more.

This leads us to another fundamental concept that integrates with the concept of the Unconscious to constitute this common ground: the psychoanalytical attitude that can provide some access to the contradictory and elusive code of the

DOI: 10.4324/9781003293392-18

Unconscious. Freud named it "evenly suspended attention", which is the desirable attitude so that the psychoanalyst could have access to the Unconscious of the patient through his or her own Unconscious. This attitude is a natural consequence of Freud's postulation which he called the "Basic Rule" of psychoanalysis: the patient's "free association".

This idea of free association as a basic rule of psychoanalysis starts to be conceived by Freud in 1900 in *The Interpretation of Dreams*, but it is in his text "Recommendations to Physicians Practicing Psycho-Analysis", from 1912 (pp. 109 to 120), that Freud proposes this joint idea of free association *and* floating attention in a more extensive and comprehensive way, clarifying his conviction that the free association of the analysand requires a floating attention on the part of the analyst in order to listen to it. The two concepts are inseparable and complementary and constitute a continuum that incorporates and transcends analyst and analysand, a transmission from Unconscious to Unconscious. In other possible words, a mutual immersion into a common phylogenetic and ontogenetic Unconscious, an infinite emotional memory, recreated between both.

The Unconscious Logic has always fascinated me and has become a search for a fundamental meaning in my clinical practice. Throughout time, my Act of Faith in the Unconscious was evolving to an almost physical feeling, almost corporeal, of my Unconscious, or I could say, of the Unconscious of all of us. I experience this feeling particularly in the presence of one analysand, but the feeling spreads to my "life outside".

There is a tendency to divide Bion's work into phases, for example: mathematical phase and mystical phase. It seems to me that they are only facets of a single phase that permeates all his work: the search for a comprehensive theory of the "emotional thinking of the human being" that covers the "Finite Conscious Logic" and the "Infinite Unconscious Logic". Bion starts from the classical mathematics of Aristotle and Euclid and Isaac Newton's classical physics, which do not admit contradiction and were the Positivist references to which Freud had access, and boldly enters the contemporary creations of a science that admits ambiguity, paradox, Infinity, and the inevitable implication of the observer.

> The historical process about the Infinite began with Aristotle, with one of the most elusive, difficult, wonderful concepts created by human thought. What is the Infinite? What do we mean, for example, when we state that the sequence 1, 2, 3, 4, 5 . . . is infinite? The infinity of the sequence manifests itself in the unassailable characteristic of "never ending", an unreachable future feature and not a concrete present trace. Aristotle called this form of Infinite "Potential Infinite". The second way of thinking the Infinite consists in seeing it as a present reality "In Act". In this case we could imagine a supernatural Being writing down all the numbers, absolutely all of them, in an act of an almost divine will. It is very difficult, not to say impossible, to grasp what that means. Are we able to represent a whole that is wholly present but never ends?
>
> Whether because it is in fact unimaginable, or for deeper philosophical reasons, Aristotle stated in his "Metaphysics" that the Infinite in Act does not

exist. Over the centuries, this rejection of the Infinite in Act was unanimously defended by Western orthodoxy, both philosophical and mathematical. The Infinite in Act, according to the scholastics, was an attribute of Divinity.

Only at the end of the 19th century, Georg Cantor revolutionizes these concepts with his Set Theory, which was his way of designating the study of infinite totalities as an object in itself. That is, Cantor admits the Infinite in Act, and that it should constitute the very foundation of a new, more comprehensive mathematics.

(Piñero. In Gödel, 2012)

Returning to the path that, from Freud, Bion traveled through transformative moments of the sciences, until then nicknamed the "exact sciences", I propose in this article that:

The Unconscious is the most striking example of the concrete existence of the "Infinite in Act", which constitutes us as human beings and that the possible apprehension of his interference in the field of the "conscious finitude" is given in an attitude of "Intuitive Attention" of the analyst.

How to judge if a new scientific theory brings something really new? We remember two propositions about it. According to the first one, "A scientific theory is NEW when it renders obsolete preexisting theories". According to the other one, "A scientific theory is new when it transforms preexisting theories in their particular cases". We extrapolate these propositions to any field of human theorization, including scientific theories, aesthetic theories, psychoanalytic theories, etc. As classic examples, Einstein reduced Newtonian physics to a particular case valid only under certain conditions, and Freud's postulation of the Unconscious reduced the Conscious to its particular case. In both examples, what became obsolete was the preexisting idea that the Newtonian physics or the Conscious could encompass the totality of all possible knowledge. Bion's ideas must be understood within this historical context in which illusory temporal certainties of conscious logic open themselves to the radical, timeless uncertainty of unconscious logic. Ambiguity and uncertainty break the limited barriers of rational certainty and confront it with the Infinite. As the atomic physicist and thinker David Bohm (1998) says, "the ambiguous is the reality and the unambiguous is merely a special case of it, where we finally manage to pin down some very special aspect".

From tradition to contradiction: from determinism to randomness

Freud lived at a time when the deterministic logic prevailing in scientific thought was being questioned, and that expanded mainly in mathematics and physics, towards randomness, contradiction, uncertainty, and undecidability. For most of Freud's life, this new vision of the world, a new cosmovision, which these and other discoveries were producing, was still confined to a limited class of scientists, having little dissemination and understanding even among cultured and informed men of the time. Bion lived at a time when these ideas were already widely disseminated and better understood by a wider audience, belonging to the most varied areas of knowledge.

Using some of these revolutionary ideas – exposed here in a very simplified and concise way – let's illustrate the changes that they produced in our way of thinking about the logic of the universe and in our own internal logic.

In 1900, at the International Mathematics Congress, David Hilbert, its undisputed leader, proposed the 23 unsolved problems of mathematics as a challenge to his peers, being sure that it was only a matter of time for them all to be solved and exhorted his colleagues with the lapidary statement: "We must know, we will know!"

At the international congress in 1931, the young mathematician Kurt Gödel surprises his colleagues and destroys further this illusion by proposing his Incompleteness Theorem. Again, in very simplified terms: any mathematical equation, besides the most trivial ones, presents undecidable solutions. The illusion of the possible conquest of the totality of knowledge is broken, but mathematics nevertheless continuously evolves by accepting its own limitation.

In short, the reality is uncertain and undecidable. Potentializing Kant: The universe to which we have access is only a possible reality among infinite multiuniverses. After the third blow to man's narcissism of psychoanalysis, this is the fourth and final blow to our arrogance, but it opens the doors of the Infinite.

Freud's Postulation of a "Psychic Determinism", which will open so many new paths, is still based on a Deterministic concept prevalent in the mentality of that time. It is interesting to remember that Freud subscribed, along with great physicists and mathematicians, such as Hilbert, Mach, Einstein, and others, to the so-called Manifesto for a Positivist Science in 1912, in the renowned German scientific journal *Physicalische Zeitschrift;* but throughout his works, not only Freud but all the names mentioned earlier let go of their certainties about a science restricted by a non-contradictory and Positivist logic and admit the inherent ambiguity of reality.

It seems to us of greater importance to point that the text "Recommendations to Physicians Practicing Psycho-Analysis", from the same year, 1912, constitutes a fundamental change in the way Freud thinks of psychoanalysis and that foreshadows "The Ego and Id" in its passage from psychic Determinism to unconscious randomness. The initial proposition of decomposing the dream in isolated elements and trying to understand the linear correlations between these elements to try to establish a broad sense still uses a conscious logic to approach the contradictory logic of the Unconscious. From the postulation of the floating attention + free association, the process is reversed: by assuming this analytical attitude, we are willing to grasp the message of the Unconscious from a totality of our informed intuition and, from it, we look for the meaning of the elements, of the fragments, of the details. From Infinite to Finite.

The characteristics of the Freudian Unconscious, displacement, condensation, etc. can be thought of as the experiential consequences of a totalizing Principle of unconscious logic. It does not obey Aristotle's *Principle of Excluded Middle*, which guided scientific thought for thousands of years and which proposes that if two elements, A and B, are different from each other, there is no third element T that equals itself to the two. It is also known as the *Principle of Non-contradiction*: contradictory propositions are unacceptable by science. By admitting contradiction, unconscious logic establishes sense bonds to any and all mental images where the emotional experiences of personal and human experiences are recorded. Unconscious logic, the dream, is an eternal return to the primordial infinite.

In the physics field, between 1905 and 1915, Einstein publishes the *Theory of Relativity* and the *Theory of General Relativity*, surprising the scientific world with the demonstration of physical concepts that contradicts established ideas and, more than that, hurt our common sense. As examples, the equivalence of matter and energy, the relativization of time and the notion of a mutant space that bends when subjected to the gravitational force of a celestial body of great mass.

In 1927, the physicist Werner Heisenberg, one of the creators of atomic physics, proposed his Uncertainty Principle: in the field of elementary particles, it is impossible to accurately determine the mass and moment (motion) of a particle; observation interferes with the phenomenon. This implies a permanent limitation of scientific knowledge, putting an end to the illusion that at some point the evolution of technology and scientific knowledge would lead us to the certainty about everything. We have to accept uncertainty as an inherent element in knowing, and that principle of physics spreads across all areas of human knowledge.

As we can see, Freud's work, from 1900 to 1939, coincides with a radical change in the scientific cosmovision, in the *Weltbild:* from Newtonian determinism to the probabilistic randomness of quantum mechanics. A new way of thinking described in an expressive way by Niels Bohr, one of the creators of quantum mechanics: "If quantum mechanics has not profoundly shocked you, you have not understood it yet". We think of a paraphrase: if the logic of the Subconscious has not profoundly shocked you, you have not understood it yet.

O the fullness of the void

Going back to the epigraphs: in his Letter on the Infinite, Spinoza intuited an idea that anticipates in 500 years Bion's proposal of an Infinite Unconscious. We use a classic illustration about the "contact barrier" between Conscious-Finite and Unconscious-Infinite. Where is the boundary between these two logics? Let us take a four-sided polygon, a square, and we will increase the number of sides. We all know that, at the limit – this is the mathematical concept of limit –, we will arrive at a circumference. But evidently, a circumference is not a polygon with infinite sides. On the one hand it is, if we imagine a lot of smaller and smaller sides, but at some point, there is a cut, I would say an epistemological cut, a logical cut, total and absolute. At some point this bunch of sides disappears and becomes a continuity, without beginning and without end. It is a way of exemplifying what happens when you go from the Conscious to the Unconscious. It is an absolutely radical change. The parts disappear, and a continuity is created. Hence the circumference is a primordial symbol of Hindu, Chinese, Mayan, and other great traditions. It is the symbol of continuity, the symbol of divinity. And no doubt Bion's *O* follows from that. It is not just a zero or a linguistic "O". It is, more than anything, the shape of the circumference, of this infinite continuity.

If we think of the Unconscious, then, as an infinity of senses and relationships, all that we have experienced emotionally will be in it, all our inner experiences and, perhaps, all the memory of the species, something that Freud called Archaic Heritage, Jung emphasized as Collective Unconscious, and Borges poetized as the Aleph.

I appeal to musical listening in an attempt to illustrate *Caesura*, a dear term to Bion, between a finite and infinite experience. We attended a concert and, stimulated by the random music of the tuning of the instruments, we prepared ourselves to listen to a piano and orchestra concert, which can be heard in many ways. Classificatory, this is a concert of Beethoven's mature phase, or, comparatively, I liked Lang-Lang's performance better, or even be led by the music to a reverie. All auditions are valid and important both aesthetically and intellectually and also emotionally. But there are times when we are captured by the *Music* and forget everything we learned before and that we know now, and we give ourselves to music in a radically pleasurable experience. It has no more composer or interpreter or listener; perhaps we are bold discoverers of a music that exists, waiting to be discovered, infinite.

In chapter 2 of *Attention and Interpretation*, a book that, in our view, represents the essence of the Bionian thinking, he makes the link between a philosophical conjecture and our clinical practice:

> The realizations with which a psychoanalyst deals cannot be seen or touched; anxiety has no shape or color, smell or sound. For convenience, I propose to use the term "intuit" as a parallel in the psychoanalyst domain to the physician's use of "see", "touch", "smell" and "hear." (p. 111).
>
> [. . .]
>
> I will use the O symbol to denote that which is the ultimate and true reality, represented by terms as ultimate reality, absolute truth, divinity, infinity, the thing-in-itself. O does not fall upon the scope of knowledge or learning, except incidentally. It may "become", but it cannot "be known". O is darkness and absence of shape but falls within the scope of K when it has evolved to the point where it can be known, by means of knowledge gained from experience, and formulated in terms derived from sensory experience; its existence is phenomenologically conjectured." (p. 112a).
>
> [. . .]
>
> One might ask what the welcome state of mind would be, since memories and desires are not. A term that would roughly express what I need to express is "faith" – faith that there is an ultimate and true reality – the "infinite devoid of form", unknown, unknowable.
>
> [. . .]
>
> The analyst cannot identify himself with O: he must be it.
>
> (Bion, 1970)

References

Bion WR (1970). *Attention and Interpretation*. Hogarth Press: London, UK.
Bohm D (1998). *Wholeness and the Implicate Order*. Routledge: London, UK.
Piñero GE. In Gödel K (2012). *Incompleteness Theorem*. National Geographic: São Paulo, SP.

Chapter 13

Observation and intuition in psychoanalysis

Carmen C. Mion

Introduction

We psychoanalysts are constantly faced with the vicissitudes of human communication in carrying out the function we propose ourselves every day, from the moment we receive a patient till the moment we decide to make an interpretation, which hopefully combines depth and conciseness. The communication in the analysis room carries great complexity, since it is a very specific communication, which serves a specific function, and about which much has been written. However, I believe that no author had devoted himself so deeply to the issue of communication in psychoanalysis as Bion did. In several of his texts and seminars, he often called attention to the limitations of the very language we use since it is not specific to our object of investigation but borrowed from sciences, religions, literature or other fields of knowledge. In one of his last seminars, Bion stated that he was not interested in psychoanalytic theories but "in the most important, which I call 'the real thing', the practice of analysis, the practice of treatment, the practice of communication" (Bion, 2005, p. 16).

I intend to develop here the concepts of observation and intuition as being part of the broader theme, communication in psychoanalysis, limiting myself to the specificity of the analyst's "listening" to his/her patients in the analysis room. The intuition and the observation through the senses and perception organs, including here Freud's concept of the Conscious as a perception organ, constitute the pathways through which we receive and perceive the sensory and non-sensory communications of our analysands.

I propose that these two psychoanalyst's functions, observation and intuition, act together similarly to the biological model of "binocular view" utilized by Bion as an approximation to his concept of the contact barrier and the interplay of conscious and unconscious. In the same way as the somatic and psychic binomial, I believe that there is no way of separating observation and intuition except artificially for the purpose of delving deeper into both. In other words, as Bion (1977, p. 55) indicates, for the psychoanalysts these questions are a matter of day-to-day practice, not only theoretical.

Before entering into the subject of the chapter itself, I consider it important to present the psychoanalytic vertex from which I will develop the theme, since

DOI: 10.4324/9781003293392-19

the different theoretical references reflect different perspectives on the human psyche, determine different preconceptions and different approaches in the clinical practice, not forgetting that, even when starting from the same theories, two analysts will still make their own transformations.

I start from the premise that the psychoanalytic meeting between analyst and analysand is impregnated by the emotions and feelings of the duo, and I see a session as a succession of movements resulting from the interaction between the two minds from the beginning of the encounter. The analyst's focus is the material for which he has evidence, that is, the emotional experience of the analytic duo at the time of the session (Bion's common "O"). Thereby, the here and now of the relationship comes to the foreground in the analytic scene, favoring a bond of intimacy, creativity and opening to the unknown for both. I consider essential the exercise of a "discipline" that takes into account the multidimensionality, the variability and the psychic complexity of the human mind so that it helps the analyst to meet his/her patient with no memories, no desires and no understanding.

I proceed by artificially separating both functions of observation and intuition to join them again at the end of the chapter.

Observation

The issue of observation remains one of the most important problems in psychoanalysis ever since Freud's encounter with Charcot in 1885: "I learned to restrain speculative tendencies and follow my master Charcot's forgotten words to look at the same thing again and again until they begin to speak for themselves" (Freud, 1914, p. 22). Bion (2005) refers to Freud when he states that observation in psychoanalysis is as close as we can get to what would be a fact in science and had devoted himself to the development of a theory on the practice of psychoanalytic observation, gathered mainly in his book *Transformations* (1965).

Departing from Kant and Hume, Bion proposes that in all communications involving the observation of people or objects, whether concrete or immaterial, there will always be a transformation of an invariant, the unknowable "thing in itself", which he denominated "O". From this vertex, the psychoanalyst's main focus, the specificity of his observation, is related to the material in which he participates directly, the emotional experience occurring between/with the duo at the present moment of the session: "any "O" not common to the analyst and to the analysand and therefore not available for transformation by both can be ignored as irrelevant to psychoanalysis . . . any appearance to the contrary depends on a failure to understand the nature of psychoanalytic interpretation" (Bion, 2005, p. 48).

But what does the psychoanalyst observe after all; what do we "look at" in the analysis room? In relation to the patient, I would say that everything that presents itself to our senses: how the patient arrives, whether he is punctual or not, his face expressions when entering the room; the way he enters and lies down, if he throws himself on the couch, if he is careful, hesitates or doesn't lie down at all; if something catches our attention, if nothing catches our attention, what emotions he transmits or doesn't transmit; if something in his clothing or his way of dressing draws our attention; if a smell is detected or not and so on. At the same time, we pay attention to what the patient says or if he does not say anything; if one sentence or another, for some reason that we do not know yet, calls our attention or causes us a discomfort. Whether the patient seems anxious or confused or frightened or, on the contrary, seems happy or triumphant or does not appear to have any feelings at all. Sometimes, we perceive a certain tone of voice or changes in the tone of voice, subtleties of his look; other times, we notice an unusual pause or a smile or a gesture with his hands: what does the patient's body communicate beyond what he says to us?

In addition to and at the same time that we make all these observations, we need yet to have another eye turned to ourselves, the analyst himself. We try to perceive, as a third party, what feelings the patient elicits in us, if some irritation suddenly arises or a feeling of drowsiness or any other unusual feeling or emotion; if you find yourself mentally reviewing the week's agenda or being absent from the session; if an undefined discomfort in relation to the patient arises, or in relation to yourself; if you are restless, if you have a sudden pain in your stomach or a headache; if a song occurred to you or an absurd thought; if an image came to your mind with no apparent relation to what is happening in the session; if you feel a sexual arousal or a sudden hatred and so on.

Bion also suggests the use of observation in psychoanalysis as a metaphor used by John Milton in *Paradise Lost,* when he claims to have the hope of being able to "see and speak of things invisible to mortal eyes" (Bion, 2005, p. 13). As analysts, we need to expose ourselves to the experience of the session in order to apprehend the ineffable, see and speak of things invisible to the eyes. It means a lively and attentive presence to what happens between/with the duo, which touches both. Who can prove or demonstrate projective identification? That the pain or fear that the analysand feels is in the analyst? As Bion points out, the concepts of transference and countertransference are useful to analysts to communicate with each other. They are experiences that we have and live in the office, but only another analyst will be able to achieve what we try to transmit when mentioning these concepts. We are hopelessly doomed to subjective apprehensions in the analysis room.

Maintaining faith in the processes of the unconscious and knowing that facts are always psychic, the analyst must be able to "lose himself" by lifting the boundaries of rational activity and logic that is proper to habitual waking thinking. Bion's recommendation to the analysts in several of his seminars (1973–1978) – "no memory, no desire" – implies detaching oneself from the protection provided by theoretical structures and the gratifying meanings of the "already known" as well as from expectations related to the patient and oneself. When we have a chance to forget everything we know about the patient, who will do his best to remind us, then there may be a chance to penetrate the astonishing caesura of the knowledge, of the reported facts and all known theories, to have a chance to hear those little subtleties, those little things hard to see, hear, feel, grasp (Bion, 2005).

In other words, we need to listen to our patients, "blinding" ourselves (Grotstein, 2007), because from time to time we may have a chance to grasp that piece of information that may become relevant and sometimes illuminating as a selected fact. Over time and with some luck, we may identify some pattern that emerges from this myriad of information gathered, a constant conjunction which recurs throughout successive encounters. Once the pattern is detected, the investigation proceeds: what leads the patient to repeat this pattern? What moves him and is not visible? What is his pain? I also refer here to the question of complementarity in psychoanalysis, the complementarity of "O", the ultimate reality. The analyst's psychoanalytic theories and the patient's own discourse can produce a barrier against direct contact, observation, the experience of the real thing, a glimpse of the patient's real suffering. Bion (2005, p. 19) proposes an illustrative model of the situation in which we find ourselves in the analysis room: "We know so much about the patient, about us, about theories, about life, that it is very difficult to see or detect 'this' that we are observing so that we can hear the faint sounds buried under this mass of noise".

It is not by chance that the fear of the darkness is atavistic: the primitive man, as soon as he had discovered fire, began to use torches to light the darkness of the night and the caves where they took refuge. This fear persists as such in young children, as well as in the grown-ups. However, in the last case it becomes "sophisticated", so to speak, expressing itself as fear of the internal dark "caves", fear of the stranger that inhabits us, the unknown: the human mind does not support the "darkness" of not knowing. Rational thinking arises then, like the torches of the primitive man, to deal with the darkness and loneliness that terrify us, as attempts to alleviate our pain and perplexity in face of life. One way found by man to give meaning and some predictability to these experiences, from the beginning, are the phantasies, mythological narratives, the stories we tell ourselves, such as who is this person with me, who I am, what is life, where I come from, where I am and where I am going to, what is death, and then we come to believe them. Thus, we acquire the illusion of conscious knowledge-ment, and as we continue to develop, the stories become more and more complex, new elements from reality are added, and they may become mythology, philosophy, psychology, psychoanalysis etc.

Intuition

Freud (1937) already refers to underlying truths not apprehended by the senses and which depend on the analyst's intuition, insight and ability to dream. The unconscious, the psychic reality as Freud postulates in "Constructions in Analysis", does not make itself known directly; we can only apprehend it non-sensorially; it can only be intuitive.

In addition to dedicating himself to the question of observation, Bion also brought an important contribution to the area of intuition in psychoanalysis, which is not surprising given his interest and his furthering the question of the different facets of communication in psychoanalysis. Through his efforts to include psychoanalytic theories not only in the Transformations group but by placing them as preconceptions in the analyst's state of mind in the sessions, Bion discriminates and specifies the intuition used in the analysis room as a psychoanalytically informed intuition by the theory we develop and build throughout our becoming psychoanalysts, differentiating it from lay intuition or intuition related to any other field of knowledge. The analyst's own analysis, supervisions and life experiences are also preconceptions which eventually may emerge in the analysis room as they find realization in the pair's experience.

The direction in which psychoanalytic inquiry moves is superimposed on Pascal's infinite spaces and follows until it reaches the deep recesses of Hades. Bion connects the analyst with the angst of living with the uncertain, tolerating mysteries and doubts; with the perception that one can be blind, deceived by one's own perceptions, choices and decisions that will inevitably have future repercussions but also knowing that this limited perception is the only instrument available to us. The emotional atmosphere of the session, the analyst's impressions, the emotional state of the analyst–analysand duo, the dreamlike thoughts themselves are the only compasses available. This state of mind of psychic unsaturation of the analyst in the session (Mion, 2017) makes us sensitive to what is not, what does not fit, difficulties, discomfort or pre-monitions not expressed or even perceived by the patient but that, once captured by the analyst, can function as "signalings" which usually present themselves as intuitions that arise in the analyst's mind as images, dreamlike memories, wild thoughts, songs, feelings, poetry.

I recall here Bion's observation that limiting ourselves to observation and inquiry of what we understand means setting aside the raw material upon which knowledge and wisdom may depend. Clinical experience continually shows us evidence of some remnant states of mind that we might find in the prehistory of some adult patients. Bion (1977) suggests that events in the womb of time may present themselves to the conscious life of a person who, however, must act and exist in the present. Memories of the future, buried in the past that cannot be (re) presented? Sometimes we need to "hear" (intuit) the remnants of what survived in one's mind, buried in the midst of all the noise that comes to us through the senses of sight and hearing, to detect the remnant of something still active in one's mental life. As Bion proposes, there are not just two people in the analysis room: "It's like having the entirety of a person at all ages and all times in one room at the same time" (2005, p. 29).

In discussing these rare moments of illumination, Bion (2005, p. 25) refers to John Milton when he mentioned *Alpheus*, in Lycidas: "Return Alpheus, the dread voice is past". *Alpheus* is a river that flows underground, hidden, and occasionally breaks into different and unexpected places. Where it appears and what effect it will have, no one knows. Bion proposes that certain ideas, which are very difficult to trace, run their course through the mind and personality like the Alpheus River, unseen, unheard nor observed. Ideas that were never conscious seem to float around and break out much later when the embryo or fetus became a sophisticated person. Where do these ideas arrive as they move along, and what apparatus can we have to grasp them beyond our senses and common sense? In another moment, I think Bion expands the subject by stating that the reason we keep dealing with things that are remembered, with our past history, it is not for what it was "but because of the marks it has left on you or on me or on us now . . . there may still be traces in the mind or character or personality, in present, of particles that have a long history, things we would expect to be fundamental, basic, primordial" (Bion, 1997, p. 38).

Binocular vision

I believe that the presence of the analyst's subjectivity acquires greater importance, with all its possibilities and limitations, as his function of observation ↔ intuition are linked to the analyst's conscious/finite↔unconscious/infinite "binocular vision". The contact barrier, which not only maintains but also gives rise to the differentiation between conscious and unconscious, is formed by alpha-elements presenting one face to conscious and another to unconscious. When Bion presented his alpha-function theory, he utilized a biological model as an approximation to his concept of contact barrier: the binocular vision. He introduced the idea that conscious awareness and unconscious capture would occur simultaneously, likewise the binocular vision. At his seminars in Tavistock (2005, p. 23) he takes up this model as an approximation to the "perception of a germ of an embryonic idea", which at first appears unfocused, somewhat confused, creates a sense of discomfort until the "focus" happens. Although Bion was not explicit, I think this is the model that best approximates the use of observation (finite conscious) and intuition (infinite unconscious) by the analyst in the analysis room. Similar to binocular vision, there is a moment when observation and intuition come together in the analyst's mind and the "focus" happens: this is the moment when the analyst "sees" (feels, captures) that the impression about the patient or what is going on at that moment, that was taking shape, perhaps growing in his mind, suddenly becomes "visible".

The development of this process will depend on the analyst's psychic qualities that will be communicated to the patient through the affective channels of communication and their inevitable impacts on the patient's mind. Welcoming the object with freedom, patience, mature compassion, respect and tolerance enables the growth of the threads forming the meshes of the continent reticulum to be filled with different emotional contents ($♀♂→∞$). In order for dreamlike thoughts and binocular perception to be possible, the analyst must have a tolerance for doubt and a sense of infinity, a certain negative capability in the conception of Keats, quoted by Bion (1967b), which refers to the ability of a man to be in uncertainties, mysteries, doubts, without any attempt to reach fact and reason.

In an earlier work (Mion, 2019), I spoke of an analyst capable of transiting between the caesuras of the multidimensional mind, crossing through transparent mirrors[1] without becoming paralyzed or drowning like Narcissus enthralled with his own reflection. That is, the analyst's function involves not only ideas in transit but an analyst with a transitive mind, a *becoming* in the sense of being able to transcend his vertices without losing sight of it, "seeing" both sides of the innumerable mirrors/caesuras which, like Alice's, we come across every day. It means an analyst being able to experience *becoming* the reality T→(O) together with the patient.

Bion (2005, pp. 62–67) brings us a beautiful image related to the analyst's resistances to *becoming* and the question of caesuras between the different psychic dimensions: Picasso's transparent glass paintings, which from the other side look like different drawings. He proposes that the analyst look at the other side of resistance, as in these paintings, to look in such a way that what is being resisted begins to shine through it, to intuit the nature of "O". "When it is clear that it is analysis that is being resisted, what is shining through it? It is not simply a matter of a change of vertex, it is also being able to see through resistance, countertransference, or whatever it may be". Bion compares us in this respect with the dinosaurs, who to defend themselves, developed a shell so heavy that they could barely walk. The problem is that man's logical capacity when hypertrophied, like the dinosaur shell, leaves no room for growth. Basically, each defense mechanism is a lie we tell ourselves about an intolerable and painful truth, "O". Bion draws attention to suffering in situations of analysis by saying that "resistance is what the patient would say if he could: I do this to survive".

This would be the domain to which the Transformations in/from "O" belong. Being *at-one-ment* with "O" describes the experience of *becoming* "O", an expression of one's being. As Chuster (2018) points out, "O" from "Onthus" and "Opus", a work in progress. Being at-one-ment with "O" depends on the ability to integrate the most primitive states of mind with the higher mental functions through which the evolution of "O" can be experienced (Williams, 2010). As beautifully summarized by Bollas (2009, p. 100): "The conscious self is now in the place of the child who does not know, who cannot think about the experiences of being, while it is the unconscious self that carries the wisdom of the self's history and does the profound work of processing the details of the lived experience through the symphony of unconscious thinking".

Final considerations

The configurations of psychic suffering we are dealing with today point to feelings of emptiness, meaninglessness, inadequacy and non-existence, psychosomatic experiences, in which objects have a utilitarian function and relationships of intimacy are absent. In the intimacy of our clinical offices, we have found fundamentalisms of all kinds, self-definitions through profession, impoverished individualities. On the other hand, technology, *Thecnos*, becomes, as it were, an ideal to which the ego is helplessly subjected, camouflaging its helplessness and fear in the face of death, indetermination, emptiness, through technological hypertrophy and its prostheses (Freud, 1930) trying to refuse chance, death and the unavoidable pains of existence. I speak of men and women for whom the aspiration to become themselves is more urgent and demanding than to make the unconscious conscious, to reintegrate the projected or even to develop thoughts from their own emotional experiences.

Note

1 At a conference in São Paulo (1978), when discussing the question of penetration of caesuras, which paradoxically separate and unite "events"/states of mind/radiations of "O" in infinite space-time, Bion suggests a very strong image: transparent mirror. A transparent mirror presupposes not only contact/separation but also movements and passages in both directions of the caesura. Bion considers the possibility of a primordial thought of the fetus, projected in caesura, to reflect itself starting from the child to its primordial levels of thoughts and feelings.

References

Bion, W.R. (1965). *Transformations*. New York: Jason Aronson, 1983.

Bion, W.R. (1967b). Notes on memory and desire. In W.R. Bion (1992) *Cogitations*. London Karnac books (extended 1994 version).

Bion, W.R. (1977). Caesura. In: *Two Papers: The Grid and Caesura*, pp. 37–56. Londres: Karnac Books, 1989.

Bion, W.R. (1973–1978). Bion's Supervisions in Sao Paulo. *Recorded, Transcribed and Presented by José Américo Junqueira de Mattos and Gisele Mattos at Scientific Meetings at the SBPSP.*

Bion, W.R. (1997). *Taming Wild Thoughts*. London: Karnac Books.

Bion, W.R. (2005). *The Tavistock Seminars*. London: Karnak Books.

Bollas, C. (2009). *The infinite question*. New York: Routledge.

Chuster, A. (2018). Intuição psicanalítica no sonho e na vigília. Cesura, imaginação e linguagem de Êxito. In: *Bion Internacional Meeting*. São Paulo: Ribeirão Preto.

Freud, S. (1914). The history of the psychoanalytic movement. *SE* 14: 22.

Freud, S. (1930). El Malestar en la Cultura. In: *Sigmund Freud, Obras Completas*, Tomo III. Madrid: Biblioteca Nueva.

Freud, S. (1937). Constructions in analysis. *SE* 23: 256–269.

Grotstein, J. (2007). *A Beam of Intense Darkness*. London: Karnac Books.

Mion, C.C. (2017). Supervision A2 commentary. In: *Bion in Brazil: Supervisions and Commentaries*, pp. 224–232. Ed. Jose A. J. de Mattos, Gisele de Mattos Brito and Howard B. Levine. London: Karnak.

Mion, C.C. (2019). Conjectures about dreams, memories and caesuras. In: *Explorations in Bion's "O": Everything We Know Nothing About*. Ed. Afsaneh K. Alisobhani and Glenda Corstorphine. New York: Routledge.

Willians, M.H. (2010). *Bion's dream*. London: Karnac Books.

Chapter 14

Intuition in Bion's colloquial words (supervisions in Brazil, 1973–1978)[1]

João Carlos Braga and Gisèle de Mattos Brito

Introduction

Wilfred Bion conducted several group supervisions in São Paulo, Brasília, and Rio de Janeiro during his four visits to Brazil (1973, 1974, 1975, and 1978). About 130 of these supervisions were recorded on cassette tapes and recovered by Dr. José Américo Junqueira de Mattos, a prior analysand of Bion who personally coordinated, took on the financial burden, and participated in a careful transcription of the tapes. For about 15 years, this precious collection has been generously shared with colleagues.

These supervisions allow a new look at Bion's ideas, as they present spur-of-the-moment communications during clinical discussions that are only possible in colloquial meetings. In addition to a privileged condition of spontaneous expression, these supervisions also offer us direct indications on how Bion thought and operated in the psychoanalytic clinic in his final years of life. Thus, the supervisions allow us to have a good sense of the ideas about the human mind and its functioning that he developed during his final years and which are related to practical situations and his own elaborations. This opportunity offers a contrast to the vision that we usually obtain of his ideas in conceptual formulations from his books and articles.

In this work, we will present a few selected moments of these supervisions in which references to the theme intuition appeared explicitly. The presentation of these moments will be complemented with some reflections that will seek to bring Bion's colloquial words closer to conceptual formulations present in his published texts. In particular, we will try to identify and correlate the presence of intuition with the different states of mind in which manifestations of intuition occur, corresponding, in broad lines, to the different evolutionary periods of Bion's thinking: the epistemological (1962–1965), the ontological (1965–1979), and the interest in the primordial mind (1976–1979).

1. Intuition in supervisions conducted by Bion in Brazil

In several of these supervisions, the theme intuition is explicitly pointed out as the fundamental resource for direct contact with the mind; in others, it appears

DOI: 10.4324/9781003293392-20

collaterally. In many other supervisions yet, it is possible to follow Bion exercising his intuition. Bion's faithfulness to the intuitive method is evident in all these supervisions: he intervenes and ponders about clarifications (questions) and elaborations of the theme that he intuitively captures in descriptions of the analyst presenting the emotional state of the participants in the group – the fragment of psychic reality attempting to evolve in the group to reach the dimension of knowing (K) and, thus, acquire the condition of thinkability by those present in the group. The discipline of limiting oneself to ongoing experiences in the group and moving away from resorting to rational conjectures is always evident. In this sense, it is remarkable to realize that this methodology for the analytical work was already present in Bion's mind since his period of working with groups:

> It will be remembered that I attempted deliberately, in so far as it is possible to psycho-analyst admittedly proposing to investigate the group through *psycho-analytically developed intuitions* (underlined by the authors), to divest myself of any earlier psychoanalytic theories of the group in order to achieve an unprejudiced view.
>
> (1961 [1952], p. 165)

In order to offer a minimal organization to our presentation, we will resort to our understanding that during these supervisions, Bion presented to us different forms of intuition, as he has done in different moments of his work. Thus, we will attempt to distinguish the following:

A Intuition evolving in a state of mind proper to the dimension of knowing.
B Intuition evolving in a state of mind proper of being in unison with reality.
C Intuition as an experience of receptiveness to thoughts without a thinker.

A. Intuition evolving in a state of mind proper to the dimension of knowing

In Supervision A16, Bion introduced the examination of the theme intuition with a question: *How does the pattern get clear to us?* He then developed some ideas, pointing out that we start with what our physical senses tell us. We can see, smell, hear, and form our understanding from there. However, when it comes to the mind, *we do not know what our intuitive senses are* (Bion, Supervision A16). We have to create imaginative conjectures from intuitions that emerge from the juxtaposition between what evolves in the analysand's mind and what evolves in the analyst's mind (*Transformations*, 1965, p. 65). In other words, following the emergence of an intuition, we need to hypothesize in a second mental movement that some work is happening in the medium of knowing to enable the emergence of imaginative conjectures. In due time, this paves the way to a rational conjecture. From our perspective, this is the idea of intuition present until *Transformations* (1965). In *Experiences With Groups* (1961 [1943–1952]), *Learning from Experience* (1962), and *Elements of Psychoanalysis* (1963) or even in chapters 1 to 9 in *Transformations*, Bion works with the ideas of his theory of knowledge.

In this epistemological period of Bion's thinking, we must discriminate experiences of intuition as thoughts that emerge suddenly and directly to the thinker, without the intervention of rational processes, from thoughts of the thinker produced by transformations of sensorial experiences and emotions by alpha function.

In the notation of the theory of transformations, this would correspond to an O=> K formulation. This experience would be the final product of a mental movement in which accumulated knowledge evolves to a point in which it is possible to be receptive to a fragment of the psychic reality that attempts to evolve; that is, the knowledge that has already developed is a continent for a content that seeks to be thought out. In Bion's terms, as present in *Attention and Interpretation* (1970, p. 26):

> O does not fall in the domain of knowledge or learning, save incidentally; it can be 'become,' but it can not be 'known.' It is darkness and formlessness, but it enters the domain K when it has evolved to a point where it can be known, through knowledge gained by experience and formulated in terms derived from sensuous experience.

These ideas can be observed in a section of Supervision A16 (São Paulo, 1978), described in what follows:

Excerpt from Supervision A16

PI: It occurred to me that – I don't know yet – but my first conjecture is: that patient aborted some capacity for love – she had some kind of psycho-infertility.

BION: This is why I was saying that from our point of view, from the analyst's point of view, the difficulty – if it has to be classified in a *grid* – needs to be a different grid from the one which I suggested, with regard to the various things. Because our problem is: how does the pattern get clear to us? Well, I'm suggesting that it starts by what your senses tell you; those in a sense, could be called *Beta or Alpha Elements*. They are facts, of a kind of which, your senses can tell you. If you put your hand out, you can touch the patient and your common senses – autonomic, sympathetic, and voluntary – can bring you the information, it can tell you *what*. So, we won't bother about that very much but. When the patient enters the room, those senses, such as being able to see the patient, see what sort of clothes he or she wore, whether there was a smell (patient are sometimes unaware of their own body odors) and so on. . . . When it comes to a question of the mind, you can't see the mind. So that's gone. We are blind!! The mind doesn't smell, it hasn't got a shape, it doesn't make a noise. So, your ears can't give you any information – it depends on something which we have to imagine, or invent we'll call it *intuition*. It's not *out-tuition* – it's not what you're taught – by what your outward looking eyes can tell you – but *in*-tuition.

T: Or *in*sight?

BION: Insight. Now, that kind of sense – as far as we know – is different from the senses that we ordinarily talk about. It may or may not be, because we do not know, what our intuitive senses are. But, as far as we can talk about it, one can say that it begins to take shape in our minds, in the form of an *imaginative conjecture*. So, first of all: it's your capacity for imagination and guessing. Now, as the patient keeps on coming, then these imaginative conjectures could become *rational conjectures* – you'd think. We could say I guess, and I think with reason: rational conjecture, that this patient is something or another. For example: With this one here, I think all of us could say what we guess. Imaginative guesses as to what's the matter. Then I'd say: "*Now, will you have another guess?*" *Do you think it would be a reasonable guess? A rational conjecture?*

B. Intuition evolving in a state of mind proper of being in unison with reality

This way of perceiving the presence of intuition is no longer limited to the historical concept of intuition as knowledge that emerges suddenly and dispenses the elaboration by processes proper of knowing. The mental experience that here receives psychoanalytic attention takes place outside the dimension of knowing and corresponds to a mental state of experiencing being at one with reality.

Referring again to *Attention and Interpretation* (1970, p. 27) where Bion illustrates the differences between the states of mind of *knowing* and *being at one with reality*:

> [T]he psycho-analyst can know what the patient says, does and appears to be, but cannot know the O of which the patient is an evolution: he can only 'be' it. He knows phenomena by virtue of his senses but, since his concern is with O, events must be regarded as possessing either the defects of irrelevancies obstructing, or the merits of pointers initiating, the process of 'becoming' O.

In the notation of the theory of transformations, this would be represented by K-> O, and we would be referring to a movement of being in unison with the origin ('O').

We cite in what follows an excerpt from Supervision D14 (probably held in Rio de Janeiro, 1973) to discuss how Bion considered intuition in his ontological period.

Excerpt from Supervision D14

A: I'd like to ask another question maybe in agreement with that, I don't know, you've changed saying about the meaning of the senses.

BION: Of the . . .?

A: The senses.

BION: Yes, yes.

A: And you have the intuition or, I don't know whether I perceive it right, but you can explain some steps of these changes.

BION: I think it became obvious to me; I might say it had always been obvious. Take something simple like anxiety: I can't smell it, I can't tell you what it's shape is, but I have no doubt at all about anxiety!! So, anyhow, although I have got no sensuous awareness – I can't take a photograph of it, I can't take an X-Ray of it – nevertheless, I'm sure that there's anxiety. Now, this is something which most people would agree about, this is hardly worth talking about, because it is clear that you can't see it, or feel it, or touch it, or say what its shape is, or what its smell is. But it exists and you could go through all the senses, all these emotional experiences, that there is no – as far as we know – sensuous evidence of it. People are angry, people are in love, people are hating, people are doing all these . . . having all these different feelings, but there's no sensuous experience of it; there's no sensible experience, no experience which is available to the senses of touch, sight, hearing, smell . . . as far as we know; or if there is, we still haven't found any words for it.

P2: Don't you think that there are some physical signs of anxiety, facial expressions, an activity of glands and so on . . . that somehow there are some senses that can capture this feeling of anxiety or other feelings like anger, pain.

BION: I think that it is so, very, very late in the proceedings. By the time these feelings betray themselves in senses, it's very late in the story; for example, somebody can be very hostile, you would certainly know that if they came with some weapon which they flourished and threatened you with – one needs to know that long before they do anything of that sort.

P2: My question is: wouldn't there be other signs that were not prominent, like a weapon, but still perceptible by the senses?

BION: I think that there probably are. That is why I think it would be helpful if one could develop the *intuition*, when somebody who's very angry, before that somebody attacks you with an ax or a knife.

P2: Perhaps some perception that would not achieve the conscious level, taking, for instance, the model of the seventh chapter of dreams, that some perceptions are like the negative of a photograph, but nevertheless, would be perceived somehow.

BION: *It's possible, but until we perceive it, it's no good talking about being analysts, or at least, it may be alright talking about it.* But it's quite a strong claim to make to say that we can do this; for example: I've known of a man who says: "*I can smell that there's a rattlesnake here and I can smell that that rattlesnake is angry.*" It is possible that so can a dog. Now, I've known – in childhood – a situation where – which is quite common and everybody knows about it – two dogs, quite ordinary dogs, quite ordinary terrier dogs, will go to the hole of a cobra. Now, the cobra is a very dangerous, very toxic snake and it is very fast, indeed, if it's traveling in a straight line! That, it can't do that fast!

[Obviously, Dr. Bion is, at this point, making a swerving movement with his arm]

Now, two dogs will get together and one of them will dig down the snake's hole and the other one stands at the side. It goes on . . . the digging goes on until the cobra is nearly reached, when the cobra will suddenly shoot straight out like that.

[Another gesture is made with the arm]

Now, the other dog, which is watching stands there. The moment the snake does that, gets it behind the neck and shakes like that.

[Another gesture]

The first dog that has been doing the digging lies down and gets his breath back. Then, at a sudden moment, the dog which has got the snake and is doing that, drops it and the second dog pounces on it, picks it up and goes on doing it. In this way, as I say, two terriers will go snake hunting – cobra hunting to be exact – and will carry it out in that successful way, for a very long time and kill snake after snake by going on shaking it, until it can't really do anything about it.

But the point about all this is: how does the second dog know that the first dog is going to drop the snake? How do these animals know that the cobra is nearly, nearly, going to strike out, as a snake, out of the hole? But they *do* know. Now, are you going to talk about the dogs' **intuition**? What is one to call it? (. . .) Yet, if it is true, an experienced hunter can smell that there's a rattlesnake about and that it is angry, then, surely, it should be possible for psychoanalysts to become, or to be sufficiently **intuitive** too – well, we call it, falling back on this very clumsy language – smell that the person is angry.

C. Intuition as an experience of receptiveness to thoughts without a thinker

In the two conditions described earlier, we identify differences between mental states in which intuition becomes accessible to us in psychoanalytic practice (states of mind of knowing and unison with reality), corresponding to consolidated forms of Bion's psychoanalytic thinking. In this third condition, we are in an investigative terrain, which Bion himself identified as *imaginative conjectures*.

We can conjecture that this is the point evoked by Bion in the excerpt reproduced earlier from *Attention and Interpretation* (1970, p. 26): O does not fall in the domain of knowledge or learning <u>save incidentally</u> (underlined by the authors).

With this conjecture, we have intuition as the ultimate experience of direct contact of the thinker with the dimension of reality not apprehensible by sensorial means, that of thought existing as a proper dimension of reality.

This was possibly Bion's effort to expand the understanding of mental states of transformations in *becoming the reality* (K-> O). In the present case, it would correspond to the evolution of a fragment of the ultimate reality that intersects with knowing (O-> K), which can be described in a series of stages. *Assuming a direction O->Tb, O can be referred to as "evolving" by (A) becoming manifest (or "knowable") TbK -> (B) by becoming a "reminder" or "embodiment" or an "incorporation" -> (C) by becoming TbO or "at-one-ment"* (Bion, 1965, p. 163). In a more summarized observation, we would probably be facing a transformation O-> O: something that exists in the dimension of unreachable reality (O) and imposes itself on the mind of the thinker as something strange, wild, often frightening, demanding great confidence from the thinker to welcome this stranger and, more than that, bear it and give it life. An *intuition without a concept* imposing on the mind of the thinker, demanding his mental work of elaborating an imaginative conjecture for the intuited thought and, perhaps, enable the thinker to elevate it to the condition of rational conjecture. This is possibly the psychoanalytic way of observing a transformation tending to O (K-> O). However, there is room for us to add that descriptions by mystic authors suggest something different: they seem to dispense the intermediate stage of the dimension of knowing and establish a 'direct line' between the origin and being at one with the thing in itself. Noteworthy in this view is the fact that the person is incarnated as the final stage of the exposure to the wild thought, which departed from the origin and was received by a thinker, ending the cycle *being* the thought. Despite this being a difficult process to think, Bion pointed this out in *Transformations* (1965, p. 139): "The phenomenon does not "remind" the individual of the Form but enables the person to achieve union with an incarnation of the Godhead, or the thing- in-itself (or Person-in-Himself)".

Bion initially explored this dimension from two conjectures: one of *wild thoughts*, an experience of receptiveness by the thinker of a thought without a thinker strayed from its origin, and another of a favorable environment in the thinker's mind for the emergence of these wild thoughts by simultaneous contact of two or more minds, as in a group (1977a, p. 47, 1977b).

This kind of intuition appeared infrequently in Bion's supervisions in Brazil, and the excerpt that we present next (Supervision D4) was the most significant we found in this regard. This supervision was probably carried out in São Paulo in 1978, as suggested by the presence of ideas that Bion only manifested with clarity after 1977 (*The Italian Seminars* [1977a], *Taming Wild Thoughts* [1977b], and *Bion in New York and São Paulo* [1977, 1978]).

Excerpt from Supervision D4

[At this point, we hear a woman's voice saying].

P1: . . . memory and . . . memory and . . .
P2: Intuition!
P1: Intuition, and what do you think about the thought without the thinker?
BION: To take the last point first, I would suggest that we imagine that when a number of people collect together, like this, there are stray thoughts floating

around, trying to find a mind to settle in. So, the problem from the point of each individual – one of us – is: can we catch one of these wild thoughts without being too particular about what race they are or what category they are? Whether they are memories or intuitions! But just get hold of any one of these wild thoughts however strange or however savage or friendly they might be. Give it a home and then allow it to escape from your lungs, in other words, give it birth. So that, here no matter how wild the idea may be.

2. Some reflections on Bion's intuitive method from his supervisions in Brazil

I. A first major point for the understanding of the seminal position of intuition in Bion's psychoanalytic thinking is the observation that this concept is always present in his work and can be found in different elaborations since *Experiences in Groups* (1961 [1945–1952]). The concept can be found in his theory of knowing (1962–1965), theory of transformations (1965), in the chapter Comments in *Second Thoughts* (1967), *Attention and Interpretation* (1970), and in his ideas of the primordial mind (1976–1979), the latter mainly in the expansions of thoughts without a thinker (*Taming Wild Thoughts*, 1977; *A Memoir of the Future*, 1991). The only part of his work without the presence of intuition is his period of fidelity to Melanie Klein's thinking (1950–1959), when his approach to mental life was mainly through the concept of part objects, in a period during which his analytical work focused essentially on schizoid mechanisms (Hinshelwood, 2018).

A second point to highlight in Bion's concept of intuition is that he follows Plato's vision, separating the achievement of human knowledge into two paths: one acquired through the senses and another from intuition through direct contact with the essence of the object. This perspective, historically taken up by Kant, is pointed out by Bion in several quotes by both philosophers – Plato and Kant – as Bion's point of reference (for example, in *Learning from Experience* [1962] and *A Key to "A Memoir of the Future,"* [1981], entry Intuition).

Sandler (2005, entry *Intuition*) also highlights this epistemological origin in Bion's thinking: *Kant's definition of intuition (Anschauung) has precision and wide acceptance: it means the contact with reality without brokerage of rational thinking.*

Although we accept this foundational concept of intuition in Bion's work, a careful examination of the way he uses this concept after 1965 (*Transformations*) shows that it has gained meanings that are beyond the limits of its concept according to Kant, and not only in terms of the difference that Kant privileged the reality possible to be sensorially apprehensible, in opposition to Bion who always privileged the non-sensuous apprehensible reality. This is the turning point in Bion's thinking that brought the proposal of a psychoanalytical dimension of *being or becoming the reality*. After *Transformations* (1965), Bion's interest became systematically focused on ongoing intuitions, moving away from references of pre-existing concepts and theorizations for the elaboration of experiences in the consulting room. From this point onward, Bion takes up the intuitive path as the privileged tool in psychoanalysis. This move by Bion expands the use of intuition beyond the process of knowledge, including transformations occurring in states of mind of being or becoming reality. Epistemologically, this expansion brings Bion's thinking closer to existential ideas in philosophy and points out to a convergence that forms between the views developed by Bion and Bergson, a fact well pointed out by Torres (2013). For example, after the inclusion of intuition as a resource for direct access to psychic reality in the epistemological period, a synthesis by Torres of the concept of intuition in Bergson (p. 26) completely overlaps with the concept that we perceive implicit in the way Bion works:

> [I]ntuition, which by an effort of imagination and in sympathy with the object, inserts itself within the state of mind of the object in order to coincide with it and what is unique in it (is absolute).

The set formed by the collection of these sparse ideas in Bion's work compose a complex vision but allows the perception that the sense of intuition changes in his thinking depending on the deductive system in which the intuition is inserted.

II. In another supervision held in Brazil (S6, Brasília, 1975), we find a description by Bion of his intuitive method to approach minimal signs of facets of psychic reality. In our evaluation, this was present in a comment by Bion on how he thought about the experience of *being in unison* with reality, but we can also observe him in the excerpt that follows stressing another very important point for the analyst: the search of being him(her)self in the analytical relationship. Descriptions of this characteristic have frequently been pointed out in Bion's personality. As an explicit example, this can be seen in his demands to Melanie Klein when he sought to start analysis with her: He insisted that it was to be in the condition that he was his own person when it comes to thinking and reacting (Grosskurt, 1986, p. 427). We can follow these ideas in the following excerpt from Supervision S6.

Excerpt from Supervision S6

PI: May I ask a question? I am considering your consideration as very interesting, but I just can't see, I'm not having the intuition . . . where did you get those contributions in the material you got?

BION: It's the impression and this . . .

PI: Tell us.

BION: In a supervision, one can hardly work out that kind of thing. I can try to answer it or try to give you an idea of what I feel about it and that is: knowing what I know about myself, this is not an experience I'd want to go on repeating. I feel that is not the sort of way that I'm prepared to spend my life and my

professional life and my time – no matter what I'm paid for it; nothing makes that worth my while. So, there's that point about it. I've got used to myself sufficiently to know that *that* is the kind of thing that does not satisfy, and I should get more and more dissatisfied and angry or hostile if I felt that I was under locks – some sort of obligation to go on behaving like that. The other thing is really dependent on the kind of experience of people, which leads me to suppose that I am familiar with this kind of behavior.
What is the . . .?

T: The second part, we didn't catch it.

BION: It's partly due to the experience which I've had, which leads me to feel that I'm familiar with people who behave in this kind of way. So, it depends on two things: partly on what I know about myself and what I'm capable of standing, tolerating, putting up with; the other thing, what I think I know about the human race, as it were, human beings. Now, this matter point is a peculiar one. I might have met one person like that, or two people, or plenty, or two hundred, like that. It doesn't mean to say that this one is the two hundredth and first. So, this general idea that people behave like that, is not really very important. It's rather silly, as to say: "I know what's the matter with you, you have an Oedipus complex." What, so what? Or "You are the kind of animal that I will classify as *Homo Sapiens*" or whatever the most usual phrase is. In short, we also theoretically or philosophically or hypothetically, believe that the human person is unique.

III. In the supervisions conducted in Brazil and analyzed by us, we were unable to identify any ideas by Bion about intuition that we have not already perceived in his written works. However, two points are new in the supervisions in terms of intuition. First, the observation that Bion used this concept in informal discussions in the last years of his life, reflecting how his concepts were already consolidated in his mind and emerged spontaneously, integrated in his way of being and thinking. Second, the examination of how intuition appeared in the model of the mind used by Bion during that time, revealing the co-existence of approaches characteristic of the transformations in knowledge (K), in becoming the reality (O), and with the inclusion of manifestations of the analyst being receptive to thoughts without a thinker. In this sense, the thesis that unfolds is that these findings reinforce the view that Bion treated the different stages of development of his thinking (groups, psychotic thinking, epistemological period, ontological period, interest in the primordial mind) as evolutionary moments that complement each other and coexist. This would be the 'onion' as a model of the mind.

IV. It becomes easy to see that no clear-cut clinical separation exists between the first two forms of intuition that we described here as occurring in the dimensions of knowledge and of being the reality. It is clear that what we are evaluating as occurring in a specific medium (knowing and becoming the reality) can easily be seen as occurring in another one of these media, contrary to initial thinking. For this problem, we will postulate the same prerogative of coexistence that Bion has already proposed to exist, for example, between K, L, and H links. The model here would also be comparable to looking to the same mountain through different cardinal points. In this condition, the observer makes a decision about which aspect seems to be prevalent or leads to more favorable developments when used for interpretation.

In an application of the model used by Bion in Supervision D14 – that of terrier dogs in their struggle with a cobra – would their intuition be anchored in a critical mass of knowledge accumulated from personal experiences or phylogenetically inherited experiences of the species? Moving to the human condition, could we carry "embryonic remains" of our animal heritage that would occasionally manifest (Bion, 1977b, p. 38)? Could we consider the possibility of the existence of primordial receptor organs, as in Bion's words "the possibility that there are other receptor organs of which we are not aware" (Bion, 1977a, p. 64)? Or the possibility of capturing sensations through "primordial senses"? (Bion, 1977a, p. 51).

V. An unavoidable question for those who experience imaginative conjectures evolving from intuition in a mental state of becoming the reality (K-> O) is to differentiate intuition versus hallucinatory manifestation. Bion sought to deal with this problem at various moments in his work, but our impression is that he was unable to reach a satisfactory formulation.

This issue was already examined in Chapter VII of *Transformations* (Bion, 1965, pp. 96, 97, 102) in which intuition shares similar aspects with hallucination: non-existent objects in search of existence. The Comments chapter in *Second Thoughts* (Bion, 1967) leaves a lingering impression that Bion identified the problem but continued to seek more consistent elements to think about it. An attempt at a solution appears in *Attention and Interpretation* (1970, chapter III p. 36) through the idea that *to appreciate hallucination the analyst must participate in the state of hallucinosis*, which implies a state of *becoming the hallucination* and, thus, being in unison with the mental state of the analysand. In this same path, in *Taming Wild Thoughts* (Bion, 1977, p. 32), Bion tells us about the process of digging up a thought buried by hallucinatory layers (treated as knowledge), indicating that thought and hallucination may coexist and are not easily distinguishable from one another. For us, the discrimination between intuition and hallucination still seems to be limited, and the elements collected from these supervisions were unable to offer us contributions to progress further on this problem.

VI. A point that becomes very accessible regarding intuition in Bion's supervisions in Brazil is that the backbone of the use of this concept in his work and his understanding of mental life are intrinsically linked to two domains of mental functioning, *i.e.*, *knowledge* and *becoming one with reality*. The first leads to a scientific view of psychoanalysis and the second to an existential perspective irreducible to knowing. With the latter, psychoanalysis must decisively include the creative dimension proper to the arts, now no longer as a model but as part of the analytical work itself.

3. Conclusion

The perspective offered by the supervisions conducted by Bion in Brazil allows us to create binocularity when combined with an examination of the same ideas in his conceptual articles. Perhaps the issue of intuition, in particular, benefits greatly from this evaluation, improving our efforts to approach Bion's thinking.

Intuition is possibly the concept most implicitly present in Bion's clinical thinking but is also the least explicit. In these supervisions, we have Bion constantly and clearly privileging the search for direct contact with the present reality but also with few explicit references to the concept of intuition.

The role of intuition in Bion's work cannot be overestimated no matter how much we value it. As understood psychoanalytically after Bion, intuition can be identified on the basis of Freud's discoveries in describing the unconscious, of Melanie Klein's formulations in describing the primitive mind, and in all the expansions present in Bion's work since *Experiences in Groups*. Intuition can also be taken as the key to our understanding of how Bion's psychoanalytic thinking expanded to integrate not only the seminal contributions of Freud and Melanie Klein but also to identify new dimensions of mental functioning until then peripheral or ignored by the psychoanalytic interest.

Even with all our observations in the present work, we must bear in mind that intuition is not part of the consolidated psychoanalytic theory. Putting in perspective, we can think that by giving intuition a central role in the psychoanalytic work, Bion has freed psychoanalysis from the shackles of a mechanistic view of science, proper to the 19th century, bringing a fresh understanding of the mind, as he observed in *Notes on Memory and Desire* (Cogitations, c. 1967, p. 293): Not a scientific paper but a super-scientific paper, i.e., a psychoanalytic paper dependent on advanced, psychoanalytic methodology. It is not sub-scientific condition.

Even after 70 years from Bion's remarks on the importance of intuition for psychoanalytical practice, intuition has received little attention from the psychoanalytic world and still awaits a greater set of experiences by psychoanalysts to be better identified, understood, and applied to clinical practice. Perhaps the increased interest in Bion's thinking and the choice of intuition as the central theme in this publication can be seen as a sign that this concept is gaining a noticeable position in psychoanalytical thinking.

Note

1 Bion International Meeting 2020. Barcelona, January 2020.

References

Bion WR (1961). *Experiences in groups*. Tavistock Publications, London, 1961.
Bion WR (1962). *Learning from experience*. W. Heinemann, London, 1962.
Bion WR (1963). *Elements of psychoanalysis*. W. Heinemann, London, 1963.

Bion WR (1965). *Transformations: From learning to growth*. Maresfield Library, London, 1991.

Bion WR (1967a). *Second thoughts*. W. Heinemann, London, 1967.

Bion WR (1967b). Notes on memory and desire. In WR Bion 1992. *Cogitations*. London. Karnack (extended 1994 version).

Bion WR (1970). *Attention and interpretation*. Maresfield Library, London, 1991.

Bion WR (1975–1979). *A memoir of the future*. Vol. I, The Dream (1975), Rio de Janeiro, Imago Ed., 1975; Vol. II, The past presented (1977), Rio de Janeiro, Imago Ed., 1977; Vol. III, The dawn of oblivion (1979), Perthshire, Clunie Press (1979).

Bion WR (1977a). *The Italian seminars*. Bion, F. (Ed.). Karnac Books, London, 2005.

Bion WR (1977b). *Taming wild thoughts*. Bion, F. (Ed.). Karnac Books, London, 1997.

Bion WR (1977, 1978). *Bion in New York and São Paulo*. The Roland Harris Education Trust, Reading, Radavian Press, 1980.

Bion WR Bion F (1981). *A key to 'a memoir of the future'*. Bion F, editor. Clunie Press, Perthshire, 1981.

Bion WR (1991). *A Memori of the Future*. London, Karnac.

Bion WR (1992). *Cogitations*. New extended edition. London, Karnac Books, 1994.

Grosskurt P (1986). *Melanie Klein: Her world and her work*. Knopf Inc., New York, 1986.

Hinshelwood RD (2018). Intuition from beginning to end? Bion's clinical approaches. *The British Journal of Psychotherapy* 34:555–561.

Sandler PC (2005). *The language of Bion: A dictionary of concepts*. Karnac Books, London, 2005.

Torres N (2013). *Intuition and ultimate reality in psychoanalysis*. In: Torres N and Hinshelwood RD, editors. *Bion's sources*. Routledge, London, 2013.

TORRES, N & HINSHELWOOD, RD (2013). Bions sources´. London, Routledge, 2013.

Chapter 15

What is your name?

The realm of Minus, half a century later

Paulo Cesar Sandler

FAUST: What is your name?

MEPHISTOPHELES: The question seems absurd / For someone who despises the mere word, / Who treats appearances as vain illusion / And seeks the truth in such remote seclusion.

FAUST: But with you gentlemen the name / And nature's usually the same, / And we can often recognize / The Liar, the Destroyer, or the Lord of Flies. / Who are you, then?

MEPHISTOPHELES: A part of that same power that would / Forever work for evil, yet forever creates good.

(Goethe, Faust, Part I Scene iii)

Bion coined a sizable number of verbal formulations to express his psycho-analytical observations, under the forms of notions and concepts (Sandler, 2005). In the sake of getting a better, for brevity communicative power, he adjoined to a few of those verbal communications a quasi-mathematical notation. One of those concepts is "Minus"; added by the mathematical sign of " - ". Half a century after this specific coining, one century after the coining of one of Bion's verbal formulations that formed a number of interlinked psycho-analytical concepts – "Minus", in which he immediately adjoined, in the sake of getting a better, for brevity, communicative power, a quasi-mathematical notation: the sign "–".

In order to didactically systematize those concepts which are scattered in Bion's written work, and to respect their origin in the history of ideas of Western civilization – as Bion did – I suggest to call them under a single verbal formulation – in linguistic terms, a syntagma:[1] "the Minus realm".[2,3]

"Minus" in Bion's parlance is by definition a non-concrete, immaterial realm that complements – but does not replace! – the positive "senseable" realm of the material reality. Philosophers call it "sensible".

The finding of this realm and Bion's coining of the word "Minus" seems to me as a scientifically precise verbal formulation of a specific transient and partial aspect (or transformation) of material and psychic reality.

I cannot stress enough the importance of the Minus realm in our everyday work of psychoanalysis. Allow me an analogy: if psychoanalysis is comparable to an aerobic exercise, the Minus realm performs the same function as oxygen. For the

DOI: 10.4324/9781003293392-21

Minus realm "is", metaphorically and theoretically, a useful "inhabitant" of the unconscious and pre-conscious systems of our psychic apparatus.

Useful to what?

To be investigated and observed in facts that occur during sessions of psycho-analysis and to be dealt with theoretically in order to mirror those facts under verbal formulations with a "language of achievement" powerful enough to perform approximations to reality as it is – both in those very same analytic sessions and in the patient's everyday life, outside the session. It is not the one and only inhabitant, but its existence must be considered if our task is to achieve "real psycho-analysis":[4]

> In the practice of psychoanalysis, it is difficult to stick to the rules. For one thing, I do not know what the rules of psychoanalysis are. There are plenty of people who will say "Don't you know the theories of psycho-analysis?" and I could say, "No I don't, although I have read them over and over again. I now feel that I only have the time to read the very, very best psycho-analytic theories – if only I knew what they were". However, that is what I would try to limit myself to. The practice of *real* psychoanalysis is a very thorough job indeed. It is not the kind of thing which should be chosen as a nice, easy comfortable way of life. Theories are easily read and talked about; practice of psychoanalysis is another matter.[5]

I suppose that some of you well know my efforts to help the study of Bion's last work, the trilogy *A Memoir of the Future*, which seems to me – since 1981, when I made its first translation to a foreign language, Portuguese – his magnum opus. And, not for a mere coincidence, it is the most misunderstood work from him, who never was an author who did not experience remarkable misunderstandings about his written work.

It became clear to me that this trilogy paradoxically subsumes and expands all of his earlier work, from 1919 to 1974. He used a quasi-dialogical mode of writing, forming imaginative characters which I suppose are, in fact, fictitious and truthful representations of his own part-objects, drawn from his real-life experiences and his practice of psycho-analysis. Among many other colleagues, Francesca Bion, Parthenope Bion Talamo, James Grotstein and Andre Green agreed with my supposition. There are many examples of his use of the realm of Minus in this mammoth-sized text. Due to limitations of time allotted to this presentation, I choose just one, in which the part-object named "Bion" attempts to talk with another part-object, named "Myself":

BION: Is there anything new in this? You must often have heard, as I have, people say they don't know what you are talking about and that you are being deliberately obscure.

MYSELF: They are flattering me. I am suggesting an aim, an ambition, which, if I could achieve it, would enable me to be deliberately and precisely obscure: in which I could use certain words which could activate precisely and instantaneously, in the mind of the listener, a thought or train of thought that came between him and the thoughts and ideas already accessible and available to him.[6]

Reality material and psychic

It needed more than two millennia, involving the authoritative work of a sizable number of thinkers – theorists of science, mathematicians, physicians, philosophers, theologists, physicists, musicians and literates – to achieve a gradually developed realization about features of human nature and its sufferings and vicissitudes, as well as a sizable number of authoritarian, deluded, clouding, darkening and disorientated throwbacks, mainly made through plausible rationalizations, disguised as if they were the only truthful reality possible to be perceived.

Freud was the first thinker who discovered a field of research hitherto unknown, even though it was dimly perceived by those ancient thinkers. In the absence of an already available name, Freud called this field of research under what linguists classify as a syntagma: "material and psychic reality".[7,8]

After forty years studying psychoanalysis, Bion offered his own version of the same observation: reality is sensuous and psychic.[9] Based in both and also in my own transdisciplinary investigation in the history of ideas under a psychoanalytical vertex[10,11,12,13,14] I propose to call it "materializable and immaterialized reality", a cumbersome but perhaps a little more precise way.

Please notice that all three verbal formulations contemplate the conjunction *and* but not the disjunction *or*.

I have no doubts that Freud and Bion tolerated this paradox: the non-splitting nature of a whole, which we, too influenced by millenary ideas in the Western civilization, call a split, two-words mode: "matter", "energy" as well as "matter", mind. Those two verbal forms entail a false split because that fails to correspond to the "whole" in reality as it is. Unfortunately, this splitting is too popular. I will not dwell on the factors that led to it now, but I must emphasize that too many members of the psycho-analytic movement,[15] due to an inattentive, misunderstood pseudo-reading of Freud's text, have the thoughtless habit of replacing *and* with *or*. In doing this, they, probably unwittingly, perform just "*little learning, a dangerous thing*"[16] in scientific and artistic activities.

Two of the common issues that merited a transdisciplinary effort are the discoveries of zero and the negative numbers. This occurred in mankind and follows on, occurring in the emotional and intellectual development of babies. Alas, a sizable number of adults (under an obstetric scale, rather than psychic scale to measure time) are greedy enough and never realize the existence of what mathematicians call Zero. And, a fortiori, never fully realize what are negative numbers: both, Zero and the negative numbers form the realm of Minus.

A definitive step can be seen in Kant's revival of Plato's numinous realm, with due help from David Hume. He was able to define the numinous realm as a negative, a "limiting concept",[17] to educe the existence of antinomy of Pure Reason. Kant showed that rationalized thought – deduction and induction – constitutes just an illusion, to the extent that pure reason cannot make real inroads toward the apprehension of material and psychic reality. Kant made a most decisive establishment of scientific methods hitherto known.

It fell to Hegel to continue Kant's work, albeit with a similar ambivalence. Like Kant, he was inspired by Ancient Greeks to develop Kant's antinomies into a new form of dialectics: each thesis enjoyed an antithesis which was "the negative".[18]

More important for us psychoanalysts is that Hegel pointed out the possibility of matching thesis and antithesis, resulting in an integrated synthesis. His ambivalence is displayed by his attributing to "the negative" the same nature that he attributed to what I proposed elsewhere to call "the positive" – to the extent that Hegel put antithesis on the same level as thesis. I collected elsewhere historical instances, matching them with clinical evidences, to display that at least part of the works of Kant and Hegel – in the extent that they were not idealistic but scientific – are intellectual ancestors of the work of Freud and Klein.

The existence of "the negative", for practical applications, can be apprehended if one tries to make observations that are before and beyond the range encompassed by the sensuous apparatus: it is pure movement, life itself transiently going on, in the "arrow of time".[19]

The negative is an immaterial counterpoint of any materialized reality. Conversely, material reality is the positive, materialized counterpoint of psychic reality. They are two forms of the same (monistic) ultimately unknowable existence.

The realm of Minus contemplates the possibilities of impossibility, and its propositional content cannot be seen on the same level of what is not probabilistic. For it does not have the same nature as what can be seen as the "Plus realm", what is affirmative; in other words, it presents to us what occupies a position in space-time. In terms of what seems to me to be the false theory of science, the "Plus realm" inexorably falls into the positivist religion, invented by Auguste Comte.[20] The Plus realm can, albeit in a restricted way, be apprehended by our sensuous organs.

Any assignment to the realm of Minus indicates "what is not" – it is an anti-positivism, so to say. **The realm of Minus cannot have the properties assigned to what would be the opposite of "what is". It is ineffable; but it is experience-able, intuitable and usable**.

The realm of Minus, negation and tolerance of frustration

Klein and Winnicott contributed to the advancement of our perception of the Minus realm; we cannot dwell on their work now but at least may quote theoretically their nomenclature: greed, envy, rivalry and their contrapuntal gratitude and reparation; false self and its contrapuntal true self; the transitional object and the real object, as well as the functions of illusion and its contrapuntal lack of illusion.

Freud, Klein and Winnicott outlined more clearly the existence of a contrapuntal negative parallel to what they saw as a destruction-bound "negative".

Bion integrates the work of Freud and Klein in almost all of his work; in what concerns the realm of Minus, Bion pinpoints out the inception of the principle of reality[21] in a newborn baby. In consequence, he draws a hypothesis about a theory of thinking[22] – based in his experiences with the psychotic personality[23] and his personal analysis with Melanie Klein. Later he developed this theory to describe our thought apparatus, learnt by experience of real events and the eventual hallucinated accompanying "minus" experiences – considering that hallucinations are perceptions with no object.

The events, in their primordial forms, are: a newborn baby, prey of the annihilation anxiety[24] faces the absence of a breast; I would say the first experience of the lacking of a materialized, sensuously apprehensible breast and its, at first, positive, because materialized realization. His or her facing of the absent breast depends entirely on his or her innate (genetically ability) ability to tolerate frustration; this ability can be enhanced or diminished, in dependent of his or her relationship with his or her mother – or, more precisely, his or her internalized and projected breast.

One may summarize it: "No-Breast", therefore a thought. Absence, lack of is the nest of thought processes; no pain, no gain – even though the quantity of felt pain depends on the individual. I propose to state this in what I suppose to be a more precise way, fully authorized by Freud, Klein and Bion's writings: the paradoxically introjected and projected Good and Bad Breast: "The domain of thought may be conceived of as a space occupied by no-things".[25]

We may state, albeit provisionally, that there are at least two kinds of Minus.

From clinical practice, it became clear that the terms "Negative" and "Minus" indicate the following counterparts in reality:

i   the nature of the no-thing that is inseparable from the thing, which I shall call the contrapuntal Minus; and
ii   a realm created out of greed that cannot tolerate the no-thing. This greedy state of mind disables one's capacity to abstract the breast from its sensuously based "concreteness". "Nothing" replaces the "no-thing"; "without-ness" replaces real lack of something.

To analyze and to live demands tolerance of a paradoxical balance between "positive" (material, sensuously apprehensible) and "negative" (immaterial, psychic, ultra- and infra-sensuous).

To describe graphically this paradoxical balance I would borrow from Bion his notion of saturation of a psychoanalytic element[26] and combine it with the double arrow that he used to describe Klein's theory of the tandem movement between the paranoid-schizoid and depressive positions:[27,28]

. . . positive ⇔ negative ⇔ positive ⇔ negative . . .

Not tolerating Minus leads to a destructive, greedy prevalence of the realm of Minus. This intolerance of Minus I propose to denote, after Green, "the realm of negative". Therefore, our attempt at a unifying theory leaves to the "negative" the expression of an imbalance of the "contrapuntal Minus" and what is real.

Clinic

My next statement may sound too haughty or dogmatic or authoritarian or like a sign of megalomania to a hostile critic – mainly to "the erudite" who, according to Bion, "can see that a description is by Freud, or Melanie Klein, but remain blind to the thing described":[29] the realm of Minus is the nest where psychoanalysis is nurtured, in a practical sense.

For what "we want to hear from our patient is not only what he knows and conceals from other people; he is to tell us too what he does not know";[30] Bion emulated Freud: "Nothing is to be gained from telling the patient what he already knows";[31] "The dominant feature of a session is the unknown personality and not what the analysand or analyst thinks he knows".[32]

We must utter to our patients that which **both of us do not know**: "thoughts without a thinker".[33,34,35] The underlying and overlying, unspoken, immaterial and non-sensuously apprehensible emotions demand that the analyst puts at the analysand's disposal his "analytically trained intuition".[36] When the negative realm obtrudes, there is an intermingling of dangerous destruction with sublime creativity, entailing the mystery of life, death, epistemophilic and group instincts. In the psychoanalytic session the insight is a kind of progeny of this creative immaterial act.

Minus K and Minus container/contained ($♀♂$)

The negative in the processes of knowing is a destructive force in knowledge: **a forceful attempt to prove that misunderstanding is superior to understanding**. He observed that some patients in which the psychotic personality is prevalent "are concerned to prove their superiority to the analyst . . . by defeating his attempts at interpretation. They can be shown to be misunderstanding the interpretations to demonstrate that an ability to mis-understand is superior to an ability to understand . . . there is a moral superiority and superiority in potency of UN-learning".

−K is not lack of knowledge. It has a meaning which "is abstracted, leaving a denuded representation".[37] It is knowledge at the service of pleasure. Its aftermath is a temporary destruction of truth or better, a destruction of the apprehension of truth, both in the individual and, a fortiori, in the group. −K is the medium of a characteristic group of unlawful lawyers, populists, demagogues and propagandists, those climbers in the political meritocracy of all human groups; in today's commonplace parlance, −K equals "fake news". It is destined to convince people of all things that are not. −K is expressed by uses of truth devoid of truthful intentions. Truth is untruthfully uttered and thus perverted. It is not intended to lead to accretions of knowledge but rather to extinguish the evolution of knowledge.

−K allowed Bion's eliciting of a Minus container/contained: Bion now resorted to a quasi-biological notation: $-(♀♂)$. It creates a sense of "without-ness" which differs from "nothingness". The latter can be represented mathematically as zero.

In clinical practice it appears as "an envious assertion of moral superiority without any morals".[38]

The contributions of André Green

Even though this is a chapter about Bion's concept of Minus, I will now take into consideration the fact that Bion quoted very few analysts in his works: S. Freud, M. Klein, H. Segal, Maurits Katan, R. Money Kyrle, J. Wisdom, D.W. Winnicott – after his colleagues' death, in two lectures.[39,40] And just one – younger than him: André Green – who, like Segal and Winnicott, wrote book reviews about Bion's works, *Attention and Interpretation*[41] and, after his death, *Cogitations*.[42]

Since 1973 André Green alone has been reconsidering under a creative rather than repetitive mode the realm of Minus as a raging generator of nothingness, first adumbrated by Bion in 1962.

Green says "the work of the negative", after Hegel, sharpens up our apprehension of this realm in the clinic. In brief, patients feel a "negativation" deeply enmeshed into pleasurable, sadistic states of transformations of hallucinosis, as described by Bion;[43] those people nourish a sensation of harboring a "hole" made of nothingness, a perverse negative object encircled by an affective vacuum, a hole. Analysis features mainly emptied concrete wording: the patient could not introject; he seems only able to "excorporate";[44,45] with this basis, I propose that one see Green's "work of the negative" as a concretised manifestation of the prevalence of the Minus realm due to an imbalance in relation to its "positive" counterparts. According to Green, the patient cannot stand the "double limit" and does not transform messages from the unconscious in a way that would render those messages suitable for verbalization. Later Dr Green observed another consequence of the "work of the negative" in a clinical case in which disturbances of thought were shaping a phobia of thinking – which precludes the obtrusion of free associations.[46]

Minus L and Minus H

With the exception of giving brief enlightening hints about what – L and – H **are not** [47,48,49] Bion did not furthered any details about what −L and −H are all about, in a stark contrast with a whole chapter dedicated to make clear some uses of −K and its relationship with Minus contained/contained.

Feeling the lack of definitions, I tried to define Minus L following a strict method that, to my mind, could give due respect and consideration to what he wrote: I applied Bion's definition of Minus K to Minus L and then to Minus L.

Minus L is an attempt to prove that to un-love is superior to love. Does that bring with it hate? Bion gave us a fundamental hint that I respected: – L is not Hate. One cannot find neither misleading hyper-simplifications nor complications in Bion's work, but one must consider that complexity is inherent to the functioning of psychic apparatus; one may find many warnings about this in Bion's work.[50] To hate is a most primitive form of to love; hate is a condition of love. In Minus Love, Hate is not the primary impulse. Perhaps this is where the problem lies, both in real life and in consequence, in real analysis.

Then I tried to define Minus H: a forceful attempt to prove that un-hating is superior to hating. The same considerations about envy precluding anything other than a parasitic relationship are valid here. The breast cannot be felt as a moderator of the dreadful and annihilating feelings; the breast that is felt as bad is, so to say, "co-opted". It is turned into a false good breast. If the baby's envy is excessive, a Minus loving Mother nourishes Minus Hate sibs. Minus H is not lack of hate. It is the triumph of hate through an absolute splitting of love from hate. There is a "moral superiority and superiority in potency"[51] of un-hating. The instinct that prevails is an excessively violent, greedy, object-damaging Love. It produces something that Freud adumbrated in 1920 as the defusing of instincts. It is excessive morality lacking any ethics.

Reports of my clinical experience are written elsewhere.[52,53]

Does the realm of Minus obtrude in the group formed by members of the psycho-analytic movement?

If you suppose that some ideas of mine merit consideration, perhaps, in social events about the scientific contributions of Bion's work, it would be opportune to put a personal observation about the possible seriousness of expressions of −K, −L and −H in the psycho-analytic movement. I tried to examine this fact before, putting forth three hypotheses, backed by clinical data – an anti-alpha function[54] of a sixth basic assumption[55] and describing the difference between political meritocracy and scientific meritocracy[56] within human groups that nourish attempts to form scientific or artistic societies – all of them wholly influenced by Bion's work.

Are there fair examples of −K, −L and −H – in the psycho-analytical movement?

I may put the general question under more specific terms, with a series of sixteen points to ponder:

1 Are ideas put forth by members of the psycho-analytic movement conducive to a group's mis-understanding, as superior posture if compared to that of understanding of earlier ideas?
2 Are there ideas that express that to unlove is superior to love?
3 And to unhate superior to hate?
4 Does the group formed by all of us, namely, the members of the psycho-analytic movement, apprehended those ideas or not?
5 It seems to me that it is high time to those members of the psycho-analytic movement to entertain second thoughts about their tendency to distort what is, in its origin, just a scientific criticism (in the Kantian sense of this term: the critical analysis of the methods used by scientists), under their feelings that such a criticism could be a disparaging comment, made to destroy the criticized one's ideas. I suppose that this is a feeling that could be better seen in a

personal analysis, and it still surprises me that certified analysts still behave like this.

6   Or not, that is, any kind of criticism, irrespective of its nature and intentions, is always took as if would as if it a just personal, disparaging criticism made to destroy the work of the criticized one?

7   Are there political uses of the scientific work of our "geniuses"?

8   If one discovers something clinically, what would be the factors making one use the same term already coined by other people to name one's discovery?

9   Why might one feel the need to disallow other people uncreatively, coining other names and, allegedly, concepts, **against** names and concepts already made?

10 Does the tendency described in item 9 above lead to confusion in the psychoanalytic movement, already pointed out by many who coined the neologism "babelization"?

11 Is the tendency described in item 9 an expression of lack of personal analysis: rivalry, envy and greed and paranoid-driven phantasies of fame at the expense of the person – usually death – who is regarded by the greedy, envious and rivalry-prone one as "famous"?

12 Would it be psychoanalytically untrue (−K) to state, as John Milton, an author dear to Bion, stated, that "fame is no seed that grows in mortal soil"?[57] Or, conversely, is it true (K)?

13 Could the case of Dr Jacob Levi Moreno be an example of K? I think so, for he thought that he had discovered a psychic mechanism in groups and coined the term "tele" to differentiate it from Freud's transference.[58] I am not appreciating scientifically either of those two discoveries in reality and their corresponding definitions but rather supposing that this is the case. Is this case rare or not?

14 Is an example of −K, −L and −H evident in the undeniable mushrooming of "schools" in our hundred-years-old movement? It already took a general name – the many "-isms" and their consequent adepts, the "ians" – "Freudism" and the "Freudians" would be the prototype of what today is a legion: Jungians, Adlerians (today unfashionable), Kleinians, Winnicottians, Bionians, Kohutians, etc. They often, similar to sporting teams, enmesh themselves in "wars": "Anyone would think psycho-analysts never quarreled? When the Wars of Psychoanalysis start we shall see something – and no holds barred. Santayana feared the day when the scientific beasts and blackguards would get hold of the world".[59] Dr Stekel, Dr Adler and Dr Jung initiated the long run of "dissidences" dressed up as accusations of a veritable row improprieties by Dr Freud – scientific, religious and social. In this long run I may quote, after Freud's death, the examples given by the "controversial discussions",[60] followed by Dr Heinrich Racker and Dr Paula Heimann's attacks on Freud's definition and use of a concept created by him: counter-transference.[61,62]

15 How many members were and are involved in the tendency to adhere to the political meritocracy at the expense of a scientific meritocracy?

16 Is the psycho-analytical movement fated to be just another establishment, as if there was a scarcity of them?

In the past thirty years, both the psycho-analytic movement and psychoanalysis as a science and therapeutic method did not enjoy its past status in our encircling society and mainly by youngsters. I am not judging this fact as good or bad; I simply try to present it. I do not think that rationalizations of the type "we live in a consumerist society little interested in emotions or art or prone to use drugs, etc." are of any constructive, durable use, as any rationalization never is. In this sense, Freud's society was as much or probably more consumerist and as prone to using drugs or as uninterested in art as ours. Bion paid a high price, personally, for this situation, which plagues all establishments from hoary times.

I see with sincere preoccupation the emerging of this tendency among colleagues who profess that they are interested in the work of Bion but and it just to achieve political ends. I have historical evidence that his work was precociously used, in some countries, by people who presented him as one who "revolutionized" our field of activity. In my country such a dubious reputation was repeated in the layman press too – to Bion's personal annoyance and refusal to agree with such a qualification, a fact reported by him in texts and recorded voice – the last one three months before his death[63]

Twenty-eight years after the appearance of the first international meeting about Bion's work – a history of them is published elsewhere – it would be timely to check if our colleagues who kindly try to make a public service work, in taking the responsibility to organize those events are – unwittingly or not, by need or by wish – collaborating in the erection of another political meritocracy – just because they are organizing those meetings. Whiffs of political leanings were felt after ten years and undeniably made more effect after fourteen years. Would it be considered statistically normal?

After Bion's death, a few colleagues tried to be faithful to Bion's original concept of -[64] Later on, conversely, most of them applied the concept to their particular areas of interest, such as, for example, child analysis; or with comparisons with other authors not exactly interested in the work of Bion who had issued new concepts – as if there was a scarcity of them; or mixing arbitrarily the concept of $-K$ with earlier concepts – like, for example, the theory of thinking, as if Bion did not take it into consideration in the development of $-K$; or making eulogies adjoined with a flurry of "new" concepts, as if there was a scarcity of them in the psycho-analytical movement.[65,66,67,68]

In doing this, they ignore or are against the many warnings given by Bion about this attitude.[69,70] In his final years (1976 to 1979), he asked publicly, in lectures [71,72,73,74] papers[75],[76] and books, "Why should not the whole of psycho-analysis be just a vast, towering Babel of paramnesias to fill the gap where our ignorance ought to be?[77,78]

With the aid of his part object named "Psycho-analyst", he tells us:

P.A.: There are no labels attached to most options; there is no substitute for the growth of wisdom. Wisdom or oblivion – take your choice. From that warfare there is no release.[79]

Notes

1 Crystal, D (1997). *A Dictionary of Linguistics and Phonetics*. Malden: Blackwell Publishing, p. 489. Disponível em http://ihjj-hr/jena/wp-content/uploads/2019/07/a-dictionary-of-linguistics-and-phonetics-by-david-crystal

2 Sandler, PC (2005). *The Language of Bion: A Dictionary of Concepts*. London: Routledge, 2019.

3 Sandler, PC (2011). Extensions in the Realm of Minus. In *A Clinical Application of Bion's Concepts*. Vol. II, *Analytic Function and the Function of Analyst*. London: Routledge, 2019, pp. 5–60.

4 Bion, WR (1977b). *The Past Presented*. Vol. II, *A Memoir of the Future*. London: Karnac, 1990, p. 510.

5 Bion, WR (1974). *Brazilian Lectures*. Rio de Janeiro: Imago editora, p. 114.

6 Bion, WR (1975). The Dream. Vol. I, *A Memoir of the Future*. London: Routledge, 2017, pp. 189–191.

7 Freud, S (1895). Project for a Scientific Psychology. *SE* I.

8 Freud, S (1900). Das Unbewubte und das Bewubtwin – die Realität. Die frage nach realitat des Unberwubtem. In Die Traumdeutung, *GW* II/III, p. 625.

9 Bion, WR (1970). *Attention and Interpretation*. London: Tavistock Publication, p. 41.

10 Sandler, PC (1997–2003). *A Apreensão da Realidade Psíquica*, seven volumes. Rio de Janeiro: Imago editora.

11 Plato (380 BC). *Parmenides* and *The Republic*. English version by B. Jowett. In *The Great Books of the Western World*. Chicago: Encyclopaedia Britannica Inc. Book II, items 131–132, 369c.

12 Einstein, A (1916–1952). Relativity: The Special and the General Theory. Versão Inglêsa, Por R.W. Lawson. In *The Great Books of the Western World*. Chicago: Encyclopaedia Britannica Inc., 1994.

13 Dirac, P (1930). *Principles of Quantum Mechanics* (fourth edition, 1958). London: Oxford Science Publications, 2001.

14 Schrödinger, E (1944). What Is Life? In *The Great Books of the Western World*. Chicago: Encyclopaedia Britannica Inc., 1994.

15 Freud, S (1914). On the History of the Psycho-Analytical Movement. *SE* XII.

16 Pope, A (1711). *An Essay on Criticism*. www.poemhunter.com/poem/an-essay-on-criticism

17 Kant, I (1781). Critica da Razão Pura Brazilian Version By V. Rohden. In *Os Pensadores*. São Paulo: Abril Cultural, 1980, p. 160.

18 Hegel, GWF (1817–1820). *Philosophy of Mind* (trans. Wallace, W. & Miller, A. V.). Oxford: University Press, 2007.

19 Eddington, A (1933). The Expanding Universe. In *The Great Books of the Western World*. Chicago: Encyclopaedia Britannica Inc., 1994.

20 Comte, A (1896). *The Positive Philosophy of Auguste Comte*. English version, by H. Martineau. Londres: George Bell & Sons. There is an electronic version by Ontario:

Batoche Books, 2000. http://socserv2.socsci.mcmaster.ca/econ/ugcm/3113/comte/Philosophy3.pdf

21   Freud, S (1911b). Formulations on the Two Principles of Mental Functioning. *S.E.* XII, pp. 221–222.

22   Bion, WR (1961b). A Theory of Thinking. In *Second Thoughts*. Londres: Heinemann Medical Books, 1967.

23   Bion, WR (1957a). Differentiation of the Psychotic from the Non-Psychotic Personalities. In *Second Thoughts*. Londres: Heinemann Medical Books, 1967, pp. 49–52.

24   Klein, M & Riviere, J (1937). *Love, Hate and Reparation*. London: The Hogarth Press and the Institute of Psycho-Analysis, 1953.

25   Bion, WR (1965). *Transformations*. London: Heinemann Medical Books, p. 106.

26   Bion, WR (1963). Op. cit., p. 24.

27   Klein, M (1946). Notes on Some Schizoid Mechanisms. In *Developments in Psycho-Analysis*. M. Klein, P. Heimann, S. Isaacs, & J. Riviere, eds. Londres: The Hogarth Press and The Institute of Psycho-Analysis, 1952.

28   Bion, WR (1963). Op. cit., p. 34.

29   Bion, WR (1975). Op. cit., p. 5.

30   Freud, S (1938). An Outline of Psycho-Analysis. *SE* XXIII, p. 174.

31   Bion, WR (1965). Op. cit., p. 167.

32   Bion, WR (1970). Op. cit., p. 87.

33   Bion WR (1961b). Op. cit., p. 111.

34   Bion, WR (1962). Op. cit., p. 86.

35   Bion, WR (1963). Op. cit., p. 35.

36   Bion, WR (1965). Op. cit., p. 18.

37   Bion, WR (1962). Op. cit., pp. 96–98.

38   Bion, WR (1962). Op. cit., pp. 95–98.

39   Bion, WR (1977c). *The Italian Seminars*. Francesca Bion, ed. Londres: Karnac Books, 2005, p. 60.

40   Bion, WR (1978b). *The Tavistock Seminars*. Francesca Bion, ed. Londres: Karnac Books, 2005, p. 5.

41   Green, A (1973). On Negative Capability: A Critical Review of W. R. Bion's Attention and Interpretation. *Int J Psycho-Anal.* 54: 115–119.

42   Green, A (1992). Book Review: Cogitations. *Int J Psycho-Anal.* 73: 585–587.

43   Bion, WR (1965). Op. cit., p. 63.

44   Green, A (1997a). The Intuition of the Negative in Playing and Reality. *Int. J. Psycho-Anal.* 78: 107.

45   Green, A (1997b). The Primordial Mind and the Work of the Negative. In *W.R. Bion: Between Past and Future*. P.B. Talamo, F. Borgogno, & Silvio Merciai, eds. Karnac Books, p. 200.

46   Green, A (2001). The Central Phobic Position. *Int. J. Psycho-Anal.* 76: 871.

47   Bion, WR (1962). Op. cit., p. 52.

48   Bion, WR (1963). Op. cit., pp. 51, 53.

49   Bion, WR (1970). Op. cit., p. 75.

50   Bion, WR (1962). Op cit., p. 43, 48.

51   Bion, WR (1962). Op. cit., p. 97.

52   Sandler, PC (2011). Clinical Sources. Op. cit., pp. 35–60.

53   Sandler, PC (2017). Wirkliche Psychoanalyse ist wirkliches Leben. *Jahrbuch Psychoanal.* 76: 181–220.

54   Sandler, PC (1997b). The Apprehension of Psychic Reality: Extensions of Bion's Theory of Alpha-Function. *Int J Psychoanal.* 78: 43–52.

55   Sandler, PC (2013). A Sixth Basic Assumption? Op. cit., pp. 249–288. The original paper was published in Portuguese, 2000.

56 Sandler, PC (2016). Toward Truth: Glimpses to the Numinous Realm ("O") and Mind-lessness: The Sensuous-Concretisation Syndrome. In *An Introduction to a Memoir of the Future*. W.R. Bion, ed. Col. II: *A Matter of Fact or Facts of Matter?* London: Routledge, 2019, pp. 218 and 301, respectively. The concepts of political and scientific meritocracy was introduced in Portuguese, 2012.

57 Milton, J (1637). Lycidas. In *The Portable Milton*. London: Harmondsworth, 1982.

58 Moreno, JL (1946). *Psicodrama*. Brazilian version by Alvaro Cabral. São Paulo: Cultrix, 1978.

59 Bion, WR (1977b). Op. cit., p. 273.

60 King, P & Steiner, R (1992). *The Freud-Klein Controversies, 1941—1945*. Londres;: Routledge.

61 Heimann, P (1950). On Counter-Transference. *Int. J. Psycho-Anal.* 31: 81–93.

62 Racker, H (1957). *Transference and Counter-Transference*. New York: IUP, 1968.

63 Bion, WR (1979). Transcription from a Tape Recording. In *Cogitations*, op. cit., p. 375.

64 Riesenberg, RR (1990). As-If: The Phenomenon of Not Learning. *Int J Psychoanal.* 71: 385–392.

65 Lagos, CM (2007). *The Spanish Journal of Psychology* 10: 189–198.

66 Hacker, A (2012). Bion, la rêverie, la contenance et le rôle de la barrière de contact. *Revue française de psychanalyse*, 76: 769–778. doi:10.3917/rfp.763.0769.

67 Levine, H & Civitarese, G, editors (2018). *The W R Bion Tradition*. London: Routledge.

68 Civitarese, G, editor (2019). *Bion and Contemporary Psychoanalysis: Reading A Memoir of the Future*. Routledge.

69 Bion, WR (1962). *Learning from Experience*. London: Heinemann Medical Books, pp. 38, 42, 86.

70 Bion, WR (1963). *Elements of Psycho-Analysis*. London: Heinemann Medical Books, pp. 1, 2, 17.

71 Bion, WR (1977c). Op. cit., pp. 7, 36.

72 Bion, WR (1978a). *Four Talks with W.R. Bion*. Perthshire: Clunie Press, (Third Talk).

73 Bion, WR (1979b). *Bion in New York and São Paulo*. Perthshire: Clunie Press (Second), 1981.

74 Bion, WR (1978b). Op. cit., p. 2.

75 Bion, WR (1976). Evidence. In *Clinical Seminars and Four Papers*. Francesca Bion, ed. Abingdon: Fleetwood Press, 1987.

76 Bion, WR (1977a). Emotional Turbulence and on a Quotation from Freud. In *Clinical Seminars and Four Papers*. Francesca Bion, ed. Abingdon: Fleetwood Press, 1987.

77 Bion, WR (1979). Op. cit., p. 540.

78 O'Shaughnessy, E (1981). A Commemorative Essay on W.R. Bion's Theory of Thinking. *Journal of Child Psychotherapy*. 7: 181–189.

79 Bion, WR (1979). Op. cit., p. 685.

Index

abstraction 31

achievement: analysis 52; creative 56; language of 11, 58, 69–73, 108, 115, 128, 162; man of 108

act: of faith 108, 125, 134; infinite in 8, 133–135; psychoanalytical and poetic 11, 69–70

aesthetic: paradigm 124; qualities 38

affect 4, 113, 116

aleph 138

alpha: anti-alpha function 103, 145, 150, 168; function 9, 18, 37, 49, 65, 122, 125, 127, 129, 145

ambiguity 8, 130, 134–136

ambivalence 24, 164

animate: communications 25; psychic reality 86; world 11, 85–86

anxiety 138, 152; catastrophic 4, 114; infant's 48, 101, 165

aphasia 87

apocalypse 62, 64

Aristotle 8, 30, 134

artificial: intelligence 29, 32, 33; intuition 33–34; voice 90n5

assertion 167

associations 41, 76, 118n9; free 19, 64, 125, 167

assumption 30; sixth basic 168

at-one-ment 6, 102, 107–108, 115, 120, 125–126, 146, 154

atonement 125–126

attention: free floating 19–20, 26, 64, 103–105, 134, 136; intuitive 8, 135; psychoanalytical 121, 125, 151

autistic 55, 90n3

awareness 8, 23, 38, 53, 87, 119; conscious 145; non sensuous 152; telephatic 93

awe 5–6

baby 40, 48, 53, 101–102, 124–125; imposter 95–98; newborn 165

beauty 11, 38, 48, 95

becoming: the hallucination 158; "O" 136, 146, 151, 154; oneself 73, 102; one with an experience 93; one with an object 92, 126; one with oneself 92, 126; one with the patient 125, 127; one with reality 86, 123, 146, 153–158; states of 51–52, 58, 115

being: alive 27, 114, 116; at-one-ment 146, 154; experience of 124, 146; the experience of 146, 154; not-me 76; O 86, 119, 123, 155–156; psychoanalyst 59, 76, 152; real 86, 124; in uncertainties 69, 100, 108; in unison 3, 149, 151, 158

beta: conglomerate 65; elements 103, 121–123, 150

Bergson, H. 120–121, 156

binocular vision 2, 7–9, 27, 49, 120, 122, 127, 140, 145

Bion's seminars 9, 140, 142, 145

boundary 77

breast: internalized 165; no-breast 165; pre-conception of 102–103; projected 165

bridge 6, 41, 47, 50, 65, 127

caesura 47–54, 69–70, 77, 101–102, 127–128, 138, 142, 147n1

capability 101–102, 108; negative 40, 49, 69, 72–73, 78, 100–108, 145

Carnap, R. 121

catastrophe 42; see also change

certainty 8, 100, 116, 133, 135, 137

change 62, 67, 94–95, 97, 124, 137; catastrophic 101, 106, 120; structural 126, 128–129

For Product Safety Concerns and Information please contact our EU
representative GPSR@taylorandfrancis.com
Taylor & Francis Verlag GmbH, Kaufingerstraße 24, 80331 München, Germany

www.ingramcontent.com/pod-product-compliance
Lightning Source LLC
Chambersburg PA
CBHW070334270326
41926CB00017B/3869